Shorthand with Champagne

SHORTHAND

with

Champagne

EDNA RUBY

THE WORLD PUBLISHING COMPANY

Cleveland and New York

Published by The World Publishing Company
2231 West 110th Street, Cleveland, Ohio 44102
Published simultaneously in Canada by Nelson, Foster & Scott Ltd.

First Edition

Printed in the United States of America.

To all my friends—
past, present, and future.

Contents

※

Chapter 1

My hand is
in their lives

I am a public stenographer in a hotel. In many ways hotels are alike—they rent out rooms, have sterilized toilet seats, bottle openers in the bathrooms, and a tipping system. But despite the similarities, each has a character all its own. One caters to residential guests, another caters to transients. Certain establishments attract businessmen, others socialites, still others attract international celebrities or playboys and their chinchilla-coated consorts. But over all, any hotel is a tight little world within the greater world. I want to talk about the workings of that smaller world, and of the life and work of a public stenographer within it. I know that world. My hand has been in the lives of thousands of hotel guests. I refer, of course, to the hand that writes the shorthand.

As a child, growing up in a small town in Minnesota, I was both fascinated and overawed by the famous people I read about. They did such exciting things, lived dangerously but gallantly.

They attracted romance and entered into it joyously. I worshipped and envied them. I am no different today. Since I never expect to be famous myself, the next best thing is to work for celebrities.

I elected to work in a hotel because I was restless. I was after something and didn't quite know what it was. I wanted to *live*, and living meant associating with a wide variety of exciting people. It occurred to me that the gathering place of the world's most exciting people was the luxury hotel. I entered the hotel world for that reason.

I work in that world, a world that needs me because of my job. I meet interesting people, I am genuinely interested in every one of them, and I become part of their lives and they part of mine—perhaps for an hour, perhaps for a lifetime. I like doing a little more for them than is required. I want them to see me as an individual; I want to be their friend.

My career as a public stenographer began at the Beverly Hills Hotel in California. One of the most gracious hostelries in the land, it is set back from Sunset Boulevard, half-concealed by trees and banana palms. Behind the main structure nestle private bungalows, surrounded by exotic foliage. The main lobby is small but luxurious, elegant in the continental manner. Here you see business magnates, bluebloods, redbloods, and people who seem to survive on white blood corpuscles. Through the entranceway come actresses, playwrights, composers and foreign dignitaries. Guests promenade, undulate, or rush about in business clothes, evening dress, tennis togs, and occasionally the flowing robes of Saudi Arabia. They are generally a sophisticated lot, either very wealthy or on an expense account.

Once when it was raining too hard to go out, I was having lunch in the coffee shop, an intimate spot seating about fourteen at the counter. It was crowded. Patrons lined up behind diners, awaiting their turns. The President of Brazil stood behind Raymond Massey. Lily Pons hummed amiably as the bell captain finished his coffee. The Shah of Iran, already seated, was studying the menu in obvious perplexity. Hedy Lamarr sauntered in, her attractive peasant-style frock wrinkled, as if she had slept in it.

I sat beside a man whose face conformed to the cartoonist's stereotype of the typical New Englander. He was thin, tight-lipped and stiff. Studying the prices on the menu, he ordered milk and a hamburger in a precise, nasal twang. The meat must be broiled, not fried, for exactly five minutes. Well browned but not charred. Light on the seasoning. No lettuce.

When his order arrived, he bent over, lifted a tiny dog from the floor and pointed its nose into the dollar-and-a-half hamburger. As the pampered poodle gobbled hungrily, the human diner's face crinkled into a smile. He lifted the glass of milk and sipped his lunch. Then he grudgingly pushed a dime under the plate and carried his dog out in his arms.

No one showed surprise. Everything at the Beverly Hills was out of the ordinary. The unexpected was expected.

My girl friend Georgette, who ran the lingerie shop in the arcade, stopped me on the way back to the office. "Edna," she said, "I just sold all my panties!"

"Oh? The Baroness, who wanted pajama tops but no bottoms?"

"No. The Maharajah. He cleaned me out! He bought those sets with a different day of the week on each pair, and those cute ones with the sayings *Don't come up any farther* and *This Seat Taken*, and the French ones with all that lace. I thought he couldn't make up his mind, but then he told me to wrap them up, all of them! I asked him if he realized he had 400 pairs there. 'Well,' he said, 'I've got a lot of women to supply back home!' "

The Beverly Hills goes to great lengths to create a homelike atmosphere, which results in the guests expecting the same attention they receive at home. A stout man with a tremendous shock of white hair summoned me to his bungalow. A black Pomeranian was barking at his heels as he admitted me.

"What is your name?" he asked.

I told him.

"This is my little dog Pilchard. Pilchard, this is Miss Ruby."

We acknowledged the introduction.

"Young lady," the man said, "I want you to take this ball and throw it toward that wall. Pilchard will retrieve it. Please keep throwing until I tell you to stop. Pilchard needs exercise but I'm too busy."

Pilchard's master worked over a mass of papers at the desk for the next two hours; I exercised the dog.

I learned to accept eccentricity without dropping a shorthand stroke. Perle Mesta sent for me to take some letters. Since she had been our Ambassador to Luxembourg, I asked how I should address her.

"Call me Madam," she said.

I was pasting an airmail stamp on a letter to Irving Berlin when she cried, "No, no!"

"Madam?" I asked.

"Put a regular stamp on it. Send it ordinary mail. I can't afford to waste money like that."

I have my own eccentricity. I eagerly do things above and beyond the call of duty, and this has involved me in some odd situations indeed.

The switchboard operator called. "Hurry, Edna! There's a woman at the pool who says she has to see you immediately."

I dropped an important oil contract I was typing, grabbed a pencil and a notebook, and ran. My client stood chin-high in the center of the swimming pool, waving to me. She worked her way to the edge, stooping lower with each step to keep the water line shoulder-high. I bent over, received her whispered instructions, and took off for her room. I got what I came for, wrapped it in a towel, and ran back. I handed her the towel. She waded into deep water, glanced about furtively, and submerged. Moments later she swam lazily to the ladder, stepped out proud and erect, and I speak advisedly when I say erect. As she sauntered past a couple of men in deck chairs, I heard one murmur, "Mmhh! Stunning figure, hmmm?"

She could thank me for that. She forgot to put on her falsies under her bathing suit, realizing it after she was already in the pool. She didn't dare come out without them, lest she lose her reputation as one of the better built women around town.

An even greater emergency broke that evening. A client-friend telephoned. "Come right up here, Edna! I need you!"

"I can't, Ted. I'm finishing a rush job for a man who has to catch a plane."

"I don't give a damn what you're doing! This is urgent. Get up here, quick!"

I rushed to his suite. He was standing in the middle of the room, bent almost double, hopping on one foot then the other. He was wearing the most fantastic space suit since *Space Patrol* quit the air waves. He grunted, grimaced, and clawed at the neckline of the ridiculous contraption, trying to yank down the zipper in back. It wouldn't yield.

"What . . . ?" I began.

"Shut up and get me out of this! I've got to go, and I can't unzip this goddamned thing!"

He was six feet two and I am four feet ten. I reached for the zipper but couldn't quite get it started. "How will I do it?" I asked.

"I don't care. Tear it open if you have to. Hurry! I can't hold out much longer!"

I got up on the couch and grabbed hold of the zipper. I had just managed to get it down past the seat when in walked the bellman with a bucket of ice. He gulped, set the bucket down, and inquired, "Will there be anything else, sir?"

"No!" Ted roared. "Just get out of my way!"

Afterward, he told me he rented the space suit for a costume party. "Shows you about these TV shows," he explained. "Suppose a man is in outer space, all by himself. He's wearing one of these blasted things. What in hell does he do when he has to go?"

Speaking of going, there was a quiet young man who, having given me some letters, was sufficiently pleased with my work to ask if I would come out to Malibu the following week so he might dictate directly to the typewriter. We set a date. He lived in a small but luxurious bachelor establishment overlooking the Pacific. He was the soul of propriety and very thoughtful. He had a hot lunch brought in at noon. He saw that the lighting was just right for me. He was patient when I asked him to repeat something he had dictated. All in all, I spent a pleasant few hours at the typewriter.

Preparing to leave, I went to the bathroom to wash up, and met a stunning surprise. The walls and ceiling were completely mirrored. Obscene effigies perched on the tub. A table was piled high with what the Supreme Court, by whatever definition, would consider pornography.

As I exited, my host smiled. "You will come again, won't you?" he murmured.

"Well——"

"Did you notice the mirrors? The one on the door is one-way. I can see in, but the person on the other side can't see out. Whaddya say, shall we set a date for your next visit?"

"Don't call me," I said. "I'll call you."

The Beverly Hills Hotel had permanent as well as transient guests. Among the former was an Austrian countess, a ramrod of a woman, about eighty years old, who emigrated when the court of Emperor Franz Joseph disintegrated. An unreconstructed aristocrat, she tried to recreate in America the life she had lived in Austria. Her past had migrated with her. Her ebony desk was cluttered with faded tintypes. The silk bedspreads bore the family crest. When I entered her room I felt as if I were stepping into the nineteenth century.

The Countess' clothes were of that vintage too. When she went calling on her many friends she wore a heavily brocaded gown, the collar scraping her chin, skirt sweeping the floor. On her bosom was an antique red-gold stem-winder, hung from a heavy chain. Her hat was festooned with birds or a waving ostrich plume. She marched regally through the lobby and into a taxicab. She owned no car, I suspect because she would have nothing if not a coach and four.

In a more commercial establishment, bellhops would have attempted to make the Countess feel cheap because she was not a tipper. It would not have done them a bit of good, but they would have tried. At the Beverly Hills they bowed when she rewarded them with two or three cigarettes. She usually offered me a few pieces of hard candy, occasionally a glass of sherry. This was neither condescension nor parsimony. In her era the mistress of a grand household demonstrated appreciation by dealing out tidbits to her servitors.

She had genuine concern for the maid, housekeeper, and maintenance man who made life comfortable for her. Periodically she invited one of them in for a few words. Puffing on a twelve-inch cigarette holder, she politely inquired about the person's health and family. When she offered advice she took for granted that it would be followed implicitly.

I admired the Countess, but for me the aristocracy of Hollywood moviedom has always been the most exciting. When I was growing up, I read all the movie magazines, kept track of who was the current mate of whom and which starlet was discovered behind which soda counter by what Hollywood scout. I fancied myself in the arms of Buddy Rogers, my very ideal, the epitome of romance. I had pictures of him on every wall of my room and even on the ceiling. I imagined him taking me out, making the rounds of the dazzling Hollywood night spots, Buddy in a white tie and tails and me in an evening gown and white fox wrap, just like his leading ladies. Now here I was in Hollywood, among the sparkling cinema personalities, and reality was more enchanting than fantasy. I actually met Buddy Rogers and that old feeling came over me, because he was as handsome and dashing as I had imagined. I felt like a gawky adolescent, nervous and ill at ease. I did manage to say I had a terrific crush on him when I was eleven, and still owned the first recording he ever made. Later, I sent it to him as a gift.

To this day, all show people are glamorous as far as I am concerned. I realize that some are vain and vapid, but it makes no difference. They are stars and all stars glitter. Even when, on rare occasions, they treat me discourteously, I still find them fascinating.

A good example is James Mason, the distinguished English actor, at whose home I once worked for several days. Typing replies to his fan mail, I questioned something. "You're paid to work here, that's all," he said haughtily. "I'm not asking your opinion about anything."

He obviously had a better side, as could be seen from his fondness for cats. The Masons, both cat lovers, had a fully equipped nursery for their pets. Certain rooms of the house were uncarpeted so the animals could scamper about and scratch to their hearts' content without getting their claws caught in a rug. There was a cat infirmary on the upper floor.

Even inanimate objects had sentimental value for Mr. Mason. He brought a spectacular, antique Napoleonic bed over from England and would sleep in no other.

In sharp contrast to Mr. Mason's manner was the informality of Norma Shearer, who lived at the Beverly Hills Hotel when I had my office there. The first letter I did for her was to one of the top officials at MGM. She wanted him to help a young man get started in movies. The aspiring actor was no special friend, and she owed him nothing. She got into casual conversation with him at the hotel pool, was impressed by him, and believed he had talent.

Once Miss Shearer asked me to deliver a letter to a studio executive. It began raining as I was about to leave her suite. She insisted on bringing out her own galoshes, kneeling, and putting them on over my shoes. It apparently did not occur to her that this was out of the ordinary for a great screen actress.

After we finished work in her suite one evening, Miss Shearer and I sat before the fireplace, talking. She was in a reminiscent mood, recalling the golden era of Hollywood and particularly her happy years with Irving Thalberg, her first husband, who died some years before. She told me he commemorated every occasion that had significance for them by giving her some jewelry.

"I'd like to show you some of my pieces," she said. She brought them in. There were gorgeous diamonds, magnificent rubies and sapphires, and a pin almost the size of her palm. She exhibited each item fondly, then placed them all in a dresser drawer.

The next afternoon, two men entered my office and identified themselves as detectives. "When did you last see Norma Shearer?" one asked.

Their impassive faces and mysterious manner had me in a dither. I began to stutter, which helped me not the slightest. I managed to say I had been with Miss Shearer the previous evening.

The detective nodded, as if to say, "Good thing you didn't lie to us. We knew it all the time."

What did Miss Shearer and I talk about? What did we do? And was I aware that the actress' jewels had been stolen last night?

I was stunned. Over and over I repeated what a shame that was.

"Does she think I took them?" I faltered.

"N-no. *She* doesn't. We asked her who knew the jewels were on the premises and she told us you had been there and she showed them to you. But she was positive you had nothing to do with the burglary. She didn't want us to embarrass you by checking you out, but we've got to do it."

There were more questions and I was extremely nervous by the time the officers terminated their inquisition. They thanked me, assured me there was nothing to be upset about, and left.

Next morning I called on Miss Shearer. She apologized profusely for being the innocent cause of my humiliating experience.

"Don't worry, dear," she said. "I am sorry those detectives bothered you."

Although the jewelry was insured, she said, she deeply regretted losing it because it had great sentimental value for her. She particularly deplored the loss of a ring in the shape of a heart, which Mr. Thalberg had given her when they became engaged.

I saw Miss Shearer on several occasions after that, and each time I asked whether the jewelry had been recovered. It had not. She and I remain friends to this day. Once in a while I see her when she is wheeling a shopping cart at the market, and we stop and chat.

In my pre-adolescent days I would not have believed that Miss Shearer or any other movie celebrity would be aware of the existence of mere mortals. Actually, they are quite approachable. They act like gods and goddesses before the general public because that is show business. In front of the people who work for them, they are more likely to relax. They are not on camera, not creating an image. They can be themselves and are relieved by the opportunity.

Like many show people, businessmen let their hair down before employees. The most eminent are likely to be most human. They aren't proving anything any longer; they have earned their position. The mark of the man who is still struggling is his posturing, his constant insistence that his importance be acknowledged.

I thoroughly enjoy working for top businessmen. They are so sure of themselves. I am stimulated while sitting beside a perfect stranger, my boss for the time being. He is preoccupied, seemingly all business. Who is he? Where is he from? What does he do? Is he married? What is he thinking about right now? Is he completely engrossed in the business at hand, or does he know I am there? Is he as curious about me as I am about him? So I study my client. I wonder as we work. We pause and chat a bit. Because of the people with whom I come in contact I may know someone he does. I can usually carry my end of a conversation on a subject that will interest him. It is polite conversation, a subtle probe. I may never see him again, but each human being has his uniqueness and I want to get the essence of this man's personality; I want him to think highly of me, not to consider me as just another stenographer.

And he is as inquisitive about me, as a rule. He is away from home. The anonymity of hotel life offers inducements. A public stenographer piques his curiosity. I am friendly, responsive, eager to please. It scarcely enters his mind that I may be married or have a boy friend. He may assume I would become interested in him, given encouragement.

The executive keeps one eye on his notes, the other on the stenographer's legs or bust. Sometimes when I work in a client's room, the air becomes charged. I can feel it. Any little thing can change the relationship. This can make it hard on both of us.

Once we become conscious of each other as individuals, a certain warmth is established. My client may ask if I want a cup of coffee. If he offers me a cocktail, that indicates he would like to know me better. Perhaps he asks me my first name or he casually mentions his wife, and I react just as casually. If I remain interested, our relationship continues on a warm and friendly level. He likes me, I like him, we have work to do, and are able to resume it in a relaxed frame of mind.

It is not always that simple, however. I remember going to a man's room on call. He was exceedingly formal. The next time I worked for him, he greeted me with a cordial "Hello." The third time, he lightly placed his arm around my shoulder as he conducted me to a chair. He dictated several letters, then interrupted himself in the middle of a paragraph to ask how old I was. He began telling me about himself, his business, his travels.

At such a juncture, the balance becomes exquisitely delicate. Almost at will, a girl can tip the scales one way or the other. If she shows considerable interest, it signifies she finds her employer reasonably attractive. What develops may be more than a business relationship, depending on the susceptibility of both. On the other hand, a courteous withdrawal will cue any but the most persistent male into a strictly business arrangement once more.

I suspect a man hopes to breach the barricades if he offhandedly asks if I am married. If I say I am, he may remark, "Your husband is lucky. You're a beautiful woman." He may not mean it. He may only be making conversation. But he has been wondering about me. He recognizes we are of opposite sexes. If I say I am unmarried, the barrier is usually removed much more quickly than if I say I am married.

We are playing with fire. Every woman likes being liked. Even if she has no intention of going further, she toys with the idea mentally. How long before he reaches that certain point? What will she do then?

She will try to please. Should the client become offensive, she will avoid displaying the fact that she is shocked, indignant, or disgusted. She will invent techniques for eluding unpleasant advances without giving offense. Above all, she will never ridicule the customer; she will never laugh at him. Nothing so infuriates a man as that. He will drop a million dollars in a stock transaction without feeling like a fool, but he cannot stand to have his ego injured by a female, especially if she suggests he is something less than a real man.

Therefore, if he makes an unwelcome pass, a wise girl's manner suggests, "Gee! You're awfully nice. I would if I could, but this isn't the time or place." Or she undertakes a delaying action. She becomes the least bit arch, creating the impression that, after all, she has to play a little hard to get. Confronted by an importunate individual who must be helped to understand that there simply is no future for him, the girl may convey the impression that it is all her fault. He is the very essence of animal magnetism, but unfortunately she must deprive herself for good and sufficient reasons.

However she handles the situation, there are certain things she must never do. She must not draw back in disgust. She must not show contempt. If she does, she figuratively castrates the boss, and no man can abide that. She will never work for him again. In dire circumstances, a girl may become downright angry with the man. He will accept that as his due. That is not contempt. That is not implying he is not the masculine type—quite the reverse. He can resign himself to rejection but not to being unmanned.

It does happen, to be sure, that ardor builds up in a man and he becomes insistent. In that event, the public stenographer takes as much as she can, then runs out. She has nothing to lose. She would not care to work for him a second time. Actually, however, should he call for her again, and should she answer the summons, she probably need have no fear. She will almost certainly find the gentleman contrite and pliable, apologizing for his earlier behavior. Having been unmanned, he has no interest in this stenographer other than as a stenographer, which suits the girl very well.

I have rarely been given a really difficult time by a big businessman. But businessmen have disciplined themselves to be discreet; or else, by the time they have reached their high position in life, they are of an age and a degree of seasoning where the sex urge is not so compelling that they cannot wait for the appropriate time, place, and companion. Whatever their reasons, businessmen usually treat me as I want to be treated. In fact, they often treat me more generously than is called for by a business relationship, even when it remains just that.

For instance, shortly after I began my career I received a call to do some work for a visiting oil man. A white-jacketed valet admitted me to the sumptuous suite, got behind the bar, and asked what I would like to drink. I took it for granted that he had mistaken me for someone else who was expected about that hour. I tried to set him straight but he didn't hear me out. I asked for a highball, which he brought on a silver tray.

As I toyed with the drink, a huge man entered from an adjoining room and in a broad Texas drawl introduced himself as, let us say, Tom Sutton.

"Would you care for some hors d'oeuvres?" he asked.

I nodded weakly. The valet busied himself over a copper steam cart alongside the bar, presenting me with a heaping plate of delicacies. Mr. Sutton ordered bourbon and branch water and seated himself beside me on the couch.

"I think there's some . . ." I began.

"Lovely day, isn't it?" he said. "Wish ah'd flown in. Ah pilot mah own airplane, y'know."

"Really? Uh, Mr. Sutton, I'm afraid . . ."

"Call me Tom, honey! Ev'body does. Where you from, little lady?"

"Minnesota."

"That so! Ah reckon a pretty li'l thing like you is married, huh?"

"Look! There's some mistake. I'm not the person you expected. I'm the public stenographer you sent for."

"Shucks, honey, there's no mistake! Ah was expecting *you.*"

"But . . . all this. . . ."

"Oh, that! Why, honey, us Texans always treat secretaries that way. We like to relax first. We'll work better afterward."

He finished his bourbon and branch water and we settled

down to work. We kept at it all afternoon. Every few minutes another Texan came in, followed by thunderous greetings, back poundings, and orders for drinks. The telephone jangled and the radio howled, but Mr. Sutton could concentrate on dictation, engage in repartee with his friends, and catch the baseball scores on the radio all at the same time.

By six o'clock there were a dozen uproarious citizens of the Lone Star State in the suite. I was doing my best to take shorthand notes despite the bedlam, when Mr. Sutton pushed my notebook aside. "You can finish that later," he said. "Let's all go down to Perino's and have us some dinner." Perino's is a plush restaurant for gourmets where $100 buys you a good dinner, half of it spent for tips.

The Texans roared through the corridor, flirted outrageously with a couple of girls in the elevator on the way down, and steamed into the lobby. Mr. Sutton's liveried chauffeur escorted us to a gleaming white monster sparkling in the sunset, and we drove away. At the intersection we became a parade. Each Texan had his own snorting Cadillac, all of them glistening white except one, which was a sickly shade of orchid. Horns blowing, they careened through traffic, waving to each other and uttering rebel yells. I held onto the window strap and prayed for a traffic officer.

At a red light, I swallowed the lump in my throat which may have been my heart, and in a feeble attempt at insouciance, murmured, "My, this is a beautiful car."

"Like it?" Mr. Sutton drawled. "Ah just got it, but ah'm right tired of the color. Ah'm fixin' to buy me a green Continental tomorra."

I have worked for innumerable Texans, and they are a breed all their own, expansive, extravagant, hilarious, and in certain respects unfathomable. In all other ways extremely masculine, they adorn their fingers with immense rings, sport diamond necktie pins, and even wear diamond-studded belt buckles. They must have company. The prospect of spending an hour alone seems to terrify them. I have almost never seen a Texan except in a pack. Businessmen from the United States make a fetish of keeping business separate from pleasure. To the man from the Republic of

Texas business *is* a pleasure, and he takes his other pleasures along with it.

It took me a while to become accustomed to Texans' ways with money. Undoubtedly, there are those who know the value of a dollar, but this is not true of the Texans who come to the luxury hotels. Hundred-dollar bills are their common currency, with a dollar suitable only for a newspaper.

I took a letter from a Texan who was writing his wife that he purchased a watch for twenty-eight-fifty. I typed it $28.50. "Ah'm awful sorry, honey," he said. "Ah didn't mean twenty-eight dolluhs and fifty cents. Ah meant twenty-eight hundred and fifty dolluhs."

Texans work, play, think, and ranch big. I had a customer who lived in a place bearing the improbable name of Mule Shoe, Texas. His ranch occupied thousands of square miles in that state and overflowed into Oklahoma. He told me he had to get a half dozen weather reports daily, because it might be raining in one section of his property, snowing in a second, and be sunny and hot in a third.

The true Texan shows a vital interest in everyone, accidental acquaintance and lifelong friend. This is so natural with him that he takes for granted that everyone else is like him.

My telephone rang at 2 A.M. one morning. Since I am on 24-hour call, hotel operators give out my home phone number without question, and I therefore assumed that my services were urgently needed. I picked up the receiver. "Hello?"

"HELLO, HONEY!" The accent was unmistakably Texan. "This is Sam Bell. You remembuh me, don't you? You did some lettuhs for me 'long about three yeahs ago? You said ah was one of the nicest men you evuh worked for, remembuh?"

"Uh, why yes!"

"Well, honey, ah'm just passin' through, changin' planes at the airpo't. Ah'm just callin' to say ah sho' appreciated what you said. Good-bye, now!"

Well, I entered the hotel world because I wanted something "different."

But this world I work in is not really *my* world. I am in it but not of it. I actually live in two worlds, the real and the unreal. I lose myself in my clients, in the luxury world of the hotel; then I go back to my ordinary, real world of the small apartment dweller in Beverly Hills.

I am torn between the two. The unreal world appeals to me very much indeed, but what happens when it ends, as it must, every night? I have come home and cried because I couldn't help making comparisons, and I have felt unhappy not being a permanent resident of that other world. I would like to belong to that other world, not for the luxury, not for the wealth, but because it is a gay world for the most part, a heady, sophisticated world. When I am in it I feel exhilarated. When I am away from it I am depressed.

I suppose, sojourning daily in this exciting world, I have taken on some values that are not altogether realistic for me. A friend and I stopped in a drugstore for a quick bite. I was in the mood for a hamburger, yet reluctant to order it. Pointing to the item on the menu, I remarked, "It's 60¢. It can't be good meat; it's so cheap."

My friend brought me down to earth. "A sixty-cent hamburger is not so cheap. It's just that you're used to seeing it on the hotel menu for three times the price. The sixty-cent hamburger at this counter is probably as good as the one that sells in the hotel for about two dollars."

In earlier years, it was particularly difficult for me to work in the hotel because I had to transfer myself from one world to another every day. Now I realize that a public stenographer headquartered in a luxury hotel cannot expect to become a permanent, full-fledged member of the society that swirls about her. I have learned to live for the day, to get my pleasure by the minute. I enjoy the delightful company and stimulating experiences that come my way, while they last. Every minute has its value, one experience leads to another, and each experience is meaningful in itself. If I were doing the same work in a private office my existence would not be nearly as satisfying as it is. My job is the most exciting in the world. It demands a lot and can be very tiring, but it is also an emotional experience.

One of its fascinations is its uncertainty. The next moment is so unpredictable. I have been called out of bed at three in the morning to notarize a document. An underworld character ordered me to come to his garrisoned home late at night to prepare an affidavit. I typed letters 35,000 feet up in the sky in a Caravelle, before jets were in commercial use. I took dictation in a speeding car, swaying from side to side as we went around curves. I stayed at my notebook aboard an ocean liner riding through a hurricane. I went with clients at a moment's notice on business trips to New York, Paris, London, Zurich. A steady customer telephoned me from Mexico at dawn, to dictate an eight-hour report, gladly paying the toll, even for time out so I could stop for a sandwich.

A French count occupied a bungalow at the Beverly Hills Hotel for a week. An imposing gentleman given to dramatic gestures, he stalked about in white jungle shorts, swinging a gold-knobbed cane as if it were a saber. One day he summoned me. I found him standing erect as a flagstaff beneath a portrait of himself in military uniform complete with epaulets. As I entered, he marched to the patio, threw himself onto a chaise longue, and commanded, "Pour me some vermouth!"

He took a sip, arose, and snapped, "*Allons! Une lettre!*" He began dictating very rapidly in French.

"Please!" I interrupted. "I can't take shorthand in French!"

"Zen you are *stupide!* My secretary in Paree, she takes ze French shorthand!"

"But M'sieur, can she take shorthand in English?"

He let that pass with only a glare. Executing squads left and right and swishing his cane, he dictated in halting English. In the process, he wheeled about suddenly, almost colliding with a little table near a window. He glared at a portable radio on the table. Tapping it with his cane, he announced, "I bought thees at—what you call eet?—Threefty Drug Store, near ze Beeltmore Hotel. Eet does not work. You weel telephone ze managaire of ze store and have heem come get eet."

"But the Biltmore is downtown! The manager of the drugstore will tell you to bring it down yourself. He just won't understand your asking him to come for it. They don't do things like that here."

He stared at me icily. "Een Paree when ze Count telephone, ze managaire come and get eet! I am ze *Count*, no?"

He was the Count, yes. I telephoned the drugstore manager and informed him that the Count wanted him to pick up the radio, that it wasn't working. There were several seconds of complete silence at the other end. Then the manager assured me, with unnecessary vehemence, I thought, that he had sold thousands of radios to thousands of people and he had never, but never, received a crazy request such as this. And as for the Count—and here his voice rose almost to a soprano pitch—there was no such thing as a count under United States law, this was a democracy, thank God! And I could tell the Count, for the manager, that he could go straight to hell, where, he suggested, French nobility might be more appreciated.

I paraphrased this for the Count, who seized the telephone and bombarded the manager with what I took to be a very purple French. When he paused for breath, the manager got his say in, while the Count listened, his eyes flashing with indignation. He flushed, hissed through his teeth, but finally relinquished the receiver.

"Allons!" he said. "We shall continue deectation."

I didn't inquire, but it seemed that aristocracy had suffered a humiliating defeat. I finished taking shorthand and proceeded to my office. Because I had another big and very urgent job to complete, I asked a bellboy to deliver the Count's letters to his bungalow.

I had just completed the rush assignment in the late afternoon when my phone rang.

"Zees iz zee Count. I leave for ze airport. Weel you pleez accompany me? Zere are instructions about some letters I must geeve you."

We left the hotel in a rented limousine, driven by a hired chauffeur. The Count gave me his instructions, then leaned back, folded his arms, closed his eyes, and commanded: "Amuse me!"

"Uh? What shall I do?"

"Anyzing!"

All I could think of was a French ditty:

Sur le pont d'Avignon, l'on y danse, l'on y danse,
Sur le pont d'Avignon. . . .

As I was about to embark on the next verse, the Count winced and cried, "Enough! Enough eez enough!"

Since I didn't think my French was that bad, I could only assume my singing voice left something to be desired. Chagrined, I sank back in my seat. We didn't exchange another word all the way to International Airport.

The chauffeur alighted to help us out. The Count waved to a skycap with his cane. Our driver blocked his path to the luggage. The Count's eyebrows shot up. The chauffeur said, deferentially, that he wanted to be paid before releasing the bags. The Count informed him that the hotel livery service would take care of the matter. The driver didn't agree, pointing out, quite correctly, that once the guest checked out, the hotel could not put the charge on his bill.

The Frenchman screamed that he would call the French consul. The chauffeur called an American cop.

The policeman heard both sides out, then said that he lacked authority to arbitrate the dispute. However, if one of the contesting parties cared to make a formal complaint, he, the officer, would have no other option than to follow regulations and invite the three of us to the stationhouse, where proper adjudication could be made. The chauffeur insisted he *was* prepared to make such complaint. The Count calmed down, extracted several bills from his wallet and stiffly extended them in the general direction of the chauffeur. The officer sauntered away.

The skycap lifted the bags. My erstwhile employer turned to me, nodded curtly, said "*merci*" and "*au revoir*" and prepared to follow the skycap.

But just at that moment, I realized I hadn't been paid for my work. "Just a minute!" I called after him. "How about paying *me?*"

He waved airily. "I weel send you a check."

"Like hell you will!" the driver exclaimed, stepping in front of the Count. "You'll pay her now—*sir!*"

The nobleman wet his lips and glanced in the direction in which the policeman had gone.

"How much?" he asked.

I told him, making no attempt to comprehend his very special language as he handed me the cash.

Yes, it's a life of adventure. Anything may happen. I complete an interesting job. The telephone rings. "This is the Governor. Would it be convenient for you to come to my room right away, please?"

A new adventure begins.

Chapter 2

What it's like

A New York attorney once introduced me to gymnasium operator Vic Tanney with the remark, "This is the best stenographer in California. Of course," he added, "none of them is worth a damn."

If they weren't worth a damn they wouldn't be willing to act as private secretary, errand girl, seamstress, tourist guide, confidante, and marriage counselor all at the same time. These are only a few of the countless duties a public stenographer in a hotel is expected to perform, sometimes for pay, sometimes out of a spirit of charity. The customer is in an unfamiliar city. Where will he buy a gift for his wife? Are there any nice girls around to take out to dinner? (One customer bluntly inquired, "What's the woman situation out here?")

A girl need not be the best stenographer in her area in order to work in a hotel. Ordinary competence and accuracy will suffice. But if a girl becomes known for exceptional ability and familiarity with a wide range of secretarial functions, such as business contracts, court papers, affidavits, and the like, she imparts overall confidence. The client seeks her out, whether he is preparing a list of addresses or a complicated legal brief.

Too many of us visualize the hotel stenographer as she supposedly was a generation or more ago—drab, probably grayhaired, wearing "sensible" shoes—the old-fashioned skirt-and-shirtwaist type. At night, she went home to a small bachelor apartment, opened up a can of soup, washed out her underthings and went to bed, alone. The next day, she had nothing to look forward to except more typing and perhaps an overdue letter from a distant relative who still cared how she was getting along.

This is of course a crude stereotype even of the stenographer of yesteryear. It is even more untrue for today's girls. Those who enter public stenography are from young to youngish, some in their twenties. They generally live satisfying lives. They are no longer predominantly products of vocational-type business schools. Some hold college degrees and a few have done graduate work. As a class, they are intellectually curious, with a wide range of interests. They are aware of the world around them, alert to issues of the day.

Today's public stenographer can wear chic clothes. She uses the best hairdressers—every luxury hotel has exceptionally creative beauty salon operators. She enjoys the first-rate entertainment and the authoritative speakers who appear at social and civic affairs held in the establishment. She works for, and is in daily contact with, informed, attractive and scintillating men.

And the contemporary public stenographer can broaden her horizon by travel. Courtesies are extended her by regular patrons, some of whom control hotels and can commandeer front row seats for top shows, and tell the maitre d' of an exquisite restaurant that she should be treated with special care. Many a vacation trip has been made more exciting and less expensive for me by influential patrons.

How can the modern hotel stenographer fail to bubble over with *joie de vivre*, considering she is in daily communication with the world's most colorful personalities? My very first client was Prince David Mdivani, of the "marrying Mdivanis." He came in to ask what I charged to do a letter. I told him a dollar. "All that?" he asked.

My second customer was Tennessee Williams, who was then working on the script of *Cat on a Hot Tin Roof*. I was puzzled by his accent. I couldn't identify it. It was not middle western, southern, or British, but seemed a combination of the three. He told me he spent most of his time in the south of France, which may have something to do with his accent. He seemed a bit shy. There were a lot of bourbon bottles in his room. His manner was so gentle that I found it difficult to believe this was the playwright who put such lurid details into certain of his works.

It took me some time to familiarize myself with the history and genealogy of entertainment people, and I had my share of embarrassing moments in the process. Once while I was at Joanne Dru's house notarizing some papers, she introduced me to her daughter. Knowing that Miss Dru's husband was John Ireland, I remarked that the girl looked just like her father, Mr. Ireland.

"Oh," said Miss Dru, "but her father is Dick Haymes!"

When I was still at the Beverly Hills Hotel, Raymond Massey asked if I would come up to run off a copy of a handwritten script. When I arrived, he handed it to me, saying, "Would you mind reading it aloud first? I want to be sure you can make out my handwriting."

I took the script and, to conserve his time, read from it rapidly, without thinking of what I was reading.

"No, no!" Mr. Massey cried. "Not like that! Put more feeling into it! More feeling! Like this!"

He retrieved the script and began reading. The effect was magical. Suddenly Raymond Massey had become a young backwoodsman before my very eyes. My scalp tingled. I sat entranced as he enacted Abe Lincoln.

Jeff Hunter once threw himself into a role which had me serving as his leading lady. He was going to produce his own picture in Europe, and was working on the screenplay himself. Dictating it to me, he got carried away by the lines written for the hero, the part he would play. Pantomiming the action, his voice booming, he grabbed me by the shoulders as he came to a love scene, looked deep into my eyes, bent over, and kissed me passionately. Then, oblivious to my reaction, he resumed dictation, pacing about, occasionally clutching my shoulder or staring into my face as he lived the scene. I must say I enjoyed it.

During those early years in my career, I became more and more conscious of the limitless variability of the human personality. Some clients were stiff and formal to the point where they made me uncomfortable. Others were just the reverse. Once a man sent for me, sat me down, and abruptly asked, "How's your sex life?"

"What!" I said. "Is that why you called me here? To ask about my sex life?"

"Why, certainly!" he told me. "It *is* important, isn't it?"

Another client was even more direct. An otherwise very fastidious and dignified gentleman, he began dictating, stopped in the middle of a sentence, and announced, "I'd like to romance you!"

At first I was stunned and ready to take offense, but then I thought better of it. "Oh, your bark is worse than your bite!" I said, laughing. "If I agreed to your proposal, you'd cut and run!"

This pleased him for some reason, possibly because he knew what I said was true. I worked for him on a number of occasions after that, and although he never propositioned me again, he always chuckled about the rebuff I had given him.

It took me a while to understand that an individual might have some minor eccentricity and yet be highly successful in business or a profession. I had one client who collected sugar. When I opened a drawer in his dresser at his request to get some stationery, I discovered it was almost completely filled with neatly stacked cubes of sugar, the wrappers carrying names of restaurants from all parts of the country. When I showed my surprise, he told me I hadn't seen anything yet. He brought a suitcase out of the closet and opened it. There was nothing but sugar inside.

"Why do you carry so much with you?" I asked.

"I drink a lot of coffee," he said.

Another unusual patron was a dowager, a permanent resident in the hotel. Deeply attached to her Siamese cat, she talked to it as if it understood the language, and lavished upon it the care and affection one gives to a child. One day she telephoned me from her suite about some work, saying she would leave the door ajar for me. As I entered, she called from the bathroom, saying that she would be right out. The door was open and I saw her holding the cat on the toilet seat, coaxing it to move its bowels. She held it gently, regarded it lovingly, and the cat returned her loving gaze with Siamese hauteur. It did not struggle but instead accommodated its mistress as she urged, "Please hurry, dearest! I have a visitor."

Permanent guests had a variety of pets, one of the oddest of them owned by a large, fuzzy-haired, dark-complexioned man. The first time I was in his quarters I was startled to hear a sort of grunting. A moment later, I discovered the source—a large, fuzzy-haired, dark guinea pig. My client swept it up in his hands as it came to him, kissing and caressing it as he dictated to me. Grunting away, the animal snuggled against his chest, eyes closed, and, so help me, a beatific expression on its face—if it could be called a face.

I asked my client whether the beastie, by its grunts, was thanking him for the caresses.

"Oh, no!" he said. "He's talking to me."

"What's he saying?" I asked. "Do you understand him?"

"Oh yes! I understand him quite well. As a matter of fact, right now he's talking about you."

This was not spoken tongue-in-cheek. He was dead serious. I refrained from inquiring what the rodent said about me.

Another lesson in my freshman year at public stenography was that possession of wealth does not guarantee that the possessor will pay for services rendered. It is curious how many well-to-do people overlook their financial obligations. Before I had been in business very long I had considerable money due me from clients, some of which I have not received to this day.

I decided, in time, that I would simply have to get tough when the occasion demanded it. After performing certain services for the Rotary Club for several months, I realized I could not break even if I continued working at the agreed-upon rate. I asked the treasurer of the club for 80¢ additional each month. My request was denied. I insisted I needed 80¢ more if I was to continue doing the work. At last, realizing I would not back down, he informed me the matter would have to be taken up at a special board of directors meeting.

"In that case," I said, "you might as well make it a dollar more a month. I'm sure it isn't worthwhile calling a special meeting for just 80¢."

Hard-fisted executives understand hard-fisted employees. I got my dollar.

In 1958, Alan Jay Lerner, for whom I had done a lot of work, wired me to come to Paris where he was writing the script for *Gigi*. This interrupted my service at the Beverly Hills Hotel, and when I returned to California I established headquarters in the newly-constructed, glamorous Beverly Hilton.

Here, my office is in a corner of the lobby. It is really a nondescript cubicle that offers no privacy. People who walk by hardly realize it is an office. They stop to ask questions—how to get to the drug store, to the airlines office, which bar is open, where a certain function is being held. Sometimes they just want to talk, particularly in the evening.

The work I get includes everything imaginable, from writing letters and reports to typing travel itineraries, affidavits, job applications, and screenplays. I have done wills, love letters, poetry, and articles in many languages.

A very important part of my work entails my duties as a notary. Many people have an erroneous conception of what a notary public is and does. They know a document must be notarized but they don't know why. Actually, the service is for the client's protection.

People come to me with documents already signed, and I patiently explain that the signatures must be affixed in my presence, or I cannot attest to their validity. Some, believing a notary public is a lawyer, ask for advice on complicated legal matters. Usually, they are Europeans. On the Continent, a person who wants to become a notary—a full-time post over there—takes a rigid examination, containing many questions having to do with law. Therefore, when Europeans drop into my office for a notarization, they generally look startled when they discover a girl. They raise their eyebrows and exclaim, "*You're* the notary?"

I think notarization should be a more dignified procedure than it is. After all, many of the documents concerned are sworn statements of considerable importance. Consequently, in accordance with law, I demand identification before accepting a signature, even though affixed before me. Otherwise, how do I know John Jones is really John Jones? I sign my own name with a flourish, and affix the raised seal with due solemnity. All of this impresses the client, and makes me feel very official.

There is romance in notarizations. Every document has a story behind it, often involving courtship, marriage, tangled love affairs, and even declarations of love.

A bellman approached me recently, obviously a little embarrassed. "Would you notarize something for me, please?" he asked. "Confidentially, of course," he added. Timidly, he handed me a small piece of paper. It contained just three words: *I love you,* followed by his signature.

I affixed my notarization, maintaining a serious demeanor and showing no surprise.

A couple of weeks later, one of the cashiers, a lovely girl, asked if I would notarize something. She gave me a small piece of note paper. On it were the words *I love you, too.* It was addressed to the bellman who had brought me the earlier note.

Late one afternoon I received a call from a man, asking that I come out to a certain address to notarize a codicil to a will. A gentleman about 35 years old met me at the door and led me to a little alcove off the hall where sat an elderly lady, perhaps 75 years of age or more, talking to a caged parrot as if it were human. Introducing us, the man gave the lady's name, but did not inform me what relationship existed between the two of them, if any. He gave her a paper and placed a pen in her hand. I watched her sign, notarized the document, and departed.

About a year later while I was having coffee at the drugstore counter, a man came over and shoved a subpoena into my hand. It had to do with the codicil to the will I had notarized. I was forced to give a deposition. The aged woman, I learned, had died, leaving her estate, worth a fortune, to the young man. Her family contested the will, charging she was forced to sign. My part in the proceedings was to depose whether to my knowledge he had used force, which of course had to be answered in the negative. I do not know the full story, nor what happened prior to my part in it. Nor did I learn the final outcome. I hope justice was done.

Wills, of course, have stories behind them. A lady arrived at my office when I was with a client. Lighting a cigarette, she paced back and forth nervously, interrupting evey few minutes with, "How much longer?" She added the usual "I have to catch a plane," an assertion I have learned to accept with a grain of salt. It is a stock expression when a client wants immediate attention.

When I was able to deal with her, she sat down, drew a four-page will from her purse and, instructing me to use paper identical with that of the document, dictated from the will, but skipping about, omitting certain sections, and adding new ones. She then took the document I typed and tore the original into tiny pieces, retaining the carbon. She asked me to try to duplicate the signatures of witnesses on the remaining copies, but I declined, pointing out this would be forgery.

Curious as I was, I asked no questions, but the story came out nevertheless. The lady had made a will several years ago, leaving all of her money to friends, but leading her husband to believe he was the principal legatee. He became dubious, for reasons best known to both of them, and insisted on seeing the document. In a panic, she had her lawyer forward the papers and, in my office, prepared a spurious document which showed her husband as legatee. She would pass this off before him as the official will. The original, official document would be returned to her attorney, to be filed for probate upon her demise.

I wonder if it worked.

Wills remind me of the very old, white-haired gentleman

who came over to me at the office. "Please don't let this throw you," he said. "I want to dictate my obituary."

"Obituary?" I stammered. "Don't you mean your will?"

"No, I mean obituary."

He dictated slowly and carefully, announcing he had passed away. He left a blank space for the date of his passing, and his age upon demise. In traditional form, he mentioned his business enterprises and civic undertakings, and ended by listing his survivors.

When he finished he grinned at me. "Now!" he said. "That should satisfy my woman!"

Noting my perplexity, he explained, "My wife's been after me for ten years to write this, and I'm just now getting around to it. I hope it satisfies her."

I never did figure out that one.

My office is a way station for a continuous flow of people who are less concerned with secretarial work than with just sitting down and geting things off their chests. They discuss matters only a dear friend—or a public stenographer—would listen to.

A woman I had never seen before came to the office with a trifling job—a two-sentence letter she could have written by hand in about one minute. This was only an excuse to discuss a problem. Out of a clear sky, she asked, "Honey, do you think it would be terribly wrong to cheat on my husband?" He was a generous man, she told me, kind and thoughtful when he noticed her, but he was so completely absorbed in his work that he seldom knew she was around. A discreet affair would be beneficial to her morale. What did I think?

While giving me some letters, a wealthy New York widow remarked how lonely she was, that she would very much like to meet a nice, intelligent man who would escort her to dinner or a show. She did not say she was looking for a husband, but I was sure that was in her mind.

I told her I knew an intelligent, respectable widower who would like to meet a nice woman.

The lady exclaimed, "If you arrange for an introduction, and something comes of it, I'll treat you to a trip to Europe!"

This was an amazing coincidence. Jim, the widower, had promised me the very same thing if I introduced him to an attractive, intelligent woman whom he would marry.

I telephoned his office and learned he was spending a month in Oklahoma. Here was another coincidence, for the lady's next scheduled stop was Oklahoma. I telephoned Jim in Tulsa and introduced them by phone. They set a date to meet there.

I got two trips to Europe out of that. Jim and the lady were married.

I am sure by now you will agree that a public stenographer is never bored. If there still is some doubt, consider this incident:

A man dictated a lengthy letter about a battery-powered machine he had invented. He was attempting to get his correspondent to finance its production on a partnership basis. The contrivance had tremendous sales possibilities, he argued. Much gratification would result from its use. The "vicarious thrills" it could provide were incalculable. The "end result" would be truly satisfying.

Dictation completed, he asked what I thought of his machine. I said I really didn't know what it was, or what it did, aside from the fact that it was operated by batteries.

"Why," he said, "it's a sex machine, of course! I'm trying to introduce it to the country! Don't you think it will be sensationally successful?"

I still have no idea what a sex machine would be; no doubt it would be sensational. But whether it would be *sensationally* successful would, it seems to me, depend considerably on how marketable it was.

Chapter 3

This is my public

Among the basic essentials of public stenography are accuracy, speed, infinite patience, tact, tactlessness when required, a soupçon of madness, a sense of humor, friendliness, and—last but not least—a genuine interest in each and every client.

Because I am sincerely interested in my customers, I rarely forget a face. I do forget a name when I have seen a client only once before and a long time has elapsed before we meet again. In such instances, I pretend I remember, hedging until he clues me (I hope).

A gentleman for whom I had worked some time back but whose name I could not recall when I met him again invited me for cocktails after I completed the letters he gave me. I ordered Courvoisier cognac.

"Why don't you order Hennessy?" he asked. "It's much better."

"Frankly," I replied, "I can't tell the difference between one brand and another."

He was miffed. "But there definitely *is* a difference! Hennessy is the very best!"

"All right," I said. "I'll order Hennessy, if it makes a difference."

"It certainly does, and I'll tell you why." He pointed to a man at another table. "See that man over there? He's just another man. I'm Hennessy!" For generations his family had been making the cognac he recommended so highly.

I am often asked about differences among clients, whether, for instance, actors are more difficult to work with than politicians. I can't generalize about clients categorized by occupation, but I have no hesitancy in saying there is a difference between the sexes. As a rule, women are more picayune than men. They will pay a $500 room bill only after haggling over a fifteen-cent telephone charge.

I did a job for two daughters of J. P. Morgan. They paid me and had four cents change coming to them, which I didn't have. They waited in my office while I went to the cashier to exchange a nickel for five pennies. A man would have waived the four cents, if only because waiting for his change would have cost him more in lost time.

Women are fussy about the stationery the stenographer uses, while men show little concern over such detail. Females demand many corrections, even to the insertion of a comma; males write in the comma by hand. Women want service, here and now, clients with prior rights notwithstanding. Male patrons are usually willing to wait their turns. Consider two contrasting incidents:

A woman for whom I had worked in the hotel came to my office as I was typing a report at the dictation of a male customer, seated next to my desk. Ignoring him completely, and without so much as apologizing for the interruption, she held out a paper and asked, "Can you notarize this? I'm in an awful hurry!"

"No, madam!" I said. "I can't right now. This gentleman is in a hurry too. He has to catch a plane. I'll be glad to help you as soon as we're through."

She waited around, tapping her foot, a deep frown on her face. A dozen times she broke in to inquire, "Are you about ready, Miss?" When the gentleman angrily told her he needed just two more minutes, she shook her head in exasperation and walked away.

After my male patron left, I telephoned the lady. "I'm terribly sorry I couldn't take care of you earlier," I said. "I'm free now and I'll be glad to bring my notary seal to your room, so you won't have to come down."

"No," she drawled. "I don't feel up to it now. I'll come into your office tomorrow, or the day after."

As it happened, another guest had been forced to wait while I worked for the man who had to catch a plane. He telephoned from his room, informing me he would like to dictate a speech.

"I'm sorry, sir," I said. "I have several calls ahead of yours. I could get you another girl, if you're in a rush."

"No," he said. "There's time."

Now, having called the lady who couldn't wait but then could, I telephoned the patient guest, a Mr. Losh, as I understood the name. "I have one more job that came in before you called," I told him, "but if you're pressed for time, I'll see if I can arrange to do yours first."

"Oh, no! Thank you very much! That's very kind of you, but I'll wait. I would appreciate your coming up when you're through with that job, though."

At 4:30, I went to his suite, determined to work any length of time to make amends for keeping this considerate gentleman waiting all day for me. He admitted me, and I almost dropped my notebook. "Mr. Losh" was Senator Frank J. Lausche of Ohio.

To my consternation, I discovered that his speech was to be given that very evening, in a couple of hours. Wasting no time on apologies, I got right to work and, happily, produced the finished manuscript in time. Only then did I express my chagrin over the treatment I had accorded my famous client. "Why didn't you tell me you were a Senator?" I asked. "And that you needed the speech for tonight? I would have kept the others waiting."

A Senator was entitled to no special consideration, he replied, and meant it. He left for the dinner he was to address.

When he checked out early next morning, he left an envelope for me at the desk, containing a thank-you note and a tip.

Between the modest Senator Lausche and the importunate lady who needed a notary immediately, I vote for the Senator.

Another difference between male and female guests is that the former keep their rooms neater than the latter. A woman's dresser drawers are repositories for a conglomeration of anything and everything, thrust into one place indiscriminately—gloves, nail polish, stockings, bills, lipsticks, and last month's *Vogue* magazine. A man usually keeps his shirts in one place, his ties in another, and you will rarely find his socks with his unanswered mail. This is significant, because the person whose room shows good organization is likely to be well organized in dictation. He does not hem, haw, and stumble, retrace his steps, and move forward again.

That is important to a stenographer, although organization, I know, sometimes becomes a fetish.

I have a regular client who checks in, unpacks, places everything where he wants it, and writes careful notes to himself recording which drawer of what dresser contains underwear, which pajamas. He sets up a schedule for everything he will do while in Beverly Hills, including what time he will have breakfast, lunch and dinner each day, when he will—well, let's forget that—and when he will get a haircut. I am not inventing when I say that I saw an entry in his log reading, "12:00—Pray for Mother."

He thinks in outlines and speaks that way even in ordinary conversation. Once he told me, "Young lady, our program for today is (a) we work until noon; (b) have lunch in the room; (c) get back to work at 1:30 and (d) finish at 5, because (e) I have to shave and get out in time to meet my daughter's fiancé at the Brown Derby at 6:30."

I have it on good authority that he makes love by the clock, terminating precisely in time to meet his next (business) engagement. According to my informant, "He'll stop in the middle of an embrace to stay on schedule!"

If I had to work with females exclusively, I doubt whether I would remain in this business. Charming as many women are, it is easier to establish rapport with a man, all other things being equal. As we begin to work, I look for clues to his personality.

I can always judge a man by his shoes. The best dressed men wear black shoes. For some reason, advertising executives invariably prefer brown. When a client wears shoes built for comfort rather than smart appearance, I know he is not trying to impress people. If he wears rounded toes, the same inference can be made. Professional men and writers are prone to wearing non-dressy shoes that accent comfort. Businessmen rarely do.

Jewelry is revealing too. When I take dictation, my eyes are usually on a level with a man's hands. I notice his wrist watch. I have a theory about watches. The gentleman who wears a conservative, conventional timepiece is probably conservative and conventional himself. The individualist, on the other hand, affects a distinctive watch, unusually large or small, square or oblong, with diamonds set into the numerals, or the face engraved with the owner's name.

I have another theory—this one about the man who wears a large diamond ring on his little finger. I don't know why it must be that finger, but it seems important, in my hypothesis. I figure he is a show-off. I have the same notion about people who put monograms on everything. I worked for a movie executive who had his initials on his shirt, belt, socks, cuff links and tie pin, all of which he wore at the same time. Even his suspenders were monogrammed. Once when he unpacked his laundry while I was in his room, I noticed that even the fly of his shorts carried his initials.

There was a Samoan chief in the hotel whose loose garb revealed he was emblazoned on the chest and both arms with explicit depictions of love in bloom. When I remarked on his visible tattoos, he broke into a toothy leer, rolled his eyes until only the whites showed, and informed me I hadn't seen anything yet. He was tattooed all over.

"*All* over?" I asked.

"*ALL* over," he assured me, and said he would prove it— when I went to Bora Bora with him. He'd been studying me and had decided to add me to his inventory of wives.

He could not understand my declination of the honor. Checking out, he notified me that the invitation remained open. Any time I wanted to see *all* his tattoos, I could set sail for Bora Bora.

It is helpful to find a customer's Achilles' heel as we begin our working relationship. Once it is located, rapport can be established. Perhaps a man is not sure of himself, or knots his tie carelessly, or wears too much jewelry. Perhaps he has a fondness for yachting, tough crossword puzzles or easy conquests. I am not looking for his weakness but for his vulnerability, and they are not necessarily the same. When I understand his particular likes and dislikes, we can communicate better. If he enjoys discussing foreign affairs, so do I. If he savors gourmet foods, I know the best restaurants. If he is an art fancier, I can direct him to the galleries.

A man's speech tells me a lot. If he dictates with a great show of confidence, dramatically, with generous gestures and exaggerated inflections, I surmise he is an egoist. If, additionally, he will not permit me to correct his spelling or punctuation, I know darn well he is. If a man slouches in his chair, dictates diffidently, uses incorrect grammar and is grateful when I correct it, he is a self-effacing individual, whom I appreciate every bit as much as the egoist. He will be easy to work for, will not demand perfection in me nor claim it in himself.

Between these two types is the average, nondescript man whose face I will not remember. He leaves little impression. He comes in, gets his work done, pays his bill, and gets out. If I should run into him again, I might wonder where I had seen his face before, but probably would not immediately recall that I once worked for him.

Clients have their individual personalities in dictation, and a stenographer needs to adjust to these quickly. Some dictate a mile a minute, spewing words like machine gun bullets, pausing not at all to indicate commas, periods or paragraphing. Others think as they speak, enunciate slowly and reflectively, and, having a mental image of what they are saying, dictate where they "see" punctuation and paragraphing. A Swiss businessman had me puzzled the first time I worked for him. He dictated, "The company informs me it chip chip does not at this time chip chip anticipate chip chip further price revisions chip chip." When he said "chip chip" he jerked his forefinger downward two times. It took a few minutes for me to realize that "chip chip" meant quotation marks.

Dictation has ethnic touches, too. Foreigners end a communication to a business associate with a remark such as "Please remember me to your charming wife Marietta." Natives of the United States eschew such amenities.

Although American businessmen rarely mention their wives to me, they do speak of their secretaries, usually in most complimentary terms. They praise their efficiency, their readiness to work at all hours, their ability to anticipate what the boss wants before he mentions it. First-rate secretaries are indeed "office wives" in the best meaning of that term. I can understand why the legal mates of businessmen are sometimes jealous of "office wives." A man's relationship with his secretary is a very special thing, extremely important to him, probably more than he realizes. This is the case even though the relationship is quite innocent of sexual overtones in the me-man, you-woman sense.

Since private secretaries are so indispensable, why don't more businessmen take them along on their trips? Because wives would resent it. And people the traveling man calls on would be shocked or jealous.

If the traveler rarely takes his secretary with him, neither does he bring his wife. If he did, his opposite number in the business negotiation might find the lady charming or as unexciting as cottage cheese, but either way, he would resent her because she might affect the negotiations, directly or indirectly. If she sat in the hotel room, boredom written all over her face as the men talked, this would put a damper on the meeting. If she got into the discussion herself, she might take over and show herself to be a tougher bargainer than her mate.

There is another possibility. The local man may deliberately set out to charm the wife. He may so seduce her with his blandishments that she unconsciously sides with him in the negotiations at hand, subtly influencing her husband in that direction. Her spouse is not going to take that chance.

There are other hazards. Suppose the local folks, Mr. and Mrs. Jones, invite the visitors, Mr. and Mrs. Smith, to dinner. Suppose Mrs. Jones takes a dislike to Mrs. Smith, or vice versa. Business negotiations will suffer. Or suppose Mrs. Smith shows up in a Paris creation, bedecked with magnificent jewelry, wearing a fur that has everyone within eyesight turning to admire. If Mrs. Jones cannot boast similar treasures, she is going to feel this affront deep down in her viscera. She will not forgive Mrs. Smith. Next day she will tell her husband "that woman" is abysmally dull, a vulgar slob, and obviously very stupid. Mr. Smith must be just as bad, or why would he shackle himself to such a hag? Does Mr. Jones really intend to do business with him?

It doesn't always work out that way, but Mr. Smith has heard enough stories to convince himself he should not chance it. So Mr. Smith comes to town alone. He needs a stenographer. Curiously, he sometimes finds it embarrassing to ask her to work in his room, and when he does, he apologizes, explains he would come to her office, but because he expects important telephone calls he must remain in his room to receive them. Frequently, when I arrive at a man's room, I find the door ajar. The client believes this is required and is self-conscious about the implication. The open door is to assure me he will be strictly business. When I take it upon myself to close it, this puts him at ease; he can concentrate better now.

Incidentally, I do not close it as I come in. I evaluate the situation first. I don't want my customer getting the wrong idea. I wait an appropriate length of time, then ask whether he would mind if I close the door, so it will be quieter. He not only approves, but usually shuts it himself.

Seating arrangement is another source of uncertainty. The client rarely tells me where to sit. He asks where I would be most comfortable. He may wave vaguely toward an armchair. Actually, in small rooms, the bed is the most comfortable place to take dictation, but no man is going to suggest that. If I casually perch myself on it without invitation, that sets everything straight. My customer scurries about for pillows to serve as a back rest.

Although some male travelers are self-conscious about asking a stenographer to come to their rooms, there are notable exceptions. Once I buzzed the most expensive suite in the house in answer to a call and was admitted by a tall man who, without so much as looking at me, pointed to a smaller chap seated at a desk. "My friend and I are alone tonight," he said. "Can you dig up a girl friend for a foursome?"

I sat down, opened my notebook to cover my surprise. "This is so sudden!" I said. "You haven't given me a chance to get acquainted with you."

"Well," he said, "you know us now. Shall I order dinner sent up?"

"You just want a date for dinner?"

"Well, we can see. *Que sera, sera.*"

The approach was too coarse. I told the men I was available for work, but that this did not signify I would accept a date merely upon request. "I wouldn't go out with just anyone," I said.

"Well, we're not just anyone!"

I was annoyed, but to be diplomatic I pleaded fatigue. The tall man said he and his companion were knocked out too, so we would make a congenial group.

I tried another expedient. The real reason for my reluctance, I said, was that I knew the management placed detectives, posing as guests, in hotel rooms to test employees' morals. "For all I know," I said, "you may be detectives. I can't afford to take a chance. In fact, to protect my job, I should report you. Just in case you are officers."

They exchanged glances. "We really sent for you to take a letter," one said. "Forget the rest."

I took the letter, typed it downstairs, and sent it up with a bellboy. They didn't offer him dinner. They didn't even tip him.

It is not that I object to socializing with clients. As a matter of fact, I have gotten deeply involved with one or two. But I am not available on call. I will have a drink or dinner with a man if I am in the mood and have known him long enough to be sure I have a choice—that I can accept or not and either way it will be all right. I enjoy stimulating people. I like fun as much as the next person, but I must call the shots.

I set few limits on the services I will render, many at no cost to my client. I will sew on a button, procure hard-to-get theatre tickets, even compose romantic prose upon request.

A very embarrassed elderly man approached my desk. "Miss, could you help me with a letter?"

"What kind of letter?"

"Well, it's a sort of unusual letter. Sort of a love letter."

"Hmm! That *is* unusual. I don't often get requests like that. Haven't you ever written one before?"

"Oh, yes! Many times. To this girl. But I've run out of ideas."

"Where did you get your ideas in the past?"

"In the public library."

Once a week he consulted a book of classic love letters, copied Abe Lincoln's passionate outpourings to Ann Rutledge. But he had run out of these and, his supply exhausted, had turned to me.

I inserted a sheet of paper in the typewriter. "Give me an idea what I should tell her."

"Oh, you know! That I love her and miss her and would like to hold her in my arms again, and maybe I'll see her soon."

I typed just that. Its simplicity and sincerity would please her more than flowery phrases.

A well-meant gesture backfired on me once. The man scheduled to be keynote speaker at a convention of gynecologists at the Beverly Hilton wired he would be unable to make it and was flying in a recording of his speech. The chairman of the evening, for whom I had done no work at all, asked if he might borrow my tape recorder. I let him take it, forgetting to remove a reel on which a client had dictated a speech he was to make before his own business colleagues. In his anxiety, the chairman of the gynecological meeting also forgot something. Instead of replacing my reel with the one carrying the other address, he played mine. And so it was that the convention delegates, assembled to hear a learned lecture on "Biological Impediments to Fertility," sat bemused as the amplifier gave out with a dynamic sales pitch for Triple Q Fertilizer.

I firmly believe that a public stenographer should say yes whenever possible. Don't misunderstand me. I mean she should accept the smallest job, even though it will pay little. You never know what may develop out of a call. Some of my most lucrative work has stemmed from a single notarization or a half-page letter. Besides, adventure is always around the corner with any telephone call or when someone stops at my desk.

It might be an adventure of the spirit, lasting only a few brief moments, but remaining with me forever. I shall never forget the day I heard a quiet, modest voice say, over the telephone, "This is Dr. Tom Dooley. Can you come up to my room, please?" I was about to meet one of the most magnetic, outstanding persons I have ever encountered. Dr. Dooley had dedicated his life to curing the sick in the tiny Asiatic country of Laos. Though he knew he was dying of cancer, he continued his work in the clinic he had established there, with little thought for himself. He occasionally returned to the United States for fund-raising purposes.

I had heard a great deal about this idealistic, spiritual man who had so much to give, and gave it without stint. Delighted at the opportunity to meet him, I came to his suite at once. When I caught sight of him, on a couch, my first thought was, "He's so much younger than I expected." He was painfully thin and looked tired, but was handsome nevertheless; his deep-set, dark-blue eyes were unbelievably piercing. And everything about him—his posture, his gestures, his most casual word—had an intensity that struck me with terrific impact.

First he asked my name. I detected an Irish influence in his accent. Then we shook hands and he showed me a small black address book lying on the coffee table. A party was being given in his honor, and he had to prepare a list of people he would like to invite. He asked me to go through the book and type out the names and addresses he had checked.

When I brought him the list, he thanked me very politely,

and said he wanted to dictate some thank-you notes to several people who had made contributions to his clinic. Even as he dictated, that intensity came through.

Later, I was to read articles about Dr. Dooley that were not altogether flattering, about his ego, his relentlessness, and other seemingly unsympathetic traits. If he had such characteristics, they certainly didn't come through to me. All I could think of in the short time I was with him was that he was so young to be so dedicated. I told him this and he was very pleased.

I asked if he would miss the modern world, the comforts of California and New York, when he returned to Laos. Would he regret leaving the many friends he had in this country?

"Yes," he said, "but the overall is most important. The poor people of Laos are my people; my heart sings when I am with them. I want to help them and I'm anxious to get back to them."

That was all I saw of him. Sometime after our meeting, I was with a writer for *Cosmopolitan* magazine, to whom I suggested that Dr. Dooley would make a wonderful subject for a magazine article. She agreed, and I wrote him, asking if he would be interested in giving an interview to the Cosmopolitan writer. He replied that I should contact his brother, who was in charge of interviews. Unfortunately Dr. Dooley died shortly thereafter.

I am very glad I said yes when Dr. Dooley sent for me. There was another time when I said yes, but only because I didn't dare say no.

I received a call from a soft-spoken man who inquired if I was a notary public and, if so, did I come to private homes to render service. When I replied affirmatively, he said, "Fine! I'm Mickey Cohen. Will you please come to my apartment?" He gave the address.

I swallowed hard. Mickey Cohen was an underworld figure, one of the most notorious in California. Reputedly, he controlled a gambling empire and other illicit enterprises. He was supposed to be a man who flew into towering rages, tearing people and furniture apart. What terrified me even more was that on several occasions mobsters caught up with Mickey, intending to plug him full of holes, only to kill and maim innocent bystanders who happened to be around, while Cohen got away unscathed. I was not eager to be an innocent bystander.

Hoping to get out of it, I mentioned that it was past 6 P.M. and that I charged higher rates for overtime.

He said, "That's just fine. Come ahead."

I tried another tack. I claimed I didn't have a car. Mr. Cohen said he would send someone to pick me up. Visualizing myself in an armored vehicle alongside a member of Mickey Cohen's set, I said I had to make arrangements to postpone other scheduled work, after which I would call Mr. Cohen back. I telephoned the chief operator at the hotel and told her where I was going, on command. That was in case I failed to return. Then I called Mr. Cohen, informing him I borrowed a car and would arrive shortly.

I drove to the Del Capri apartment hotel in nearby Westwood, and telephoned from the lobby to announce my arrival. Mr. Cohen informed me he was sending someone down to escort me up. A handsome, dark-haired fellow arrived, gave me a comprehensive once-over, and bade me enter the elevator.

Mr. Cohen was dressed in pajamas bearing his monogram on the pocket when he opened the door of his apartment. He was tiny, stubby, quiet-spoken, with a sort of questioning look on his perky, heavy-jowled face. Four men lolling about on the couch and easy chairs of the living room stared glumly at me. Mickey immediately deserted me to attend to his beloved pet, Mickey, Jr., a fierce-looking bulldog. I have seen cartoons depicting dogs that resemble their owners, and I assure you this is altogether possible. When the human Mickey noticed I was afraid of the bulldog, he told me that despite his sullen expression, Junior was docile. He had been trained in a special school. No matter what happened, he would not bite, except upon one provocation. Let anyone utter the word "Parker," and the dog would leap to the attack. William Parker was Chief of Police of Los Angeles. He and Mr. Cohen enjoyed a cordial distaste for each other.

Mickey conducted me to the bedroom. I supposed he wanted privacy, but I felt very ill at ease. He showed me the documents to be notarized. I told him the form in which they were drawn up for signature was incorrect, and suggested I use a typewriter in the manager's office downstairs to make changes. Unwilling to entrust the papers to my exclusive care, he motioned to one of his men to go along with me.

I amended the papers and returned to the apartment. Mickey signed them and I notarized them. He did not ask what my fee was, but instead placed $6 in my hand. Perhaps he considered that amount generous. Actually, I normally charged $10 for such a job during regular working hours, when travel was required. But I had no intention whatever of so informing Mr. Michael Cohen. I thanked him for the $6 and got out of there.

I saw Mickey the next day, when he happened to be in the hotel. He stopped at my desk, a surprising courtesy, it seemed to me. I mentioned I had read an article about him in a magazine. It was far from complimentary, and I was a little reluctant to give details, even though he pressed me for them. When I did repeat some of the statements, referring to him as a tough mug, a mad little thug, he puffed up like a pouter pigeon. I think he would have been unhappy had he been pictured as a gentler soul.

He gave me his business card, carrying the address of the Carousel, an ice cream parlor in Brentwood. "Here, Miss," he said, "drop in any time and have a soda." To authenticate the card, he wrote on the back: "Michael Cohen."

Mickey Cohen and ice cream sodas just didn't seem to go together, but one never knows. At any rate, Michael Cohen's name no longer makes me tremble. I am glad, today, that I didn't say no when he telephoned. Meeting him was worth the trip.

Because I derive satisfaction from even a frightening experience doesn't mean I'm a Pollyanna. I have pet peeves, things about customers I don't like.

I don't like smelly cigars. When a client with one in his mouth asks if I mind cigar smoke, I say yes.

I don't like a man who wears shirts so tight that the buttons pop off, exposing his stomach. He wears expensive suits; his nails are manicured; he can afford a shirt that fits.

I know it is unreasonable, but I don't like clients to borrow my pen. It is precisely broken in for my stenography. The least bit of unusual pressure might spoil it for me. And too often a borrower walks away, forgetting to return it.

Another thing that annoys me is the customer who is in an awful rush. I must hurry, hurry, hurry! He must have the letter by such and such an hour and minute. This keys me up, makes me tense, and yet when the letter is ready and I call the customer, what do you know? He isn't in his room. He left word he would be gone until midnight. I'll know better next time, I tell myself. But next time never comes. It seems that most of my work has to be done in a hurry, with someone standing over me, waiting to grab it, hot off the typewriter.

I am annoyed by the customer who goes on and on about price. It is a habit with some. I have customers who demand a lower price no matter what I quote. They enjoy making a bargain. For these people, I have learned to hike my regular price up, after which I allow myself to be argued into a lower one, which is actually what I meant to charge in the first place. I get my accustomed fee and my client is happy.

I know an elderly man who is rich but constitutionally unable to give up a dime without a struggle. He gave me a big argument when I charged him a half dollar to notarize a paper. Oh, he cried, he could get it done at the bank for a quarter. There was no use arguing over such a trifling sum, so I said, all right, I'd accept the quarter and let's forget about it.

He paid, and as he left I sighed to a friend standing nearby, "Gee! I sure hate to work today." I didn't have the parsimonious customer in mind when I said that, but he may have assumed that I did. He caught the remark as he was walking away, turned back, and told me, "See? If you had married a rich man, you wouldn't have had to work."

I was about to make a sharp retort, but my friend got hers in first, remarking she would rather be married to a nice man than to a rich man.

That stung him. "But a rich man can be nice, too!" he declared. "And it's just as easy to marry a nice rich man as a nice poor one!" With that he plunked down 25¢ more on the desk and walked away.

My pet peeves are counterbalanced by pet likes. Above everything else, I like the client who treats me as an equal, who shows respect for my judgment, who makes me feel I have helped him and contributed a service he needed for which he is grateful. Some customers say "Thank you" so automatically it doesn't mean anything, doesn't sound sincere. Others say *"Thank you!"* and I know they mean it, and it makes me feel very good.

The greatest rewards are the friendships I develop. And the freedom that comes with a job that has no hours. I am answerable to no boss. I can run off somewhere for a month, leaving a replacement to handle the work. If I want to do something I can do it. My chosen career makes that possible, within reason.

Chapter 4

The society
of employees

A young lady registered at the hotel, presumably to stay a day
or two, but a week passed and her bill became inordinately large,
so the credit manager asked her to settle her account up to that
date.

When the guest did not settle the account, the manager called
her again. She said she expected a check in the mail, that the
hotel would have to wait until it arrived. She stayed several more
days, then came down to the lobby to check out. Presenting a
good-sized check drawn to her by a gentleman, she asked the
cashier to deduct what she owed and give her the balance in cash.
The cashier referred her to the manager, who explained that inasmuch as she had not established credit in advance, and this
was a two-party check and he did not know the man who wrote
it, he could not honor it.

The young lady was very annoyed. The credit standing of

her friend was perfectly good, she said, and she would inform him how rudely she was treated. The manager insisted, nevertheless, that the bill be paid in cash.

She left, to return a couple of hours later, accompanied by a man lugging two large canvas sacks. He heaved them onto the cashier's counter and announced, "This lady is checking out. She owes $437.02. There's $500 in here. I'll wait for the balance, but I'm in a bit of a hurry."

The cashier opened one of the sacks and poured out a flood of nickels and dimes. The man had taken the trouble to go to a bank and get $500 worth of small coins, loose, mind you, not in rolls. The cashier was furious, but there was nothing she could do except to start counting. Soon there was a long line of fretful guests at her window, waiting to check out. The manager came to find out what was holding up the line, and when informed of the situation he asked another cashier to help count the loose change. He remained beside the two of them, grimly observing the proceeding. It took a long time to complete the transaction. The cashier finally pushed the left-over coins toward the waiting man, who snapped, "Maybe next time you'll know better!" Triumphantly, he and his girl friend stalked away.

The cashier had to take the next day off, to rest.

In any first-class hotel, personnel are trained to take all sorts of problems in stride. They will go to almost any lengths to keep a guest satisfied and encourage him to come back. Rare is the issue they cannot resolve, if only by a mutually acceptable compromise.

There is that rare exception, though. A group of Englishmen were having dinner in the hotel dining room. When the waiter presented the check to one of the guests, that gentleman pointed to a figure at the bottom and inquired, "What's this for?"

"State sales tax, sir," the waiter said. "We turn it in to the government."

"But we're not residents of California. We're not even citizens of the United States. You can't tax British subjects, y'know."

The waiter explained that the hotel was obligated by law to charge the tax. The diner, abetted by his fellow Britons, insisted that he was not concerned with California law, that he didn't vote here, that he was a citizen of another sovereign nation, and that forcing him to pay a California sales tax would be tantamount to taxation without representation. Damned if he would be taxed by a foreign nation.

The waiter appealed to the head waiter. He sent the case up on appeal to the manager, who ruled that the tax had to be paid. It was, but only after police were summoned.

When a guest precipitates a ticklish situation, invisible machinery begins whirring. First, second, and third lines of defense are deployed. A dozen staff members are on notice to stand by and be prepared to settle the difficulty as expeditiously and painlessly as possible. They are charged with satisfying the patron, if this is at all within reason. But the fact that they do so as representatives of the hotel, not the guest, gives them a feeling of unity.

And this is the primary source of the *esprit de corps* which exists to a greater or lesser degree among personnel. The hotel world consists of two separate societies, one of staff, the other of guests. The first society serves the second, but at the same time it must safeguard the interests of the establishment.

Staff societies are ruled by a government which differs only according to size and type of hostelry. What I will describe is a fairly typical pattern in the larger organizations.

The general manager, sometimes called managing director, is chief of state. His immediate aides usually include a resident manager, a reservation manager, and one in charge of credit. A banquet manager books and arranges private luncheons, dinners, and other affairs run by clubs and civic and social organizations.

Other managers are assigned supervision of the auditing department and the food and beverage department, which keep tabs on inventories. The bell captain, in charge of the bellboys, reports to a manager, as do desk clerks.

Desk clerks are an intriguing lot. Mostly males in the lower age brackets, they accept their modestly compensated posts because they like white collar work which permits them to wear nice clothes and deal with interesting people.

A crucial functionary in any hotel is the executive chef, or head chef, as he is sometimes referred to. Nominally subject to the authority of the manager, he is fiercely proud of his profession and guards his prerogatives zealously. He and he alone commands the small army in the kitchen. Only he decides what will be on the menu. He does defer to the banquet manager when the bill of fare for a private banquet is planned, but that's as far as it goes.

The lord of the kitchen has earned his role of authority. The fact that he reigns in a luxury establishment proves he is a superb, not merely an excellent, chef. He thinks, breathes, lives and dreams the life of his profession. Once when I was in the kitchen, the chef came on duty, remarking on the storm outside.

"Is it raining hard?" I asked.

"Medium to rare," he answered absently.

All the chefs I know are foreign-born and have worked in distinguished hostelries all over the world. They are highly temperamental. I have known them to throw up their hands when something upsets them, slam their chef's hats to the floor, and go home in the middle of the working day. And why not, they ask? A man must be given his head and have his way as he lovingly prepares a special order of *Pigeon en Cocotte Petits-Pois* or *Troncon de Turbot Grille Bearnaise.*

Your genius chef knows that no one can concoct an exotic dish as exquisitely as he. My friend Louis told me that when he was forced to eat outside his own hotel kitchen he carried a bag of spices with him and flavored the dishes he ordered to his own taste. I conjured up an image of this roly-poly man with the dark mustache, who hails from Marseilles, coming into a proud French restaurant, setting up his cartons of spices on the table, ordering dinner, sampling it, suppressing a shudder and proceeding to season it as it absolutely must be seasoned to be edible.

What does the waiter think? If he reports the insult to his own chef, will that excitable artist grab the nearest meat cleaver and storm in to redress the grievous wrong done to him?

Under the chefs are sous-chefs, his subordinates. The pastry chef is in a department of his own, and can be as temperamental as the monarch of the kitchen. Pierre, for instance, is as sensitive as a matinee idol upstaged by the ingenue. Strikingly handsome, the light-haired Frenchman designs cakes that belong in a museum of fine arts. He is as mercurial as quicksilver. I have seen him melancholy, gay, boorish, genial, and sullen, all in an hour. In a sentimental mood he is as sweet as his patisserie, in anger as awe-inspiring as the Alps.

Pierre need only glance at a woman and her knees wobble. He has been married three times, and two of his wives attempted suicide when he broke up with them. His last mate was a Hungarian girl whom he met in South America—hotel folk get around—and she slashed her wrists when his ardor cooled. She survived, but the shock forced a firm resolution on Pierre. Never, he told me, would he go out with European women again. They were too emotional.

Another pastry artist, Francois, came from the South of France. At age seventy, he had a forty-year-old wife and a mistress of eighteen, both so jealous of his attentions you would have thought he was being courted by Miss Universe. Francois was a virtuoso in more than one line. His pastry gun could transform the top of a layer cake into a flower garden of riotous colors. For a royal couple visiting this country shortly after their marriage, he spun out the intricate curlecues of an Arabic love poem atop a cake compounded of ingredients native to the land of the guests he was honoring.

I once called him at home for help in translating a passage in French. Francois was gracious and very helpful, but the next day he stopped in my office and asked me please, *please* not to telephone him at home again. His wife became very suspicious when he switched from English to French in our conversation. She didn't understand French.

The chef commands only the kitchen personnel, not waiters. They report to their own manager. Waiters rank themselves above dishwashers and busboys, who are at the bottom of the prestige ladder of the hotel class system.

The Beverly Hilton busboys are almost exclusively foreign, most of them coming from Spanish-speaking countries, although one, a most unusual gentleman, is Russian. A health food addict, he drinks Rose Hips tea from Yugoslavia, which he claims is good for just about anything that ails a person.

Once, he noticed I looked tired. "What bothers you?" he 'asked.

"I'm not feeling very well."

"Why don't you get yourself some leeches? They'll suck out the bad blood. I'll bring you some. I sell them."

Proceeding along the hierarchy of employees from lobby and kitchen to the upper floors, the housekeeper is an important figure in hotel government. She manages chambermaids and housemen, the former taking care of guest rooms, the latter handling general maintenance such as cleaning corridors and polishing bannisters.

Carrying the responsibility she does, a housekeeper wants her status and authority recognized. I learned this the hard way. I happened to look up from the typewriter, in my office, when I saw a houseman collapse on the lobby floor, the victim of a heart attack. Shaking with fright, I telephoned the house physician, met him when he arrived, and conducted him to the already dead man stretched out on the floor. The housekeeper was now standing over him, looking very annoyed. Turning to me, her voice frigid, she said, "This is my department! You should have contacted me first. I will handle this!"

The maids at the Beverly Hilton are foreign born and bring their customs with them. Walking through a corridor, I heard a girl, recently arrived from the French provinces, call to a houseman, "Hey, Jacques! Bring me a box! I want to make pipi!" Where she formerly lived, either there are no toilets, or they are of the portable variety. The houseman, who must have known about Old World sanitation, shrugged and walked on. The maid muttered to herself and hurried down the hall.

Rarely seen by the guest, but essential to his welfare, is that segment of employee society housed in the telephone room. The operators are the lifeline of the plant. All the crises, all the dramas of joy and tragedy, flow through the switchboard. The operator is first to hear when a guest needs a doctor. She receives the urgent call for police. Anything can happen, the telephone is the first thing a person in trouble reaches for, and the operator acts accordingly. A garbled message transmitted to a guest may cost him a business deal. An impatient word to an outside caller can render a traveler's stay useless. Many a guest has checked out of a hotel never to return because he failed to receive a message, had to wait too long to get telephone service, or didn't like the attitude of the operator.

She helps set the tone of the place. A warm "Good morning, Mr. Smith" makes him feel welcome—she took the trouble to address him by name. Many hotels now ask operators to follow this practice when operating the switchboard.

Because of my work, the operator is of utmost importance to me. Since I am away from my desk so much, taking dictation in various parts of the hotel, I must depend upon the switchboard girls to handle calls that come in for me. They transmit messages, know where I will be when I leave my office, and get in touch with me if necessary. Without the switchboard, I couldn't stay in business.

Where, in the small hotel, *esprit de corps* stems from intimate face-to-face associations and is reflected by a feeling of camaraderie among all employees as a group, the good feeling that develops in larger plants is more likely to be found in individual cliques, the membership of which is determined by function and rank. Waiters are a prime example. A waiter is a waiter, hence a brother. Some serve in hotel dining rooms, others are assigned to room service, and still others are temporary employees, brought in for big banquets. It makes no difference. They fraternize with each other, seldom with outsiders. Every waiter seems to know every other waiter in the region, and considers him a friend unless and until he proves otherwise by behavior bringing him into disfavor. A man says he saw John the other day. "Oh, yes!" his companion says. "He's at the Roosevelt now. He used to be at the Waldorf before that."

Where a man works or worked is important. A waiter says, "I was at Chasen's for four years." He is proud of it. Working at Chasen's gives him more prestige than working at Sam's Grill.

Ninety-nine percent of the waiters I know are distinctive personalities, and the rest are characters. They don't seem to run to colorless types. They are basically friendly, but under such unremitting pressure that they cannot display it while working. Every minute of their day is devoted to giving the customer "service." This makes the waiter nervous and high-strung. He bangs into the kitchen, raps out the order, and slams out, to render more "service." He is brusque because he is in a hurry.

I am friendly with a good many waiters, and despite their harried existence they find time to be nice to me. A room service waiter will pass my desk, wheeling a serving table from a guest's room to the kitchen. He hands me a piece of cake. "Here!" he says. "Eat it! It wasn't touched."

I am particularly fond of Sam, who is about 60 and treats me as if I were his daughter, inquiring after my health, telling me I am working too hard, suggesting I take a day off and rest.

Once when I was working late at my desk, I telephoned room service for some dinner. Sam delivered it to me. "What did you want to order a steak for?" he asked. "It's too expensive. Look! Next time, order just a steak sandwich. It's the same thing, off the same piece of meat, only a little smaller." He didn't know that I was going to charge my client for the dinner bill. When I signed the check I wrote in a dollar tip. "You don't have to do that!" Sam exclaimed. "Save it for yourself. I'll make it up on the next customer."

I explained that I was going to charge it to one of the rooms.

"Oh!" Sam said. "Then put down a dollar and a half. What do you care? He's paying for it."

I made it $1.50. My client wouldn't mind, and I owed Sam more than that extra half dollar. It made up for the rather slim tips I gave him when I paid for my own dinner.

Occupational cliques are not so self-contained that all association with members of another clique is hindered. A clerk may make friends with a maid, or a secretary with a bell captain. There is some interdepartmental dating, romance does result, and there is even an occasional marriage.

As in any society, folkways develop among hotel employees,

eventually to be incorporated into the protocol of the establishment. One example is the tipping system. You will find no written, enforceable rule on tipping. An unseasoned traveler suffers uncertainty and embarrassment because of it. He wants to know the rules, but it would be indelicate to inquire. He may under-tip or over-tip but one thing is certain: so powerful is the tradition established by employee society that he will not fail to tip.

A guest tips the doorman, bellman, waiter, shoeshine boy, bartender, valet, maid, gent's room attendant. Which reminds me of the story that is told about the man who telephoned from his room and asked to have a deck of cards sent up. The bellboy, it is said, delivered them one at a time, in 52 trips!

The smallest tip I know about was one penny, donated by a Japanese diplomat to the doorman. The largest gratuity was a pastel mink stole and an all-expense trip to Hawaii, given to a beauty operator by an appreciative customer.

What about a public stenographer? Many of my clients are not sure whether I expect a tip. I think it's nice to be tipped, but I don't want it to be on the basis of compulsion, subtle or direct. To me, tipping indicates that the customer is pleased with my work, that he recognizes the extra effort I have made on his behalf. And I am not hurt if he overlooks the gratuity. His appreciation of my efforts is sufficient. And clients can be extraordinarily kind in other ways. I have been taken to lunch and dinner and have received gifts from satisfied patrons.

The mere fact that I work in one hotel makes me a member of the family in another. I receive special courtesies in New York's Waldorf, Chicago's Ambassador, San Francisco's Mark Hopkins. I can use a typewriter, cash a check, and get a room at special rates merely by identifying myself as working at the Hilton. Favors are generally extended everywhere, even internationally. When I wanted a vacation in Mexico, a hotel man in Beverly Hills arranged part-time work for me in Mexico City to help finance it.

This informal understanding that special courtesies will be extended to any member of a hotel staff breaks down when bureaucracy takes over. Vacationing in New York one summer,

I did part-time work helping the public stenographer in a hotel so I could stay longer. One hot afternoon, sitting at the typewriter, I became thirsty. Drinking water is one of the hardest things to find in a hotel. Ordinarily there are no fountains, since they would reduce bar business. There are no drinking glasses in the washrooms; and if an employee goes into the cocktail lounge to ask the bartender for a glass of water, he is busy, and may be annoyed.

I knew that in the manager's office, next to where I worked, there was an inverted jug of iced spring water on a stand inside the closet of the anteroom. I asked the receptionist if I might have a drink. She wrinkled her brow, hesitated, and walked into the next office, where I heard her conferring with a secretary. She returned, still dubious, and told me, "I'm sorry. I don't think the manager would like it."

"Why not?" I asked.

She could see I was offended. "Well," she said, surrendering protocol to common decency, "I'll let you have a little, this time. But I know the manager wouldn't like it."

Chapter 5

The society
of guests

Let me take you on a tour of a large luxury hotel, not a particular one, but a composite of all in that class. Think of it as Everyhotel, where Everyman comes to spend a night, a week, or a year. I would like to introduce you to the society of guests.

Let's begin in my office, located in a foyer leading to the main lobby. It is just large enough to accommodate a desk, chair, typewriter table, and storage space for supplies. It has no door, only a gate attached to the counter, over which I transact business. I can look across the counter into the lobby.

The lobby itself is in continuous activity. Day and night, the electronically controlled glass doors at the main entrance swing open to arriving and departing guests. Through those doors pass some of the most influential, powerful, wealthy, famous, happy, sad, excited, fortunate, tragic people in the world.

Generally, the procession is orderly, but there are dramatic exceptions. A rumor spreads that the Beatles are about to check in. Other aspirants to theatrical fame get the idea of cashing in on the expected publicity. A singing group, also English, shows up in Beatle wigs. A dozen local boys from the lesser nightclubs, and a score of young men not yet off the ground as entertainers also arrive in similar attire. It is a staggering sight. The lobby is jammed with long-haired Beatle-top youths, jockeying each other to get into what they hope is television range. To add to the insanity, several hundred squealing teenagers scurry about, autograph books in hand, not quite certain which are the real Beatles.

What with all the rush and bustle of a hotel, it is possible to overlook the more quiet nooks and people. Let's walk through the lobby. Here you will see tired businessmen returning from a hard day's work. Here, too, people come to consult medical specialists and divorce lawyers, prospective employers and employees. That sad-looking couple near the bell captain's station have come to California to bury a relative.

The aged, heavy-set lady wearing a suit reminiscent of the Gold Rush Era is Mrs. Calverton, one of our permanent guests, formerly of San Francisco. Often, when I go to the drugstore for a sandwich, I find her having lunch at the counter and we sit together. She likes to talk about her former home in San Francisco's elite Nob Hill section. She loved it, but when her husband died, and her children married and moved away, she sold her home and came to the more equable climate of Southern California. But she cannot forget the good old days and ways. "I wouldn't want to be of the younger generation," she told me. "I am so glad I lived in the Golden Era, in the days of elegance." Saying this, she sighed, smothered her hamburger and onions with mustard, and nibbled at it listlessly.

The lady over there, reading a magazine, comes to the lobby occasionally to regain contact with a life she no longer participates in actively. A gentle little woman, a native of Washington, she took a suite in the hotel shortly after her husband passed away. I did some work for her at the time, when she was settling her husband's estate. One day she remarked, "Oh, dear! I have to go back to Seattle next week, and I really don't want to go."

"Must you?" I asked.

"Yes. I promised my husband I would. He made me promise that when he passed away, I would have him cremated and would scatter his ashes in the Pacific Ocean, at ebbtide."

She seemed so unhappy at the prospect of going north that I suggested, "Why don't you scatter his ashes at Santa Monica? It's the same ocean."

She considered it a moment. "Do you think he would mind?" she asked.

"I really don't think so."

"Maybe I'll do that. I really hate to go all the way to Seattle. It *is* the same ocean, isn't it?"

The man and woman over there on the couch against the wall are from Canada. They come here every winter, to escape the cold. They sit all day, gazing idly at the passing throng. They don't do much of anything, don't go anywhere. They don't even talk to each other. I once asked them why they didn't go sightseeing. They said they were too tired. They will remain in the hotel until the weather changes back home. Meanwhile, they sit in the lobby, watching life pass them by.

But we had better be moving along. This is the coffee shop, a cosmopolitan spot. Yesterday I sat at the counter between an Iranian and a German. The day before I sat between a Briton and a Belgian. You won't find a better place to get the flavor of international guest society.

Mr. Edgar eats here every day. He receives a handsome monthly stipend from relatives back East, and can afford to dine in the main restaurant, but he is lonely and prefers to sit at the coffee shop counter and talk to people. He is a rather sad human being. His remittances are provided on one condition— that he stay away from home. When he lived with his family, he was co-owner of a large business enterprise, but was so inept, by his own account, that he made himself a nuisance. His family decided it would be more economical in the long run to send him a liberal monthly check in California, far enough away to prevent his interference in business affairs. He dabbles in stocks simply to pass the time. For several months now, he has been having lunch with one of the girls who works in the hotel, but there is no romance there. She told me she knows the man is lonely and invites her only to get a human response; she has a nice lunch and he has her company.

We will just peep into the bar and the dining rooms. And this is the drug store, where guests get a quick bite to eat or buy a toothbrush.

As you have seen, in establishments of appreciable size there are both transient and residential guests. Most of the latter live in a hotel by choice. It offers the comforts and conveniences they require without imposing upon them the responsibilities of a householder. Other residents are not there entirely by choice. They may be elderly folk, with neither kith nor kin. Or they have kin but no love. Their children have their own busy lives and don't want to be bothered with them. Grandma sensed she was unwanted and went to live by herself, on her own means if she was fortunate, or at the expense of children willing to pay to get rid of her.

I notice that these older folks rarely talk to one another, although they see each other all the time. They could become acquainted, but for some strange reason they don't. They merely exchange a "good morning" as they meet in the hallway.

There is nothing quite like the panic that spreads through the floor when an older resident dies. Others in the same age-bracket shut themselves up in their rooms until the body has been removed. When they emerge, they shuffle past the vacated room, not daring to look in that direction. When the maid comes in, they say, over and over, "Isn't it terrible about that poor old woman in Room 705? I saw her only the other day, and she looked so full of life!" They keep repeating, "Why, she wasn't old at all!"

As a substitute for human response, these oldsters adopt pets that they can love, and from whom they can expect affection. One lady kept to her suite most of the day, leaving it only for her meals. She was willing to take a chance on the hotel's restaurant fare, but her dog was another matter. She refused to give him food prepared in the kitchen, behind her back. The chef might slip in meat scraps instead of premium grade. Therefore, she ordered room service for her pet. Every day, a waiter brought up a platter of raw, freshly ground sirloin. The lady inspected it meticulously, and, if it passed muster she made it into patties, placed an electric grill on the lid of the toilet seat, and prepared hamburgers for her beloved little animal.

But not all permanent guests are elderly. Some are middle-aged, and some much younger. The New York parents of one young woman sent her to live in California. She was accompanied by a female companion charged with keeping her out of mischief in the West and out of contact with the East, lest her predictable habits cause the family embarrassment. In the eight years she remained in the hotel I never saw her in anything but one suit. The valet told me that when she sent it out for cleaning, she remained in her room until it was returned on the same day.

This lost soul rarely spoke to anyone, and people seldom spoke to her because she seemed so strange. She never left the grounds. For exercise she took brisk constitutionals along the hotel walks.

Sensing her loneliness, and being curious about her, I went out of my way to break the barriers she erected around herself. Occasionally I shared her walks. She talked mostly about the birds perched in trees lining the paths. She had become an expert at identifying different species, and would point them out to me. She recognized individual birds and gave them pet names. Many times I came upon her, standing beside a tree, peering up at a bird in a bough, murmuring unintelligible messages to the feathered creature.

I asked her why she didn't go to a show, or sit in the lobby, just to be with people and talk to someone. She said she had all the conversation she needed.

"With whom?" I asked.

"With the birds."

She had settled for that.

Whether permanent or transient, guests differ widely in the

degree to which they understand that the management wants them to be comfortable. It is surprising how many are reluctant to ask for things they need. They are often unsure of themselves in the hotel environment.

In the restaurant, they may toy with a napkin uncomfortably, unable to begin lunch because they have no fork. They will not stop the waiter or busboy to ask for one—that would embarrass them. They have not learned that the more service a guest demands (within reason), the more he gets, and the greater respect employees will have for him.

As I left a room where I had been taking dictation, a maid asked if I knew why the guest, a businessman, kept his bedside lamp burning day and night. I told her I had no idea, but would try to find out.

The next day I asked him.

"The bellboy turned it on when I checked in," he told me, "and I can't figure out how to turn the damned thing off!"

It worked by a new type of button. The maid did not turn the light off because she assumed the client wanted it on. He definitely did not, and for one whole week slept with the light shining in his face, covering his eyes with a towel.

"Why didn't you call the housekeeper?" I asked.

He shrugged.

Just as incomprehensible is the man who must have groped around in the dark throughout his stay. After he left, it was discovered that a failure in the electrical outlets had shorted out all the lights in his room.

Many guests cannot master the mechanism of the air conditioner. Unable to turn it on or off, they swelter in the heat or freeze in the cold, but they will not call for assistance.

I delivered a batch of work to a woman and found her drinking water out of a Coke bottle.

"Did the maid overlook putting glasses in the room?" I asked.

"Oh, no! I've got my medicine in one and I broke the other."

She wouldn't ask for a replacement.

In newer hotels, telephones have a small red light which flashes to indicate that there is a message for the guest. It keeps blinking on and off until he calls the message operator. When she transmits the message, she shuts off the light. Some guests do not understand the purpose of the light, yet they will not ask about it. A telephone operator told me about a businessman who stayed in the hotel for three days. Before checking out he finally asked about the red light, adding that he found the continuous blinking most disturbing. At night he had to cover it with a towel, so he could sleep. For three days he put up with the thing, making neither inquiry nor complaint. Throughout that period he failed to get his messages.

Incidentally, an operator tells an amusing story about Jack Paar and the message light. Checking into the Beverly Hilton, he told her he didn't want to be disturbed—no calls, please.

"Should I put the red light on for your messages?" she asked.

"What for?" Jack cracked. "I couldn't read them by that little light anyhow!"

Where some guests are timid about asking for things, others go to the opposite extreme. A man called for six pillows, tested each for hardness and softness, explaining he had figured out scientifically what made for the most restful slumber—two hard and four soft pillows. Some guests ask for two mattresses or king-sized beds.

A chef told me about a very particular guest who ordered two potatoes with his dinner, specifying that they were to be boiled in their skins in sea water. The chef had a dishwasher drive all the way to the ocean, about fifteen miles each way, to fetch a pail of water. He made quite a picture, sloshing through the corridor to the kitchen. The potatoes were very good indeed, the chef said. They were salted just exactly as they should have been.

Employees do not consider it their business to check on guests' morals, but occasionally they have to act to prevent mayhem in a matter of morality. A famous movie star escorted a lady, whom every columnist knew to be his mistress, into the beauty salon. The star's wife was one of the few people in town who did not know he had a paramour. This was a blessing, for his wife was extremely possessive and fiery tempered. And she was at that moment in a booth, having her hair done. The mistress, who was fifteen minutes early for her appointment, was about to sit down in the section reserved for patrons waiting their turn. A hairdresser sized up the situation and expertly steered her to a vacant booth, shielding her from view en route by placing himself between the lady and patrons in occupied booths. Advising her of the hazardous situation, he placed a heat cap over her hair, completely hiding her face. The actor, quietly informed of the reason behind the maneuver, departed quickly. His mistress sat in the booth, incognito from the neck up, until the star's wife left the salon. The actor paid both bills—$7.50 for his wife and $80 for his girlfriend.

Management does not police the morals of the millionaire who periodically checks into a world-famous hotel for a week, takes over the penthouse, and throws one wild party lasting the seven days. Gossip gets around, and I received a report on one of his wingdings. He provided female companionship for his guests. He himself enjoyed the company of a string of girls, at staggered intervals. One of them told a maid, who told another maid, who told me what happened. The host insisted on washing his lady friends in the bathtub before taking them to bed. He used a fresh washcloth each time. He himself showered three times a day and went to bed—alone—at 10 o'clock every night. The showers and many hours of sleep, he told a bellboy, sustained his virility.

This man, incidentally, carried his hygienic habits beyond showers and healthy slumber. He had a phobia about germs. He carried one white and one blue handkerchief in his pockets at all times, the white one for his nose, the blue one to clean his ears. A room service waiter filled a glass of water for him while he was out of the room. When he returned, he asked just how the waiter had held the glass. When it appeared that a finger had touched the rim, the glass had to be replaced. He always wiped the silverware before using it; and he threw away the top piece of Kleenex in a box.

Aside from questions involving personal morality, hotel employees become inured to all kinds of eccentricity. I often see a particular patron of the coffee shop lick the ketchup bottle after he pours some on his hamburger. I had a South American client who ordered cracked crab for breakfast every morning, washed down with champagne. A Russian count, who wore a red smoking jacket as he dictated, ordered wine brought up, filled a wineglass, drained it, and sent it crashing into the fireplace. He repeated the performance every time he took a drink. By late afternoon the fireplace was heaped with splintered glassware.

An Englishman who uses my services as he shuttles back and forth between the two continents indulges in an interesting fancy. Wherever he goes, he brings along a huge, stuffed teddy bear. He sits it up on the dresser, costumed according to locale. When he had a room near the pool, teddy wore bathing trunks and sunglasses. When Mr. Teddy came in from the Orient with his master, he was caparisoned in a high-collared Chinese silk mandarin tunic, especially tailored for him in Hong Kong. This was not a case of arrested development. Teddy's owner conducted business in a mature, realistic manner. His personal relations were on an adult level. He just happened to love his teddy bear.

Affection for a toy animal can be an endearing trait. Less endearing and much more puzzling was the pattern of one client, who traveled about the country restlessly and called no place his home. He lived well on a large inheritance. Wherever he spent a night, he brought out a military helmet, a pair of command boots, and a flashy military jacket. He placed the boots outside his door at night, to be polished. The jacket hung in a conspicuous place in the room all day and night. The helmet lay on the bed. From time to time as we worked, the client picked it up and fingered it lovingly.

He told me he would love to be an army general, and make arrangements for war and death.

His sense of humor was bizarre. He played what he considered hilarious practical jokes on friends. I considered them an expression of his sadism. He sent for me once, solely to inform me that as he passed through Denver he had learned that a very dear friend of mine had murdered a girl and then thrown himself from the window of a hotel. He told the story so convincingly that I picked up the telephone, in tears, to call the suicide's mother, at which point the client confessed that the story was a hoax.

When I exploded in wrath, he said, "You're worse than I am. I lied about your friend, but you believed the terrible things I told you. You didn't have faith in him. Otherwise, how could I have fooled you?"

Taken as a whole, hotel guests are about the same, year after year. There is always a monomaniac, a teddy bear lover, and someone who must sleep on six pillows. What does change is the hotel itself. It goes through continuous evolution. It has been more than a century since this country has seen the tavern or inn, gracious precursor of the modern high-rise steel and concrete edifice. An inn was small, intimate, individualistic, taking on the character of its innkeeper. The true inn feeling has almost completely vanished, victim of the industrial revolution. We have found ways to erect magnificent structures, reaching for the sky.

Today's guest does not know the innkeeper, who is not in fact an innkeeper but a bloodless corporation. The traveler cannot be sure he will find his accustomed stopping place as it was when he was there last. I hear guests remark that they do not feel at home when there have been changes. They add to the traveler's comfort, but too often depersonalize the establishment one step further.

There is a limit beyond which the hotel cannot go in modernization without sacrificing the friendly, homelike atmosphere. True, rapid growth cannot be avoided. It is part of the contemporary scene. The roadside inn multiplied a thousand times couldn't begin to take care of the available business, and no inn can operate as economically as the large hostelry. But even the faster-paced traveler of today wants more than modern conveniences. He wants to rest in a reasonable facsimile of a home, not a factory.

Hotel owners recognize this. They do all they can to create a congenial atmosphere. The inn effect is furthered in some hostelries by a blazing open fireplace in the lobby. Tables, chairs and couches are placed so that people, brought into more informal contact, can talk to each other and come to know one another easily. There are flowers at the reception desk and on tables. Music is played all day long in the lobby. Room radios connect with a special station which provides good music while eliminating the commercials. While it used to be necessary to order ice for drinks, some hotels now provide an ice-making machine in every room.

Not all establishments succeed in regaining the tone that suggests that mine host is interested in each and every traveler, and probably when a structure reaches a certain size it cannot be transformed even into a pseudo-inn. But imaginative management does wonders in the select establishments.

A good example is the rustic Bel Air, a thoroughly modern hotel, which is at the same time an inn in the finest sense of the word. It is set into a canyon close to Beverly Hills, a fact which in itself seems to draw its guests together, separate from the outside world. As you enter the lobby, employees greet you with a smile and a friendly word.

The rooms at the Bel Air Hotel are large and furnished in a warm, homelike manner. They do not have that "hotel" look. There are paintings on the walls, large lamps. Some rooms have fireplaces, with a supply of logs alongside. There are fresh flowers in all the rooms. When a guest checks in, the manager sends candy or fruit or nut corn—sometimes champagne—depending upon how well he knows him. Most of the guests have stayed there before, and they ask for the same rooms each time. They come so often that the clerks and other employees know them and greet them like old friends. There are gardens everywhere, and a small pond with swans.

The maid comes in, toward evening, to turn down the bed. She lays out pajamas, robe and slippers.

The loveliest touch of all at the Bel Air, so far as I am concerned, is in the lobby, meeting the eye as one arrives. To one side of a huge fireplace is a wooden standard carrying a sign: MY NAME IS KITZI. PLEASE DON'T DISTURB. Kitzi is a yellow, white and black tabby cat that, almost any time of day, will be found luxuriating on a soft rug before the fireplace.

Kitzi is as much a part of the charm and warmth of this gracious inn as any employee or fixture. She leads so comfortable a life that guests who believe in reincarnation remark that they would choose to be the Bel Air mascot in their next life.

Kitzi is an established institution, loved by everyone. Whatever she wants is provided by her human confreres. She has her own chef, who prepares her breakfast bacon. She will settle for nothing else, and it must be very crisp, else she refuses it disdainfully.

Her noon meal is always the same, a bowl of rich cream and a plate of freshly prepared shrimp, steamed exactly the way she wants it. She eats no beef, pork, or veal, and would not bother to lap up milk—only cream. She lunches regally, then settles back for a siesta.

Promptly at 3 o'clock, the chef sends out an afternoon snack of shredded turkey, which Kitzi adores. That is her final repast for the day. She never eats between meals, no matter what tidbit is dangled before her nose by fascinated guests. And although she patently enjoys the adulation she receives, Kitzi dislikes being touched by anyone, which is the reason for the PLEASE DON'T DISTURB warning.

Currently, the Bel Air feline has her eye on a bird that lives in a cage across the road at the Greer Garson mansion. Not a predator, Kitzi has no evil intent. She merely wants to admire the bird. Several times a day, tabby ambles across the road and seats herself at a convenient distance from the cage. She eyes her friend steadily and the bird returns her stare, showing no uneasiness. After a half hour of silent communion, Kitzi strolls back to the fireplace of the hotel.

She takes an evening airing, too, stepping gracefully across the hotel grounds to a pond, where two lovely swans skim over the water effortlessly. They ignore her. They know she cannot reach them with her paws and will not swim out to them. Kitzi sits and stares. What is she thinking?

When she has feasted her eyes sufficiently, Kitzi sashays back to the lobby and settles down for the night, with a leave-me-alone expression on her face.

Neither employee nor guest would dream of disturbing her slumber. They love that cat, and pamper and spoil her disgracefully. Kitzi was run over by a car once, and the Bel Air, from guest room to kitchen, went on disaster duty. People ran hither and yon, summoning medical assistance and making Kitzi comfortable. Word-of-mouth bulletins were issued on her condition. The hotel spent over one hundred dollars caring for her. Everyone was dreadfully disturbed until she was on the road to recovery.

When an entire establishment can be welded together by a cat, you may be sure that, whatever it is called, it remains an inn.

In the inviting Bel Air as well as in a colder, more businesslike hotel, there have been changes induced by the acceleration of modern existence. For one thing, a certain kind of business has declined. Years ago, the average stay of a businessman was between ten days and two weeks. During weekends, he found himself at loose ends, away from his family, with time on his hands and no business to be transacted between Friday and Monday. With business appointments set up for the following week, he could not take a train home and return Monday if he lived at some distance.

Today, weekends are slow in hotels. Aviation, and particularly the jet, accounts for it. The businessman flies home for not much more than it would cost for lodging, meals and entertainment over the weekend. He spends most of the two days with his family, and flies back to keep his appointments. Some businessmen fly coast to coast twice in one week rather than stay in the hotel over the weekend. As a consequence, public stenographers get little work and playgirls get less play on weekends.

Compensating for slower weekends is the fact that there is no longer a tourist season, reaching peaks and collapsing periodically. Air conditioning makes the hottest region comfortable in summer. Thermostat-controlled heating renders the coldest area habitable in winter. Tourists pour in the year around.

I have noted other changes in hotels, some of which are related to technological progress. Years ago, business deals were entered into and concluded with great deliberation. The incom-

ing negotiator took a train and, therefore, he had plenty of time
to plan his campaign as he traveled. After arriving in California,
he discussed his proposition with the parties concerned. No final
decisions were reached; this was only a ground-breaking operation. There were few contracts or letters to dictate to a public
stenographer.

The out-of-towner went back to his office and from there
continued negotiations. When he had agreement and a firm deal,
his secretary drew up what papers were required, he returned to
California, and the deal was officially consummated. A public
stenographer played little part in the proceedings.

Today a man flies in for a day or perhaps for only a few
hours. The deal must be clinched during that time. Negotiations
are conducted at top speed. The interested parties want to exe-
cute a legal contract immediately. A public stenographer is
essential.

In the final analysis, what is any hotel but an idea inside an
individual guest's mind? For some it is a happy place, for others
a sad one; some come to find peace, some to gird for war; some
are virtually oblivious to their surroundings, some find the hotel
a wonderland.

It was a wonderland for John. Every September, unfailing as
a homing pigeon, he came and stayed exactly two weeks at the
Beverly Hills Hotel. Enchanted by the celebrities, he stalked them
in the lobby, introduced himself, begged outright strangers to
have dinner with him. Let a movie personality pause for breath,
and John was upon him, backing him to the wall, buttonholing
him into the lounge. Since, as he unfailingly pointed out, he was
an important man back home in Illinois, he usually found someone willing to accept his invitation to dinner or cocktails, albeit
at the cost of hearing John's small talk about his estate and the
hometown politicians who sought his advice.

The lobby would be abuzz. John would ease in between two
people and, in a voice he made certain would be heard a block
away, exclaim, "Man, did I have a time at Sam Goldwyn's last
night! I told him, I said, 'Sam,' . . ."

While in the pool one afternoon, I saw John walk self-consciously past the sun worshippers lounging in deck chairs around the rim. Passing Hedy Lamarr, he did a double take, turned back, bowed. She returned a weak smile, pretending she recognized him.

Encountering me in the lobby that evening, he boomed, "Did you see me with Hedy at the pool?" He pivoted his eyes, to calculate the effect on others within earshot. "Where on earth has she been? I was telling Joan Crawford the other day, I said, 'Gee, Joanie, where on earth is Hedy? I don't see her around any more!' "

One of John's prize catches was an English lord, with whom he became quite friendly during one of his annual pilgrimages. He wined and dined him, took him to night clubs and sporting events. The night before he was to check out, he invited the Englishman to La Rue's for a final bottle of Pomerey '28. At dinner his guest remarked he would be leaving for England in a week, that he would enjoy stopping over at John's estate on his way east. As I got it later, John's face lit up. Then he groaned, "Oh, hell! I forgot. I'm due in Washington that week. Friends of mine have been named in an anti-trust action the government's bringing. I gave them my word I'd drop in on the Attorney General and see if I couldn't get him to drop the suit. He's an old friend from 'way back, and I've been in position to do him a favor now and then, y'know. So that week's shot. How about some other time, though? I'd be delighted!"

The Briton took John's address and said he'd try to visit next time he was in the United States.

It was the Englishman who related the denouement some months later when he was in Beverly Hills again. On his way west from New York, he stopped off in the Illinois town where John lived. The address, in a decrepit neighborhood, was of a ramshackle building. John, his wife and two children shared an apartment with relatives, who paid the rent.

John, it turned out, was an assistant buyer in a "junior department store," in charge of men's underwear. He took as good care of his family as his modest funds permitted. He scrounged and scratched all year, putting aside every dollar he could for his vacation. When September arrived, he would set out for the intoxicating climate of California. Precisely what those two weeks in the hotel meant to him, only he can say, but that they meant a great deal I have no doubt.

He has not returned to Beverly Hills after the visit he received from the English nobleman. I have a feeling he cannot face the possibility that the people he hungers for have learned who he really is, and having discovered his true identity, will decline his wine and ridicule his dreams.

Chapter 6

The lonely ones

A young woman whom I met casually at the drugstore counter came to my office, sat down, and in a calm, unemotional voice, asked, "Do you think I ought to kill myself?"

Attempting to be equally casual, I replied, "No, I don't think so, because if you do, you'll never know what tomorrow would have brought."

She was very attractive. She had money. She dressed well. Why should she think of suicide? The reason she gave was that she was desperately unhappy, having discovered that the man she loved, who claimed he loved and wanted to marry her, was already wed.

We talked for over an hour, and she felt much better at the end, so much so, in fact, that she asked if I knew a bachelor who wanted to get married.

A hotel is a place in which to be lonely, and hotels can make a person lonely. The little old lady who lives in her comfortable suite year in, year out, is lonely because she remembers a real home and family she once had. The transient guest is assailed by loneliness because he is an alien in this society, removed from his kind of people. For him, hotel people are faceless automatons. They are there, as he is, to get something done and to get out.

A woman came up to me in the office. "I hope you won't mind my asking," she said, "but would you come to the bar with me? I've seen you around, and you seem friendly. I'm dying for a martini, but I can't go into the bar by myself." She stopped short and grimaced. "Oh, hell! Why kid myself, or you? I'm lonely! I want somebody to talk to!"

I meet lonely folks everywhere in the hotel. They come to my office as clients, and in the process of giving me work reveal their need for warm human relationship. I find lonely people in the coffee shop. I see them at the drugstore counter, drinking coffee and munching sweet rolls. They could sit at a table, but if they go to the counter someone is likely to seat himself on the next stool and start talking.

Look in the lobby. Men and women sit hour after hour, watching others go by, wondering about them, wishing they could somehow participate in what they are doing.

Look in the bar. Men and women sit twisting their glasses idly. They don't particularly want a drink; they want conversation, and the informality of a bar is conducive to it.

There used to be a retired businessman living in the hotel who sat in the lobby with a Polaroid camera in his hands. At every opportunity he snapped pictures of guests, many of them total strangers, and presented them to his subjects. They were his calling cards, a way of getting to talk to people.

The lonely ones often think of the public stenographer. She is alone, too, available on call, and she seems pleasant. I consider it part of my obligation to sit and talk with a guest when he is in the mood.

An elderly gentleman walked slowly into my office, sat down, and asked me to take a letter to his lady-love in Palm Springs. It was an impassioned plea that she meet him in Beverly Hills, where they would get married. I received a telephone call from him less than an hour after he left my office. "Miss, would you be interested in having dinner with me?" It surprised me greatly that he should be trying to date me immediately after proposing to another woman. I told him I was sorry, that I promised my mother to have dinner at her house, which was a fact.

He flattened my ego by asking, "Maybe I could go with you? Maybe your mother would enjoy meeting me? Talking to me?"

Now I understood. He was not interested in dating me, nor was he particularly eager to meet my mother. He did not even need a wife. All he needed was a friend, someone who would give him a bit of companionship.

I invited the gentleman to accompany me to my mother's house, since I thought she would enjoy meeting him. I am sure he was very pleased to sit down to a home-cooked meal.

Another man, Jack, moved to California for his health. He was frightfully lonesome and bored, wandering about in the lobby, talking to bellboys, to passers-by. He had no family left, and his social life had to be derived from inside the hotel. He and I developed a speaking acquaintance, in the course of which he once boasted that he could give me a daily weather report for every major city in the United States if I wanted it. I asked how he got his information. Simply to hear someone's voice, it appeared, he would ask the switchboard operator to connect him with Information in another city. This cost nothing. He would give the Information operator an invented name of someone who presumably lived in that city, and ask for the telephone number. While the operator was checking, he would casually say, "By the way, how's the weather there?" She would tell him. If she was friendly, he would ask her name, merely to prolong the conversation. Occasionally, an operator not only gave her name, but mentioned a relative she had in Los Angeles, whereupon Jack would ask if she would like him to call the relative to say hello for her. If so, he was delighted. It would give him an additional contact.

Calling Information was more than a hobby for Jack. It consumed time and reduced boredom, but even more important, the operators became his friends. He got so he could recognize many by their voices. He dropped into my office one afternoon when I was with a client, who was debating whether to call a certain man in Mexico City. "Maybe it's too late in the day," he said. "I wish I knew what time it is in Mexico City."

"Mind if I butt in?" Jack asked, beaming. He turned to me. "Hand me the phone!"

He got our long distance operator to connect him with the Information operator in Mexico City.

"Hello!" he said. "Consuela? I thought so! This is Jack. You know! Jack! In Beverly Hills. *Como esta usted?*" After an exchange of greetings he asked Consuela what time it was in Mexico City, said "*Muchas gracias*" and hung up.

"It's 5 o'clock," he announced. "Two hours difference in time." He was very proud of himself.

Loneliness respects neither man nor woman, neither rich nor poor, and a public stenographer encounters it outside the hotel as well as inside. Early in my career I received a call from a woman who spoke in a low, subdued voice. Almost in a whisper she asked whether I could come to the home of the Princess Troubetskoy to notarize some papers.

I drove to the address and found a huge, isolated Beverly Hills mansion that at one time must have been the scene of many a gala occasion. I rang, and the huge front doors were opened by a butler. In a barely audible murmur he invited me to come in. From the entrance foyer I could see a large winding stairway, and as I looked up I saw a footman, lighting tapers. When the footman descended the stairs, the butler addressed him in almost a whisper, and it was the footman who ushered me upstairs to a large reception room. Here he asked me—in a whisper—to wait a few minutes.

Presently the Princess' secretary emerged from an adjoining room. Speaking very, very quietly, she said, "Will you come this way, please?" She escorted me into a bedroom, where I found the Princess, in a nightgown and peignoir, propped up in bed. I recognized her immediately. The Princess was Barbara Hutton.

She greeted me quietly, explaining that she had been ill—and she looked at it. As she got out of bed to bring the papers that required notarization, I caught sight of the bracelet she was wearing. I had never seen one with so many huge diamonds. They were not only set into gold, but also they were hanging from tiny chains all the way around the bracelet. At the dresser, she picked up an address book to look up a number, and the book was jeweled, too.

When she attempted to sign the papers, her hand shook so that she could hardly hold the pen I gave her. I placed my hand over hers, lightly remarking that the pen wasn't very good; it had to be held a certain way before the ink would flow. In this manner, I guided her fingers as she affixed her signature. She understood what I was doing, and threw me a grateful smile. Then she returned to bed.

Instead of paying my $5 fee, she had her secretary give me $10. As I prepared to leave, she thanked me over and over most graciously.

My heart ached as I left the room, in tow of the secretary. Miss Hutton had a look about her as though she had been whipped, a look which reminded me of a sweet little cat I once saw after it had been beaten. It sat cowering in a corner, no fight left in it. Its expression seemed to say, "Thank you for letting me live." I felt a great wave of sympathy sweep through me for the gracious lady with the sad face. I thought, "Here is one of the richest women in the world, yet she doesn't seem happy."

The secretary conducted me to the door. "Thank you very much for coming," she whispered.

Automatically, I started to whisper a reply, but stopped short. "Is somebody ill here?" I asked.

"What do you mean?" she asked.

"You're whispering. The servants were whispering. I find myself whispering."

"No," she said. "There is no one ill here. We always talk that way in this house."

I let it go at that.

I met Miss Hutton again, this time in her bungalow at the Beverly Hills Hotel. She was now a baroness, by another marriage. I was to notarize several documents concerning her son, Lance. Again she was in bed, again she wore jeweled bracelets,

and again she seemed very sad. She greeted me politely but listlessly, put down the book she was reading, and handed me the
papers she wanted notarized. Doing so, she glanced at a book I
was carrying.

"What are you reading?" she asked.

"The autobiography of the Duke of Windsor," I told her.
I said that I was fascinated by his version of the romance that
led him to abdicate the throne of England rather than give up
"the woman I love."

"Have you read it?" I asked.

She leaned back against the pillows and replied, "I couldn't
care less about how the Duke met Wally Simpson."

I said I thought it was a wonderful thing for a king to have
abdicated rather than give up his beloved. "And," I added, "how
wonderful for her, to become a Duchess!"

Miss Hutton looked at me wanly, smiled wryly and remarked, "Wonderful? I don't know. Things are never what they
seem."

After I handed her the notarized papers she did not dismiss
me, but seemed inclined to talk further. I stayed awhile and we
chatted. She asked how I liked my work. I said I was very happy
in it, and that it enabled me to meet famous people, such as herself, who was a legendary figure to most of us. She gave me a
quiet little smile, as if deprecating her fame.

I mentioned that I was attending classes at the University.
"I envy you," she said.

"*You* envy *me?* What for? I don't have anything."

"Well, you go to college. That's something. My son doesn't
want to go to school, and I want him to go, more than anything
in the world. All he wants to do is race cars."

Before leaving, I did something that I am sure will appear
strange to some readers. I have always had a compulsion to give
things to people I like. I wanted to give Miss Hutton something.
Not only would it afford me the rare pleasure of presenting a gift
to a fabulously wealthy woman, but, I thought, it would be an
agreeable reversal of roles for her to receive something instead
of doing the giving. I wanted to show her I liked her, which I

really did. I held out my ballpoint pen. It was a beautiful shade of blue, and it had my name on it.

I said, "I would like to give you this because it matches your bed-jacket."

Her face lit up. She showed more animation than at any other time during my visit. "Oh, thank you!" she said. "I appreciate it so much!" The wistful look returned. "I don't often get presents."

I walked slowly back to my office, feeling sad and contemplative. Here was this fine, lovely woman, whom one would consider indeed blessed by good fortune, lying in bed, looking far from well, showing appreciation of a gift worth all of thirty-five cents.

I hoped she would some day find lasting happiness and good health.

Chapter 7

The man who was himself

Undoubtedly, when I began my career as a public stenographer in the Beverly Hills Hotel, I was more impressionable than I am today, but I do not believe this accounts entirely for the fact that I can think of no other individual who made quite the impression on me that Serge Rubinstein did.

A secretary, like a valet, sees her employer as he really is. For that reason, the secretary may see a kinder or nobler or more sensitive man than the public sees. Or she may see one who is meaner or baser or cruder. I don't quite know how to characterize Serge Rubinstein, for whom I did a great deal of work. I have been told so many ugly things about him, yet I found many admirable traits in him, as well as some that were not so admirable. My theory is that he was two people, that he had two distinct characters, one warring against the other. I do not pretend to understand the person the public said he was. I knew him only as a man who, in the course of our work, revealed himself in off-camera moments. It is this image I am presenting.

I once watched him playing tennis with a South American

financier. It was as if his very life depended on winning. As the ball came his way, he swung viciously, not to return it but to murder it. When he succeeded, his face was illuminated by a broad smile. When he failed, he spat vile imprecations.

His moods changed with lightning speed. He hated his opponent, loved him, destroyed him, forgave him. He exuded warmth one moment, cold fury the next.

As he catapulted over the court, it was obvious that, dedicated as he was to the sport, his mind could be on other matters at the same time.

"Seven million!" he cried.

The South American shook his head and returned the ball. Smash! "Eight million!" Serge snarled.

He was negotiating a business deal over the net. He walloped the ball and grunted, "Nine million! Final!" Then "Ten million! Absolutely final!" Crash! Smash! "Eleven million! Game! Take it or leave it!"

Thinking back on Serge Rubinstein, it occurs to me that I saw all of his traits that day on the tennis court. There was the furious drive, the keen mind, the inexhaustible energy, the complete absorption in self. There were the split-second mood changes, from charm to frigidity to warmth to cruelty. He was hard, yet sentimental. He loved life, risked death, was both cynic and romantic. His enjoyment of the game, be it tennis or business, was of the flesh. He was a libertine on and off the court. He had to win dollars and females, and if necessary he would wrest victory from defeat by assault. He took what he wanted, brutally, coarsely, considerately, inconsiderately.

My friends, puzzled by this complicated man who died as violently as he lived, ask me, "What was he like?"

I tell them, "I'm not sure. He had a dual personality, to say the least."

The key to Rubinstein, if there is one, lies in that duality. One of his friends told me Serge was essentially a sado-masochist. I think he was correct. Serge Rubinstein was driven by demons. He may have derived real gratification from hurting people. And certainly he derived pleasure from being hurt. He was neither consistently evil nor good, but some of both. I understood him, which is why I liked him.

He was Machiavelli, Casanova, Nero, Midas, family man, and Sybarite.

I met him about 1947. The manager of the Beverly Hills Hotel told me that Mr. Rubinstein wanted a stenographer; would I come at once? I first laid eyes on him as he sat in the manager's office, in tennis shorts, a racket in his hand. He was about five-foot-six, of stocky frame, and blue-eyed. His brown hair was matted from perspiration. I was most conscious of his protruding lips and flaring nostrils. His nose was flattened, like a boxer's and I was to learn that he sometimes had difficulty in breathing because of a bad sinus condition. He was not handsome, nor did he look particularly Russian. I think of Russians as dark. Serge was light complexioned and looked more like a Pole.

In an urgent, high-pitched voice, he told me he wanted some documents typed. I said I was in the midst of other work, but would send another girl. He grunted agreement to this.

I sent in a temporary assistant. When she finished the work and Mr. Rubinstein wanted to pay her, she explained that since she worked for the hotel except when helping me out in emergencies, she could not accept payment directly from a guest. She asked him to send it to me; I would pay her when it arrived.

It didn't arrive, and I called on Mr. Rubinstein in his suite, to ask why.

"Her work was no good!" he said gruffly. "I don't think I'll give her anything."

"Oh, give her something," I urged. "Pay her something. She did put in the time."

Without further argument, he went downstairs to the specialty shop and ordered a huge bottle of perfume sent to the girl. It cost a good deal more than he would have had to pay for the work.

There was my first indication of his dual nature. He wouldn't recompense her, but he would. He wouldn't pay a $10 fee, but he would spend $50 on a gift.

If I had an initial resistance to working for Serge Rubinstein it was dispelled soon after this incident. To begin with, he was a customer. But also, something about his brusqueness and coarseness fascinated me. Without any preliminaries, he treated me as if we were lifetime friends. That was one of his talents. He could be friendly and unaffected with anyone.

He had leased quarters at the hotel for an extended stay, and I did a good deal of work for him in the next six months. At times I found myself liking this enigmatic man, yet I was also repulsed by his coarseness.

He seemed to like me and also to respect me—and respect was something he seldom had for people. We had unpleasant incidents, but they were momentary.

Our business relationship quickly ripened into a sort of friendship that lasted until his death. He considered me indispensable; he would have no one else work for him when he was in California. He would even telephone from New York, ordering me to fly East for some work. He was very generous, paid me well, and told me I could come to New York any time I wanted at his expense. When working hours called for it, we often dined and went to parties together, always with others. Serge was forever with a crowd. He needed people around him. Those about him were parasites—he knew it—but it made no difference. He got what he wanted from them just as they got what they wanted from him.

Everything was done frantically, sometimes hysterically. Wherever Serge was, there was excitement, a lot of noise. Most of his entourage consisted of strays, people he met one day who would be gone the next. There were a few steady hangers-on, however. There was a constant parade in and out of his rooms. Half the time he was unaware when people came and went. Waiters eternally trotted to and from the suite with food and drink. No one asked Serge's permission; everyone ordered extravagantly from room service; and Serge picked up the check and tipped generously without a murmur.

I have wondered why a man who could be satisfied with

mere acquaintances should have maintained his friendship with me. I think it was because he needed me and liked my work, and recognized in me someone who understood him.

He was not a religious man, but, incongruously, wore a mezuzah, a Hebrew talisman, around his neck. He liked talking Yiddish to me. He treated me as a sister, not as just another girl. By contrast, one of his New York secretaries told me that he treated her very indifferently, that he was cool toward her, often brusque. He didn't socialize with her or anyone else in that office. He was the boss and they were employees.

I doubt whether I would have remained with Serge had I not discovered how to handle him. He treated me very rudely once, and I flashed back at him. Immediately his behavior changed. I realized that the way to keep him in reasonable check was to talk back to him, although it was not my nature to behave that way. I noticed that if someone gave in to Serge readily and took a lot of browbeating, that person lost all influence over him. So far as he respected anyone, Serge respected people who gave him back as much as they took. In fact, there were times when I was sure he expected abuse. He appeared to take delight in being humiliated.

I saw casual acquaintances to whom he owed nothing insult him, show contempt for him, berate him viciously. Sometimes Serge didn't seem to understand he was being mistreated. But on other occasions he laughed appreciatively, as if admiring the technique.

If Serge wanted to be humiliated, I didn't give him much satisfaction. He did not hurt me often and I did not lose my temper except on rare occasions, and then only to get a matter settled expeditiously. He took it for granted that since he paid me well he had first call on my time—any time. He had no compunction about telephoning in the dead of night to bother me about the most trivial matter.

After a business session, Serge occasionally asked what I thought of the men with whom he had conferred. Could they be trusted? Why? He learned that a certain divorcee, who frequently came to the hotel, had a fortune in a silver mine. Did I think she was reliable? I did? Then I knew her? Did I believe she might be interested in investing in a corporation he was putting together? I introduced him to the woman at the pool, they chatted, played tennis, and it turned out that she was, indeed, willing to invest. I felt very good about having brought them together, because I thought they would both benefit from the relationship. Several months later I picked up a paper and there she was, suing Serge for a million dollars, charging misrepresentation in a business deal.

One reason why Serge remained an enigma to me was that I was never entirely certain about his background. He told me a great deal about his life but I could not be sure what was real and what was invented. Although his mother, Stella, was with him a lot, she rarely had anything to say, and I gleaned nothing from her.

Some of the stories he told about his childhood and youth were difficult to believe. This much, however, I accept as fact:

He was born in St. Petersburg, in Tsarist Russia. His father, a member of the nobility, was financial adviser to the Romanoffs, and reputedly a pretty sharp fellow at turning a fast and illicit ruble. When Serge was about four, the Rubinsteins escaped Russia one *verst* ahead of the Bolshevik Revolution. They did not leave as paupers. Serge told me he had jewels and negotiable securities sewn into his clothing.

That much is documented. Of the rest I am not positive. The family lived in France for a time. Then, Serge claimed, his mother sent him off to Vienna to study under Freud. This was on his thirteenth birthday!

On another occasion, he told me that he studied at Cambridge. Then he apparently lived in Portugal and other European countries. He was also in China, Japan and Korea. He headed the Bank of Korea. He also was engaged in gigantic financial operations in Europe. They were so complicated I could make no sense out of Serge's description of them.

Not from him, but from other informants, I heard that he

manipulated the French currency, producing a financial panic. As the value of the franc plummeted, the French government invited him to get out.

He was 28 when he arrived in the United States with his mother. Already he was a legendary figure, a boy wonder of finance.

I have heard that Serge was in some way responsible for the death of his brother, that it had to do with finance, but I don't know. If that were true, would his mother have come to New York with him?

I never really understood his kaleidoscopic dealings, but I do not doubt that they were spectacular and spanned the globe. To one person or another he was a genius, a financial wizard, a pirate, a confidence man, a draft dodger. He could manipulate stocks and bonds the way a little girl handles a ball and jacks. He smelled out money, sensed a company was going on the block before its officers did, bought it for thousands, then sold it for millions. He was great at figures. With almost lightning rapidity he could estimate what a corporation was worth and what it would earn.

Once he had me take notes at a business meeting, since a great many figures would be involved and the conferees would want an accurate record kept. When the meeting was over I prepared to read back the intricate mass of data. It was unnecessary. Serge repeated all of the figures from memory, without a single error.

Serge had a talent for rubbing people the wrong way and his reputation suffered for it. There was little suavity in Serge. His voice had an irritating quality. When he treated people rudely or coarsely, they called him a scoundrel. When he wined and dined his parasites, they ridiculed him behind his back. Since Serge died I have encountered many of the good-time Charlies who sponged off him, and not one had a kind word to say about him.

He usually didn't give a damn, but when he did he showed no sign. He was too busy. Dictating to me, he paced back and forth, greeted a sycophant, picked up the phone, fired away in

English, Russian, French, Portuguese. He screamed his arguments, spat his decisions. Momentarily charming, he would become a maniac before my eyes.

No matter how busy he was, he had to have girls around him. They telephoned him, or he would interrupt work to call one of them, cooing salacious messages into the mouthpiece. Sundry females, many of them unattractive in my opinion, trooped in and out, day and night. Almost always, one or more remained until morning. Serge liked a crowd, even in bed.

Finance, like women, intoxicated him. He shivered ecstatically when buying a transit company, selling an oil company, or manipulating the market. As negotiations reached a climax, anything could upset him. After working for days on a deal that had him keyed up to a high pitch, he telephoned me at 3 A.M. and demanded I come immediately. I found him pacing the floor in pajamas, actually trembling. He held up a box of pills.

"Do you think I should take some more of these?" he asked.

I stared. I had never seen him so overwrought.

He seemed like a little boy. "Do you think it would help?"

I felt sorry for him. "Don't take too many," I said, preparing to leave. "Good night—or good morning! I have to be back in a few hours."

He didn't want to be alone.

"Oh, no! Please!" He turned crafty. "What about that letter I gave you? The one I absolutely must have first thing in the morning?"

"I'll do it first thing in the morning, as I promised."

"No, please! I want to make sure! Do me just this little favor, Edna darling. Like a good girl, give me that one little letter."

Wearily, I took my notebook, went to my office upstairs and typed the letter. I brought it to him ten minutes later. He barely had it in his hand when he began screaming hysterically. I was so frightened I began to cry. "What's wrong?" I asked. I had never known him to carry on like that.

He screamed and screamed, jumping up and down. It was no common rage, but that blend of fury, anguish, pain and frustration one sees in an animal caught in the teeth of a trap.

The night maid banged on the door. "What's going on in there?"

This cooled Serge down a bit. "The date!" he said. "I distinctly instructed you to put yesterday's date on this letter, don't you remember? You've got today's date on it! TODAY'S!"

I remembered no such instructions, but I wanted to appease him. "I'm sorry," I said. "All I have to do is erase this date and put in the one you want. It won't show. Calm down! All the money in the world isn't worth working yourself up into such a state."

His response was odd. Staring into space, he said, "It isn't the money. This deal will break a lot of people, and I don't want to hurt that many people."

"What's the date got to do with it?"

"It might turn the whole deal." His mood changed. "Now go and change the date and come right back. I want you to go with me."

"Oh? Where are we going at this hour?"

"To the airport. In case."

I didn't ask why the airport or in case what. I said I was too tired to accompany him.

A pathetic smile suffused his face. "Do me this one little favor, Edna dear. You're a notary and I need you."

"No! I need my sleep."

"Look, Edna! This is the most important thing I've ever done. I'll give you a hundred dollars."

"All right. It's not the money, but if it means that much to you, I'll go."

"Thanks! Now let's get going. We haven't any time to lose. Hurry, for God's sake!"

He was to meet a representative of the corporation involved in the deal that had him in such a tizzy. The plane was due in from San Francisco at 6 A.M. The representative would depart on the next plane.

En route to the airport in a chauffeured car, Serge fidgeted, muttered to himself, and gazed unseeing into the distance. To get his mind off what worried him I remarked, "You know, you're getting thinner."

"Shut *up!*"

The chauffeur called back, "Pardon me, sir, shall I take Sepulveda or . . . ?"

"Shut *up!*"

When we arrived, Serge accompanied me to the Sky Room bar and instructed, "Sit at that table in the corner. I'll meet the plane. When I get back, pretend you never saw me before. Keep your eyes and ears open. Don't speak a word. Don't do anything unless I give you a sign."

It was about 5:45 in the morning. I sat tensely over a cup of coffee until Serge returned, piloting a tall, heavy-set man carrying a large briefcase. They sat down a few tables from me. I sipped my coffee and lit a cigarette. They conferred in normal tones. I heard nothing extraordinary. The recent arrival took some papers from his briefcase. Serge looked them over, then offered his own. The visitor studied them, signed, shook hands, departed. Serge came over to me and said, "Let's go. Everything's O.K."

A few months later Serge telephoned from New York. "Edna, get on the next plane."

"What for?"

"I need a deposition from you. Remember the fellow at the airport, that morning when you sat near us? You were there. I want you to make a deposition about what happened."

Serge told me later that my deposition saved him millions of dollars. I have no idea how.

Serge had a Napoleonic complex. He kept a bust of the Emperor on his desk in New York. When he attended masquerade parties it was invariably as Bonaparte. One evening I was answering the telephone for him in his suite while Serge dressed for a party. There was a knock on the door. The caller, who had never met Serge before, entered just as the Little Corporal emerged from the bedroom, cocked hat, epaulets, sword and all. The caller gulped, muttered a few words and left hastily.

I ran into him in the lobby later. "What's with him?" he

asked. "I heard he had a Napoleon complex but I didn't know he was that nuts! I wouldn't do business with him if he threw Josephine in with the deal!"

Serge was exceedingly vain. He would admire himself before a mirror while dictating. He worried over a line in his face, studied his waistline apprehensively. He wolfed his food, always had a drink at hand, yet was terribly weight conscious. His dresser was loaded with exotic toilet waters.

When he returned to the Coast after a brief absence, his invariable greeting was, "Well, how do I look? Am I fat? Did I get thinner? Do I look pale?" I would, of course, assure him he looked fine, whereupon he would pull in his stomach, puff out his chest and kiss my cheek lightly, saying, "Boy! It's good to see you!"

His dual nature came through in so many ways. One day he was chintzy, the next he threw his money around. The hotel, not having wanted him as a guest to begin with, notified him that his rent would be raised $10 a day. He bellowed he wouldn't stand for it, that he would move. Three days later he telephoned from New York, instructing me to lease a house for him.

"How much do you want to pay?"

"Well, use your judgment, but don't go over $5,000 a month."

He would not have his rent raised $300 a month, but he would spend much more than that in new quarters.

Sometimes he complained about my charge for a letter; on other occasions he paid me double and triple what I asked. At times his generosity really seemed to come from the heart. He remembered me on every holiday, either with a gift or a telegram. The last New Year's greeting I received from him from New York, arrived with a magnificent bouquet. Attached to it was a card reading, "Thanks for your wonderful work. Let's work together for many years to come. Wishing you a Happy New Year. Serge Rubinstein." I still have the card.

He kept me working at all hours, but continually interrupted with, "Hungry? Eat something! Order room service!"

His generosity stemmed in part from his need for company.

He half-hypnotized himself into believing the sycophants liked him. They satisfied a need for him and he let them share his liquor, his women, his tips on business. Serge couldn't make friends; therefore, he had to buy people, cynically, deliberately.

I used to ask him, "Serge, why do you fool around with those girls? They're only interested in your money."

He would answer, "I know, but they give me what I want, so what do I care?"

He bought his girls, if not by outright payment, by entertainment and gifts. He had a penchant for very young ones. He would locate them at dinner parties, in cocktail lounges, hotel lobbies, and through business acquaintances who wanted to get on his good side. He once financed a beauty contest so that a particular girl would be able to enter and, hopefully, win. He even bought into movies to get girls.

From what I heard, his sexual demands were inordinate. He craved variety, yet never had enough. Girls meant nothing as individuals. It made no difference who or what they were, so long as they were there when he needed them and gave him what he wanted. I never knew him to have an intelligent girl friend. His former wife was an exception.

He could be as rude to his lovelies as to anyone else. I was taking notes at a business conference in his suite when an exceptionally stupid girl knocked at his door and sauntered in, strumming a mandolin.

"Hello, honey!" she crooned. "Am I on time?"

Serge nodded curtly, pointed. "Be quiet! Sit over there!"

He returned to business. She continued plunking her mandolin.

"You dope!" Serge shouted. "Stop that goddamned racket!"

She giggled and plunked her mandolin. The conferees exchanged glances. Serge turned to me. "Take that idiot into the bedroom and shut the door! Lock it! I'll see her later."

Once an acquaintance asked him to help a South American girl get her career started.

"What does she do?"

"She's a singer. Acts, too."

"I didn't mean that. *Does* she?"

"She does."

"Bring her to dinner at the Marquis Restaurant tonight."

I was there, too. The chanteuse sat beside Serge. She was beautiful, and Serge brazenly admired her attractions. During dessert he told her, "Get up on the chair and sing."

She was about to refuse, thought better of it, and got up on her chair, teetering on spike heels.

As diners gaped, the ambitious young lady faced Serge, smiled seductively, and opened her mouth. What came out wasn't good, but it wasn't bad, either, at least not bad enough to merit what happened before she completed two bars. "Sit down!" Serge yelled. "You're terrible!"

Needless to say, the outburst disrupted the gaiety of the party. The poor girl descended from her perch in tears. Serge ignored her the rest of the evening.

This same chameleon-like man called me one night, insisting I drive Peggy, an eighteen-year-old whom he particularly liked, to her home in San Pedro. I pleaded that it was late and foggy, and that she could take a taxi. He would have none of that. Peggy was young and inexperienced, he argued. He wouldn't have her in a taxi, with a strange driver. He offered me $100 to take her home. I refused, suggesting instead that he rent a chauffeured car. Serge finally settled for that.

Although he indulged his girls, he did not neglect his own welfare. During one of his frequent sieges of insomnia, he flew out of Los Angeles for New York each Friday, returning on Monday at noon. He had no urgent business in the East. The droning of the plane engines put him to sleep.

Because he was Serge Rubinstein, wealthy, of dubious repute, a man who served a penitentiary term for draft dodging, everyone felt free to exploit him. If he bought a suit, he usually paid more than anyone else. When he registered in a hotel, he was charged premium rates to discourage his coming again. Turned down altogether, he would shrug and try the same place next time.

It was strange that a man who could be so calculating in some ways should be so impulsive and unpredictable in others.

He sent me to buy him a plane ticket to Kansas City for a flight departing that evening. When I delivered it, he asked if I would like to go to San Francisco with him instead, to attend a wedding. As we discussed the matter, two acquaintances phoned and he invited them, too. Kansas City and business forgotten, he took off for San Francisco.

Serge was engrossed in a deal, scarcely aware of anything else, when he heard over the radio that the United Nations had committed itself to sending troops into Korea. He put his papers aside and immediately dictated a letter to the Secretary of Defense, stating that he knew the Korean people, that he had once controlled the Bank of Korea, and that he would be happy to serve the United States Government in any capacity suited to his abilities. The offer was declined, and he was very disappointed. I don't know what Serge had in mind. Maybe he wanted to redeem himself for his draft-dodging record in World War II.

Serge demonstrated his inconsistency when his ex-wife who lived in California, wanted a dishwasher. He phoned me from New York to ask, "Will you please locate a discount house and get me a special price? I'll call back."

When he did, the price didn't suit him, and he asked me to try further. He telephoned five times that day, and continued calling all of the following week, by which time he probably had spent some $300 in long distance calls.

"Oh, hell!" he said at last. "Forget about it!"

I heard later that he had his ex-wife buy the machine she wanted in a local department store. She paid full list price, which still was less than what it cost Serge for toll calls trying to locate a bargain.

He seemed to love his children, Sandy and Diana, and had them stay with him as often as possible. Yet in his will, he specified that they were not to come into the money he left them until they reached age 50!

Some of Serge's help in his New York home treated him disrespectfully, in my opinion, and got away with it. He and his mother lived in an impressive Fifth Avenue mansion, once the residence of the financier Bache. It was a huge structure, next to the home of William Randolph Hearst, Jr. A heavy iron door barred the front entrance. There were two elevators inside. The rooms and hallways were hung with priceless paintings. Serge worked in an office-study on the third floor, adjoining the bedroom.

His butler-chauffeur, William, had been with the family many years. He was a caustic Irishman, about Serge's age, very likeable. I was present once when Serge told him to take care of something.

"I can't do it now," William said.

Once when he failed to do something he was supposed to do, I remarked that his boss would bawl him out. "Well, he'd better not!" William growled.

We were working one afternoon. Serge asked William to bring us some lunch. A half hour later he brought in delicious tuna sandwiches.

"Thank you, William!" said Serge.

"Oh," his man said, "I didn't go to all that bother for you. I did it for her."

I was in San Francisco, having breakfast in the Hotel Maurice, when I happened to see the headline on a newspaper another diner was reading. It struck me full in the face: SERGE RUBINSTEIN MURDERED. I uttered a cry, sank into my chair, in near-collapse from shock. As soon as I could manage, I ran to the newsstand and bought a paper. I locked myself in my room, terrified. I took it for granted that Serge was killed in reprisal for some business machination. His slayers, I thought, might come after me, believing that I knew enough to incriminate them.

With the illogic born of grief, I thought: "Now Serge won't have to be worried about getting old." He was so vain! Now at 42 he was dead.

When I regained some composure, I read the details of the homicide. They were revolting. He was bound, gagged, strangled. I visualized the bedroom where William came upon the body. On several occasions I had been in the study next to it. The house was large, but it seemed improbable that no one heard Serge cry out. The stairway was not far from the bedroom. There were windows all around. How could this have happened without anyone overhearing the struggle that must have ensued? It would have been possible only if his killers had crept up behind him, taken him by surprise, gagged him before he could utter a sound, tied him up and murdered him.

Guests in the hotel dining room heard me cry out when I read the headline. Someone apparently discovered that I had worked for Serge, and now reporters began telephoning, demanding interviews, insisting on a statement over the phone. They asked for my theory as to motive. I told them Serge had many enemies. They asked why, and I suggested that perhaps it was because of his business manipulations. What they printed was that I believed Serge had enemies because he had so much money. I didn't say that. At least I didn't mean that. What I tried to say was that, as a man of wealth, Serge was involved in a great many financial transactions. Naturally, some led to enmity. The homicide, I felt, was the climax of a vendetta, based on a business operation. Someone was taking revenge for a real or fancied injury. I told reporters that Serge had a knack for antagonizing. I meant to point out that his relationships were very bad in many quarters. Perhaps someone, outflanked or double-crossed by my erstwhile employer, got his revenge this way.

I still hold to this theory, although others have been advanced. One theory maintains that he tried to extort blackmail from a victim, who then turned on him. That is fantastic. Serge didn't need money. And if he had damaging information about anyone, he could scarcely have used it as a threat, for all of Serge's private life was known to his associates, and a victim would have plenty of juicy stories to use as a counter-threat.

What about William? He was questioned at length and exonerated. William was loyal and, as far as I knew, had no motive for murder.

Then could this actually be plain robbery? Not in my judgment. The iron door barring the entrance was locked to all but expected callers. Entry through a window would have been almost impossible. Besides, neither door nor window was breached.

Only a senseless amateur would have tried to burglarize such a house, and if robbery were intended it would have been easier to waylay Serge on the street. Moreover, nothing seemed to have been taken from the Rubinstein home.

The logical conclusion, it seems to me, is that someone known to Serge was admitted by him. There may have been more than one caller. Whatever the reason for the visit, a quarrel ensued. Then murder. The slayer or slayers departed quietly.

There was one hush-hush theory going the rounds that has not yet come to an end. It was whispered that this was not a homicide at all, but rather that it was an accident. According to this rumor, Serge derived sexual gratification from being bound hand and foot, subjected to indignities, whipped, and tortured. This story maintained that Serge invited several girls and perhaps some men for such a party. They bound and gagged him at his own request, left him in the bedroom to flavor the ultimate in helplessness. Trussed up as he was, he had difficulty breathing. His flattened nose would be a factor. As he struggled to extricate himself, the rope about his neck choked him into insensibility. His body sagged, the rope tightened, shut off his windpipe entirely, and he strangled.

I have already suggested Serge was masochistic. He may have been masochistic enough to experience sexual satisfaction from being tortured. There were dark recesses of his character which people never knew about. Yet I think that I understood Serge better than most people, and it is difficult to believe he could have had a compulsion as deep-seated as this without my sensing it. If Serge died in the course of such a ritual, it has not been established. Undoubtedly all his known associates in New York were interrogated by police, yet no supposed participant in such a rite came to light as far as I know. The riddle of Serge's death remains unsolved.

In death, the vultures hovered over his body. Firms sent bills for expensive dinner suits he had never ordered. He was billed for legal and medical service he had never received.

Of all the men I worked for, Serge Rubinstein stands out as the most flamboyant. I often think about him, and really feel bad. He loved living. He might have been a better man in the conventional sense had he been born in different circumstances. Perhaps he would have lived longer. He could have done so much if he had been pointed in the right direction!

Reviewing his life, I realize there was a basic consistency in Serge's many inconsistencies. Good or evil, generous or picayune, gentle or coarse, he was never anything but himself.

Chapter 8

Life with
Lerner and Loewe

Alan Jay Lerner and Frederick Loewe were among my early
clients. In 1950, Mr. Lerner, who with his wife Nancy Olson
occupied a suite at the Beverly Hills Hotel, asked me to come
up for dictation. Curiously, Alan Lerner's name was unfamiliar to
me at that time. And I had never heard of Frederick Loewe,
although the two collaborators already had a smash hit to their
credit, the musical *Brigadoon*. At the time he called, Mr. Lerner
was working on the screenplay of *Royal Wedding* for MGM.

I was surprised to be greeted by such a young fellow when
I entered the suite. Short, slim, wearing glasses, he looked like a
college boy, although he was in his early thirties. There was an
intensity about him, a certain nervousness. He was straining at
the bit, anxious to get working. I found him appealing.

A painstaking craftsman, he dictated slowly, laboriously.
Rarely did he have to revise anything once dictated. He was

pleased with my work, and continued using my services throughout the preparation of the script.

He rented a large house high up in Beverly Hills when he was writing his new musical, *Paint Your Wagon,* in collaboration with his music man, Frederick Loewe. Again he called on my services.

As I entered the library with a cheery good morning, both men jumped to their feet. They were in rumpled sleeping pajamas, and barefooted. Their hair was tousled. They remained standing until I politely asked them to sit down, and in the meantime deposited my portable typewriter and stationery.

Loewe, whom I was seeing for the first time, was short and of slight build, with large eyes that bulged somewhat. Although Austrian by birth, he retained only the slightest trace of a Germanic accent.

The partners were of different temperaments, I soon noted, Mr. Loewe being more outgoing and direct in conversation than Mr. Lerner. Lerner seemed impersonal; Loewe was quite friendly.

We worked relentlessly, sustained by innumerable cups of coffee drawn from an electric percolator. The partners worked well together, had the same feeling for things, were sensitive to each other's moods. Although Loewe was considerably older than his collaborator, this difference in age was no impediment to their creative undertakings. I liked them both very much, although at the time I felt more *en rapport* with Mr. Lerner, perhaps because I had worked with him before.

We struck an informal note from the beginning. They called me by my first name and I addressed them by theirs. In the days that followed, Alan and I enjoyed excellent working relations, but rarely discussed personal matters. Fritz and I, on the other hand, frequently did. I am not suggesting that Alan was insensitive to people's feelings but rather that he concentrated so intensely on his work that other things were of lesser importance. He could and did emerge from his retreat, displaying warmth and consideration.

There was the time I arrived at the house highly disturbed.

An hour before, I had been in the suite of a South American client who apparently believed a girl willing to take dictation in a man's room must be willing to take something else. He became insistently amorous, and when I rebuffed him he only increased his importunities. When I suggested that he bank his fire, he went berserk, pulled me to him, tore at my clothes, and dragged me toward the bedroom. I managed to break loose and get out of his room.

I was still so badly shaken when I got to Alan's house that my hand trembled when I started to write shorthand. He noticed this and asked what was wrong. When I explained, he brought me a glass of brandy and said, "Here! Drink this! You'll feel better." Then he remarked, "I don't see why you should be so shook up. I'm sure it isn't the first time a thing like that happened to you." There was no innuendo in the comment. He merely took for granted that a personable public stenographer inevitably is the object of uninvited advances every so often.

The brandy did calm my nerves, and Alan's kind gesture made me feel a little closer to him.

With the completion of the *Paint Your Wagon* script, Lerner and Loewe returned to New York. Their next collaboration was *My Fair Lady*, the biggest hit Broadway had seen to that day. It made them world famous.

I did not see Fritz for quite a long time after he left Hollywood. I did spend an agreeable evening with Alan while visiting New York. He invited me to see the show we worked on in Beverly Hills. Afterward, I met him at Sardi's for a drink, and it was a thrill indeed to be seated beside the famous Broadway playwright in the gathering place of the most successful and scintillating folk of the theatre.

I did not really know Lerner and Loewe well until I went to Paris to work for them on the MGM film, *Gigi*. The opportunity came my way by sheer accident. In the dining room of the Bel Air Hotel I caught sight of Alan's wife at a table with her father. She and I had become rather friendly during the time I worked in her house, and she now invited me to join them. In the course of conversation she remarked that Alan was in Paris, doing a movie, and when she spoke to him last, by telephone, he complained that he was in great need of a competent secretary and unable to find one in France.

Paris is to me the spirit's fountain of replenishment. Nancy's remark fairly set me aquiver. "Do you suppose I could work for him?" I asked.

"Why don't you wire Alan and tell him you're available?" I did, and he cabled back, "How soon can you get here?"

No one informed me what I would be paid, or by whom. I didn't want to ask, and besides, it didn't much matter; I would be in Paris. I flew over, and since I would have to lay out my own money for the time being, took a room in a cheap little hotel a few blocks from Alan's suite in the Hotel George V, where I was to work.

Neither Lerner nor Loewe brought up the matter of salary at any time. I did not ask them about it. They did not inquire why I was living in another hotel, and I did not volunteer an explanation.

We had a miserable heat wave that summer, my room had no bath, and it was impossible to cool off. The one bathtub was two flights up in a room that was locked at 8 P.M., when the maid went home. Since I never returned to my hotel before then, I forfeited that modicum of comfort. I could stand it just so long. One day, when the humidity was unbearable, I explained my predicament to Alan and asked if he would mind if I took a bath in his suite when he was out. He was agreeable, and I appreciated his kindness. He still did not inquire why I remained in my uncomfortable quarters.

About that time, a knowledgeable acquaintance told me that MGM was paying the living costs of other Americans working on the film, and no doubt would pay mine as well. Acting on that, I moved into the cheapest room I could get at the very expensive George V, a type reserved for maids and chauffeurs.

Alan Lerner ran a tight schedule. We began to work around mid-morning, stopped for a late lunch, and then returned to our labor and kept at it until Alan called a halt for dinner, at about eight o'clock. We frequently returned to work after dinner. Alan seemed at his creative best late at night. He asked if I minded putting in such hours, and since he needed me, I answered in the negative.

The strain of keeping up to schedule made Lerner tense and nervous. He chewed his fingernails to the skin. It seemed to annoy him if I interrupted his dictation to ask him to repeat something. His nervousness communicated itself to me, and yet I felt drawn to him. I may have had an idealized crush on him. He was handsome, educated, successful—but also aloof. If he was aware of my existence it was only because I was his secretary.

Throughout that terrible heat wave I did my typing in a tiny room without air conditioning. After being cooped up for hours, I would escape to the outdoor patio of the hotel for lunch. It furnished such blessed relief that I began taking an hour and a half or even two hours. Lerner said nothing for awhile, although I could tell he was displeased. Eventually he asked me to have lunch in the room where I worked. He justified the request by saying that he had failed to get several phone calls because I was out to lunch, and there really was no reason why I couldn't eat in the suite.

I wanted to get away for some sightseeing, and when a friend from the States arrived in Paris, we decided to spend a weekend in Belgium. I notified Alan, saying I would return on Monday. Unfortunately, I came down with flu on the trip, and had to wire him that I would probably not return until the end of that week.

When I returned to Paris, still shaky, Alan seemed very cool. I suspect that he believed I feigned illness to prolong my vacation, for he interrupted dictation to ask, rather pointedly I thought, just what had been the trouble. When I told him I had the flu, he remarked that I picked a mighty poor time to contract it, inasmuch as he needed my services more than ever during the past week.

Alan's nervous temperament showed itself in a mild hypochondria. The medicine cabinet of his bathroom would have passed for a pharmacist's shelf. Because he was so concerned about his health, I suggested that he try a certain vitamin pill, highly advertised in the States and supposedly beneficial for anything from pip to pellagra. It was quite a fad. I myself used it and was convinced that it helped me, I told Alan.

"O.K.," he said, "get me a bottle."

I ordered one from the San Francisco distributor, asking that it be shipped airmail. This must have suggested urgency, for to insure speedy delivery the firm stamped MEDICINE on the package. The pills cost $27. Airmail charges added to that. French law fixed a special duty on medicinal imports, in this particular instance, $54. The bottle of vitamins cost almost $100 in all. This did not upset Alan, but he must have been disappointed in the pills, for he did not reorder, which was just as well. The Food and Drug Administration subsequently charged the manufacturer with making exaggerated claims for the product.

Once in a while Alan would relax and tell me something about himself. His family owned a nationwide chain of dress shops, and he could have taken them over had he so desired, but he was disinterested in business, turning to writing musicals instead while still in college. His parents considered this a waste of his time, but Alan was not deterred. At a comparatively early age he proved that his faith in his talent was justified.

I got to know Fritz Loewe better during the *Gigi* period, although I spent most of my time with Lerner. The contrasts in their personalities seemed based at least partly on their dissimilar backgrounds. Lerner traveled a great deal and was by no means insular, but Loewe was even more sophisticated, a real continental European. Lerner was born to great wealth, where Loewe had to work to acquire it. The money Alan made in show business did not alter his living habits to any appreciable degree; accustomed to luxury, he took it in stride and continued much as before. Loewe enjoyed high living once he could afford it, but since this occurred comparatively late in life, he was less casual about it. He surrounded himself with all sorts of luxuries and indulged in them with great gusto.

When I saw Fritz during my stay in Paris, he was very

friendly. He asked about my personal life and my work. He regaled me with details about his own experiences and people he had met.

I had gone to his suite on an errand one afternoon and was preparing to leave when he surprised me by saying, "Stay a little while longer." He seemed to be in a lonely and talkative mood. We went onto the balcony, overlooking the roofs of Paris. Fritz talked about Europe, its culture, its meaning to him, the charm of Paris. He reminisced about his childhood in Vienna, his first introduction to music. As we stood there, we heard music from the score of *My Fair Lady* coming up from the patio below.

"Listen!" I said. "Your beautiful music! It follows you even here, in Paris."

He was very pleased. "Yes!" he said. "It is everywhere. Wherever I travel, I hear my music." He hummed "I Could Have Danced All Night" to the music reaching us from below, and though he was proud of it, he had to be modest. "Ach!" he exclaimed. "I'm tired of hearing it!"

As if to divert my attention from the music, he changed the subject, asking if I had had any affairs in Paris. When I answered in the negative, he expressed surprise. "You should," he said.

"It doesn't happen like that," I told him. "I have to care a lot for a man first."

"Hah!"

A few days later, he asked me to exchange some francs for English money. "I need it for the BBC," he explained. I took that to mean he was leaving for London to do business with the British Broadcasting Corporation. When I delivered the money, I heard him instruct his chauffeur to be available to drive him to the Orly Airport that evening, where he was to pick up a friend flying in from London.

"Did you change your plans?" I asked. "I thought you were going to London."

"No, I'm not going to London."

"But you said you needed English money, for the BBC."

He chuckled. "Oh, that! She's Big and she's British and all the rest of it."

Ever since then, I cannot refrain from smiling when the British Broadcasting Corporation is mentioned.

I had something of a resentment against Lerner and Loewe in Paris because neither of them invited me anywhere. They dined in the finest restaurants with their friends, but never took me along. I had told them that I didn't know many people in Paris, and that the few I did know were out of town for the summer, yet at day's end, they went their way and left me to go mine. To be sure, they were not obligated to entertain me, but I thought it would be nice to be included in a party now and then, since I was alone.

I hinted shamelessly. Many times I mentioned I had had dinner by myself. I remarked I had never been to Maxim's the famous restaurant where a scene in *Gigi* was being shot. Neither Alan nor Fritz took the hint.

But, I discovered, they were not altogether impervious. When I arrived for work one afternoon, I found Alan in deep conversation with Fritz and Arthur Freed, the producer of the film. They stopped short when I greeted them, leading me to suspect they had been discussing me. In a casual *non sequitur*, Mr. Freed inquired if I was having a good time in Paris. Since he had never thought to ask the question before, this seemed curious to me. I told him that merely being in Paris excited me. But, I added, I hadn't been around much.

Freed glanced at Lerner, and Lerner at Loewe, as if my response bore on their previous conversation.

"Why don't you get yourself a date?" Freed asked.

"I don't know anyone to go out with."

Lerner picked up. "We've been talking about you."

"So I gathered."

"We decided you should have a date."

"That's nice of you! But I don't see how I can get one. I usually leave here so late, I can't meet anyone. I can't just go out on the street and pick up the first man who comes along."

"Well, not at night," Alan said. "But you could take the afternoon off, and go over to one of the restaurants on the Champs Elysees, sit down at a table on the sidewalk, and order something. If you're alone, some man is bound to start a conversation and he may invite you to go out. Try it! This afternoon."

"O.K. I'll try it. Let's see what happens."

I sauntered over to the Champs Elysees, sat down at a table at Fouquet's and ordered tea and a strawberry tart. Sure enough! A very attractive fellow was sitting at the table next to mine. We exchanged glances now and then. The waiter brought the check and I asked if his tip was included. He said it was not. I handed him some francs to pay the bill, and left several coins for him. At this, the fellow at the next table jumped up, came over and told me the waiter was not telling the truth, that a 15% service charge was added to every bill. He scooped up my coins, returned them to me, ignored the waiter glowering from a distance, and asked if he might sit down.

I was American, was I not?

Oui, m'sieur.

He introduced himself as a duke from one of the provinces, and as proof, displayed the ring on his finger, bearing the family crest. I told him what I was doing in Paris and that I had not seen very much of it.

He pointed to a blue, high-powered sports car at the curb. Would I care to visit Versailles?

Would I!

Off we went. Arrived at our destination, the Duke looked toward the gates of the Palace and remarked, "It's closed. I'm sorry. We're too late."

Seeing how disappointed I was, my companion suggested we drive a few miles farther, to where he kept his private plane. He would like to show it to me. Flying and automobile racing were his hobbies.

He had been charming, I had nothing else to do, so I said I would be delighted to inspect his plane.

After about a fifteen-minute drive, the Duke pulled up alongside a wheat field, which was just about ready for harvesting.

"Where's the plane?" I asked.

He pointed into the field. "We go down that path. You can't see it from here."

We got out and walked into the field some two hundred feet. Suddenly I hit the ground with a shuddering thud; the Duke was on top of me, transformed into a snarling madman. I screamed, scratched, but the weight of his body immobilized me. Then I began sneezing. I have hay fever, and the dried vegetation sent me into convulsions. Defending myself became almost impossible. Certain that this maniac would rape and perhaps murder me, I summoned all the force at my command, heaved upward, and got him off balance just long enough for me to get out from under him. The next moment I was on my feet and racing off, the duke in hot pursuit. If I got onto the open road, perhaps a car would come along and save me.

No such luck. The duke caught up, grabbed me, pressed me against his car, panting. He wasn't like an American man, he snarled—a fool who allowed a girl to lead him on, get him all excited, then tell him to cool off and forget it. A Frenchman wouldn't stand for such nonsense. The Duke was a man, a real man. I accepted his offer of a drive, I led him on, and he would show me. . . .

In my desperation it occurred to me that if I could get him to believe I had indeed led him on, because I found him terribly attractive, I might avoid being dragged back into the field. Stalling for time, I coaxed, "You scared me, back there. That was the trouble. You don't want me like this. Suppose someone comes along? Why don't you come back to my hotel with me? It will be much more pleasant there."

He studied me, undecided whether this was a trick or an invitation.

"You're very handsome," I said, attempting what I hoped was a seductive smile. "I would enjoy having you make love to me in my room. I've never had a Frenchman."

He loosened his hold. "Very well," he mumbled. "I will drive you back and we will go to your room. Yes?"

"Yes!"

It was my only alternative. Once at the hotel, I would be able to manage the situation somehow.

We got into the car and drove back to the city. The Duke must still have been fuming, for he stepped up his speed until the needle trembled at 120, with me swaying from side to side and begging him to slow down. He paid no attention, uttered not a word, and just clenched his jaw and kept zigzagging in and out of traffic, his hand on the horn. Motorists honked, shook their fists, shouted imprecations. He kept roaring along. I am sure that only his experience in racing cars was responsible for the fact we were not annihilated.

By the time we reached the city, his mood had changed, whatever the reason. He came to a stop not far from the Arc de Triomphe and barked, "Get out!"

I complied with alacrity, and tramped back to the George V, a bedraggled figure, sneezing, my dress and stockings torn, face scratched. Just as I arrived, Alan Lerner walked into the lobby.

"My God!" he cried. "What happened to you?"

I certainly couldn't boast that I'd made a conquest at Fouquet's. All I could say was, "Achoo!"

When I described my harrowing experience to the three men, they considered it hilarious. I think they were disappointed in me, too, for having passed up what they thought should have been a thrill for me—a roll in the wheat with a duke. Or perhaps they believed I hadn't passed it up. I detected skeptical gleams in their eyes now and then.

Alan and Fritz finished their work and returned to New York. I remained in Paris, working for Mr. Freed a while longer.

Unbelievable as it may seem, I still had no idea what was due me in salary when I was ready to leave for home. Having moved into the George V on faith but no francs, I asked the cashier to advance me some money, to be charged to my room. Since she accommodated me without hesitation, this confirmed in my mind that MGM would underwrite living costs. From then on I handled everything I could that way—meals, valet, hairdresser, even a doctor. That was how I managed to get along.

And now, preparing to leave Paris, I asked the auditor of the production company about salary. He assured me that I would receive it after he figured out what was due me, but that would take some time.

When I returned to Beverly Hills, I began what promised to be an endless negotiation for the money due me from my stay in Paris. It took almost a year, but at last I received a check for slightly more than $100—my net for three months. It didn't much matter. I had had a memorable stay.

The following year, Fritz and Alan won Oscars for *Gigi* and I wrote them separate letters of congratulation.

Alan was now living in New York. I saw him only once, when he came to Beverly Hills for an Academy Awards banquet. I called to him as he walked through the lobby, he turned, said hello, and went on.

I have seen Fritz Loewe more often, since he lives in California. Several times, when he visited Beverly Hills, he asked me to his hotel, for dinner, or just to talk. Despite his sophisticated existence, a yacht on the Riviera, a Rolls Royce, and a mansion in Palm Springs, I think Fritz is lonely. He has few intimate friends; indeed, he is a bit cynical on the subject. To explain his cynicism, he told me about a man with whom he had been very close for years, whom he had loaned considerable sums. When Fritz was hospitalized with a heart attack, this good friend telephoned to wish him well—collect.

Although Fritz thoroughly enjoys what money will provide, he claims it is a botheration. Once when we were dining in a hotel and the orchestra struck up a medley from *My Fair Lady,* he found it necessary to say, "I wish they'd stop playing the darn thing! Every time they play it, it's only making more money for me, and I've got enough to worry about already!"

"Were you happier when you were poor?" I asked.

"Hell, no!"

If Fritz lives regally, he gives the same way. He contributes to many charities, his favorite being Palm Springs Hospital, which receives a substantial percentage of his royalties.

I asked, "Why Palm Springs Hospital? Why not some great medical center in Los Angeles or New York?"

"I spend more time in Palm Springs than anywhere else. Suppose I have a heart attack in Palm Springs. I'd rather be in a hospital that will have the best of equipment, where I can get good care. Besides," he added, "when you contribute to a small hospital, in a small community, you get big notices in the papers. If you contribute to a large, world-famed medical center, it goes unnoticed."

I think he injected that materialistic note so I wouldn't consider him a sentimentalist.

Many people who love musicals ask why such a nonpareil team as Lerner and Loewe broke up. Fritz gave me his version one night in the Escoffier Room of the Beverly Hilton. He sounded bitter, declaring that he wanted nothing more to do with Lerner, that he didn't want to hear his name mentioned. People who knew them had urged them to get together again and Alan had made overtures through friends once or twice, so Fritz said, but he had no intention of becoming reconciled with Lerner. In fact, he told me that he no longer cared to write music.

According to Fritz, Micheline, whom Alan married after he was divorced from Nancy, was responsible for the rupture of their relationship. She wanted Alan to herself, and isolated him from his friends. He became very nervous, irritable, and impossible to work with.

Fritz pinpointed an incident for me which, he said, finally convinced him that further partnership with Lerner was untenable. President Eisenhower invited them to dinner at the White House, and they accepted. Then Alan pulled out, explaining that he would not attend because his wife was not included in the invitation. Fritz felt in his own heart that it was Mrs. Lerner, not Alan, who made the decision. The incident was of little importance by itself, but it convinced Fritz that Alan's wife dominated him, had driven a wedge between Lerner and Loewe, and had effectively stifled any further opportunity for continuing the intimate collaboration they had formerly enjoyed and had to have if they were to be a working team.

I cannot, from my own knowledge of the two men, say who or what was responsible for the breakup of this highly talented, spectacularly successful team. I can only say I admire and respect them both, and wish they were together again, so the world might thrill to more of their magnificent collaborations.

❊

Chapter 9

The champagne
never stops bubbling

We were taking a breather in the Peacock Alley Lounge of the
Waldorf-Astoria in New York, following a long afternoon's
work. I had a glass of sparkling champagne at one elbow, my
notebook at the other. My client, an author, had a faraway look
that suggested he was thinking his way through a writing problem. He had not touched his glass.

"Don't you like champagne?" I asked.

He grinned. "Work is my champagne." His problem was
solved; he was impatient to get back to the room to continue our
work.

Fortunate indeed is the person whose work is champagne.
Mine is—and the champagne never stops bubbling. But sometimes the cork pops with an extra bang and the bubbles are bub-
blier than usual.

There was the world premiere of the Cinerama film *Mad*,

Mad, Mad, Mad World. The company that produced it took over the Beverly Hilton as headquarters for the promotion. Reporters, columnists, critics and publicity men from all over the world were invited, and a press room was set up near the pool for their convenience. Among the many show people on the invitation list were Russia's top actress and actor, Margarita Volodina and Viatcheslav Tikhonov, who were to be accompanied by Philip Yermach, a film critic from a Russian news agency. Before they arrived, an executive of the film corporation asked if I could furnish an interpreter. I volunteered the services of a friend, Helga, who met the Russians at the airport, only to discover that they had brought their own interpreter, Vitaline Noval.

I wanted very much to meet the foremost film stars of the USSR, and Helga introduced us upon their arrival at the hotel. We established rapport immediately, despite the fact that we could communicate only through the interpreter. I spent a great deal of time with them during their stay.

I watched the girls unpack, curious to see what clothes were available in Russia. They brought out simple, black cocktail dresses, which they planned to wear to a banquet that evening. Their clothes were modish, more so than those I had seen in the Soviet Union when I visited there a few years earlier. The girls told me they had excellent dressmakers in Moscow.

Their shoes were attractive, too—nicely fashioned sandals with short, slim heels. They owned wrist watches, and very attractive jewelry. When I admired the long amber earrings Margarita had dangling from her ears, she took them off, put them in my hand, and indicated that she wanted me to have them as a gift.

Considering their otherwise abundant finery, I was surprised to learn that neither girl owned an evening wrap.

They had good makeup and used it generously. The mascara and powder were of Russian manufacture, the eyebrow pencils and nail polish French. I made a gift of my own eyebrow pencil to Margarita when I noticed how its built-in sharpener fascinated her.

The girls had not yet departed for the banquet when the two men of the party knocked and entered. As we all conversed, it was obvious to me that our Soviet visitors were more nationalistic about their country than we are about ours. Mention of anything or anybody Russian struck a responsive chord immediately. When I told them my father had come from the Ukraine, each of them hugged me.

My Russian friends invited me to sit with them at the banquet, and I kept Vitaline, the interpreter, very busy, trying to carry on a conversation with the other three. The girls appeared blasé, uninterested in the obvious show of wealth all about. It did not seem to bother them that they were wearing their regular coats whereas the other women were decked in luxurious furs and evening coats. Vitaline remarked that all our evening dresses looked like theatrical costumes.

They also seemed unimpressed with the dinner. The filet mignon and Baked Alaska failed to excite them, but they were delighted when the waiter, who spoke Russian, brought them extra portions of potatoes. They engaged in conversation with him and came near embracing him when they learned he spent some time in the Soviet Union during World War II.

I spent every available moment with the visitors in the days that followed and liked them very much, but at times I couldn't help feeling that they considered themselves superior to us. But despite their understandable favoring of things Russian, they could not conceal their delight in certain of our goods and conveniences. They would have been content to remain in their rooms all day and night, I do believe, so fascinated were they by American television. They kept their sets going continuously. They loved our fresh fruit, of which they ate a great deal. The winter season was almost upon us, yet in Russia they could get fruit only at the height of summer. One thing they didn't care for was our cigarettes. Viatcheslav smoked a very strong Albanian brand. He refused American cigarettes. He tried one of our brands once, he said, and that was enough. He had no desire to try another.

Before they left, I gave the Russian visitors some remembrance gifts. Because they had told me artificial flowers were unavailable in their country, I presented them with a selection of these. I gave them a huge box of toys for their children, having been informed there was a shortage of toys in the Soviet Union. The actors were so intrigued with the cowboy stuff that they kept playing with the six-shooters themselves.

After I gave them the presents, they led me to an easy chair, gently pushing me into it. They surrounded me, the girls at each side, the men at my feet, and handed me a pin emblazoned with the hammer and sickle emblem and some hand-carved, lacquered wooden art objects. We all kissed and hugged, and made plans to get together in San Francisco a few days later, where they were to attend the Film Festival. However, once in San Francisco, they had to withdraw their invitation, since they feared the Russian attaché would question my presence among a group of Soviet citizens. Incidentally, I did not hear from the Russian show people after they returned to their native land, although they promised to write me. However, I enjoyed them, and feel I did my part for Russian-American relations while they were on our shores.

An experience I did not enjoy, but one I would not have missed, was visiting Caryl Chessman, who spent years on San Quentin's Death Row, making appeal after appeal, only to die ultimately in the gas chamber.

While working at my desk I happened to overhear a Frenchman at the car rental counter next to my office, trying unsuccessfully to make himself understood. I came over and helped him complete the transaction. He was, I learned, François de Montfort, a journalist for the French newspaper, *Ici Paris*, which his father owned. In addition to other assignments in this country, he was going to interview Chessman and he asked if I would accompany him to San Quentin, to act as interpreter and take notes. I quickly accepted.

When we arrived at the prison, I was not so sure I had done the right thing in coming. Just being behind those walls scared me, and it didn't help matters when I had to stand on a platform to be photographed from various angles for identification purposes, in case, I suppose, I tried to smuggle Chessman out in my purse.

We were conducted to a double-barred, guarded interview room, the door was closed behind us, and the key turned in the lock. I broke out in a sweat. Never in my life had I felt so confined.

Mr. Chessman entered from another door, on the other side of which sat an armed guard. The prisoner greeted us courteously, shook hands, seated himself at the table, and motioned us to sit opposite him. He looked fresh and clean, in blue prison garb, his straight black hair slicked down on his head. He spoke quietly, even if vehemently at times, always in a gentlemanly manner. It was difficult to visualize the Caryl Chessman who, according to the judgment of a court and jury, committed vicious acts.

I was surprised at the range of subjects he could discuss knowledgeably. Chessman seemed very well read, commenting on authors as varied as Victor Hugo and Simone de Beauvoir. He remarked that his favorite was the 15th-century poet François Villon, and I wondered whether Chessman saw himself as somewhat in the role and position of this outlaw, thief and murderer whose poetry, written from prison, made him a hero with the people. Chessman wrote two books about himself while awaiting execution.

At one point, he glanced over at my notebook and asked what shorthand system I used. I told him Gregg. He took the notebook and read back part of what I had inscribed. Noting my surprise, he said, "I studied Gregg. You see, I have lots of time on my hands."

I was wearing a fairly heavy suit, in anticipation of the cool weather of Northern California, and now in that stifling room, I did something stupid. I took off my jacket and draped it over the chair. François glared, but I didn't understand what he was trying to communicate until he directed his gaze toward my chest. I was wearing a transparent, white nylon blouse through which the outline of my brassiere was clearly discernible. It was certainly not a thing to do before a man in confinement, especially a convicted sex offender, but it would have been too obvious to replace my jacket, so I kept working. François continued to glare, but Chessman kept his eyes fixed on my face as the interview continued. I was grateful.

When we were about to leave, the condemned man rose to his feet. I took his hand, looked into his eyes and told him I hoped everything would work out all right for him. The words sounded inane, but he thanked me.

Not long after our visit I read the horrible details of Caryl Chessman's execution, and the mental image of him strapped to the chair, awaiting the drop of the gas pellet, haunted me for days. They say he died unafraid and arrogant.

Fortunately, it has not been my lot very often to have any connection with a situation as horrifying as the Caryl Chessman case. I am content to stick to the more normal chores of my position, official and unofficial.

By the latter, I refer to the many voluntary services I render clients. Without premeditation, I seem to have become a shopping service, a counseling bureau, a lost-and-found department, an information booth, a stopping-off point for sad sacks, and a loan company. People take it for granted that I am there to serve the public. I enjoy it; besides, it pays to be nice to people. It enables me to meet people, find out who they are, what they do. I know that some will show no appreciation, but that does not discourage me.

When a bartender wanted a job in an electronics firm, I helped him prepare a summary of his background and experience. When a bellman's daughter started giving him a bad time, he came to me for the name of a psychiatrist. A shop clerk sued her boy friend because of a loan he failed to repay, then consulted me on how she could win him back after the settlement. Guests inquire where to get a movie star's address, a Jewish meal, a distant relative's telephone number. I am asked whether it is all right to wear a sport shirt in the bar and if the night maid should be tipped. Men have asked me to refer them to a masseuse—not a masseur, mind you—stipulating that she must be pretty. A long-time client called my home from a Sacramento hotel and had me turn on my TV and roll it to the telephone, so he could hear the program he usually watches—he didn't have a TV in his hotel.

Men ask me how they can meet a girl, and they make it clear they don't mean for a taffy pull. They would be embarrassed to ask a bellman, they explain, but are sure a woman will understand! That is one business I am not in, and I say so, very politely, and sometimes not so politely.

Client friends think nothing at all about calling in the dead of night to ask me to come clear across town to perform a two-minute service. Ted, for example. I very much doubt that in his lifetime he can possibly spend the fortune he has acquired manufacturing Fourth of July fireworks, of all things, but he does his best. He is an indefatigable playboy. He owns an ocean-going yacht and a score of oil wells. He maintains several homes on three continents, and for all I know several more establishments he keeps secretly. I visited one of those homes. He had a television set in every room, including the bathrooms. He had one installed on the wall along the stairway so he could follow a program as he walked up to his bedroom.

One night he telephoned from a hotel in Hollywood, asking me to come right over. I found Ted in bed, a cigar in one hand, a highball in the other. A pretty girl sat alongside a paunchy man on the couch. I had seen her around. From what I heard about her, she was familiar with every room in that hotel.

I no sooner was introduced than Ted ordered the girl to stand up. She looked uncertainly at me, then toward the man on the couch. I looked blank. He looked imperturbable. She stood up.

"Pick up your skirt and let Edna see your legs," Ted commanded.

Taken aback, she looked to the man on the couch for guidance. He opened his palm, jerked it upward meaningfully. She giggled nervously, and gingerly lifted her skirts above her knees.

"Higher!" Ted commanded.

She complied.

Ted turned toward me. "What do you think of them?" he asked.

Embarrassed for all of us, I studied them briefly, assuming an air of nonchalance. "They look very nice. They're pretty legs," I said.

"Pretty enough to invest a million bucks in?" Ted inquired.

The girl hoisted her skirts still higher, flashed the artificial smile of a fashion model, and sent me a pleading look.

"What's this all about?" I asked.

"I'm thinking of investing a million bucks in a movie for this kid to star in, that's what it's all about! But I won't unless she's got what it takes. Not *nice* legs, not *pretty* legs. Has this gal got the goddamndest, sexiest, bitchiest legs you've ever seen? Or hasn't she? Which?"

He was infinitely better qualified to pass judgment on the allure of feminine legs than I was. This girl's endowments were not bad, but not earth-shaking either, in my opinion. On the other hand, many movie starlets had made the grade on less, and I didn't want the responsibility of having terminated the young lady's career before it began. I delivered my verdict. The under-pinnings were first rate. The girl lowered her skirt, and flashed me a grateful smile. The man on the couch scratched his ear. Ted said, "O.K. I'll make a deal tomorrow."

I never did learn the identity of the gentleman on the couch, or whether the million-dollar investment was ever made. In any event, the girl with the legs has not become one of America's top stars.

Sometimes I get a fleeting notion to quit doing things for people beyond the strict call of duty. If that happens, it will be partly because of the swarthy Arab who came to my office with a speech to be typed. As I looked it over, I caught him staring at a medallion I was wearing around my neck, depicting Moses and the Ten Commandments. I turned it over so he could see the Hebrew letters on the other side. He remarked that it was a nice medallion, and I asked if he had ever seen one like it before. Oh, yes, he replied, he was from Cairo, a government official of the United Arab Republic, and of course he had seen one.

I typed his speech. He paid me, but didn't leave. He wasn't interested in Moses; he wasn't studying the Ten Commandments. I figured that he liked my looks. There's no law against that.

I asked, "Was there something else you wanted, sir?"

He coughed, cleared his throat, said he was leaving in the morning, and his deepest regret was that he hadn't had a chance to see "your Pacific Ocean."

It wasn't mine, but I told him I would be delighted to show it to him that afternoon. I had to make a call in that direction, and if he would accompany me, I would drive him to the Pacific after taking care of my business.

He joined me in the afternoon and away we went. My call was to Temple Sinai, where I had an appointment with the Rabbi. When I pulled up in front of it I told my Arab friend this was a Jewish temple, that I was going in but I imagined he would prefer to wait for me in the car. To my surprise, he indicated he would like very much to accompany me.

When I introduced him as a highly placed Arab in the Nasser regime, the Rabbi was nonplussed. Nasser, after all, was not the Jews' best friend. Nevertheless, the Rabbi welcomed his visitor and offered to show him through the temple. The Egyptian official courteously accepted the invitation.

The Rabbi showed him the Ark where the Torahs are kept, explaining their meaning and purpose.

"Our Mohammedan religion is not much different from yours," the Egyptian said.

At this point, a man came up to the Arab and asked, "Are you here for a minion?" (A minion is a group of ten men, the minimum necessary to conduct a religious service.)

The Arab looked at us, perplexed. The Rabbi laughed and told the man who asked the question, "Do you know who this is?"

"I don't care who he is! We need him for a minion."

He didn't get him. I finished my business and the Arab and I proceeded to the ocean.

After he had had an opportunity to take in its beauty I asked if he would like to stop somewhere for a drink.

"Oh, no," he said. Arabs didn't drink.

As we got into the car he tried to pull me into his arms and kiss me. He gave me a few bad minutes but I pulled loose and admonished him.

"You're just a woman!" he said. "And a woman is like a dog in my country."

I replied, "Maybe in your country—but in this country I'm your equal."

He didn't like that at all. End of American-Arab relations.

Chapter 10

From absolutely to zany

My work provides adventures running the gamut from A to Z. It subdivides into three categories—Absolutely Business, Business, and Zany. Let's talk about Zany first.

Chatting with a customer, I happened to remark that he was an enigmatic man.

"Does that have anything to do with sex?" he asked.

Later, I put through a call to a newspaper plant to talk to a friend whose family owned the paper: "Mrs. William Randolph Hearst, Junior, please!" I said.

"How do you spell it?" asked the switchboard operator.

On another occasion a sweet old man I know dropped into a seat alongside me at the coffee shop. "Mm, mmh!" he said. "I had a wonderful morning! Bought four suits at Gus May's! I love that shop!"

Inasmuch as the suits he buys from Gus May's run to about $400, I could well understand that he would love the shop.

I noticed him fingering something in his hand.

"What have you got there?" I asked.

"Pieces of cloth. From Gus May's."

"What do you want them for?"

"I might need them for patches."

A favorite client, a handsome and very eligible bachelor, was in town and I thought it would be nice to have him meet one of my girl friends, so I invited her along when I went to his room for dictation. I introduced them and as she reached out to shake hands, her finger caught in a long strand of beads she was wearing, and it broke. We got down on our hands and knees and began picking up beads. After collecting those on the carpet, the three of us crawled under the bed for more. There we were with only our legs sticking out when the room-service waiter appeared at the open door with my client's lunch. He almost dropped the tray, but his sense of humor restored his equilibrium.

"It's O.K., sir!" he chuckled. "I'm not the husband of either of these ladies."

Situations have a way of developing. I was at my desk, expecting the arrival of three oil executives. Taking advantage of a few free minutes, I opened an English literature text to catch up on a reading assigned in a class I was taking. I was scanning the stanzas of a verse by Shelley when a shadow fell across the page. I looked up. There stood a tremendous fellow, leaning down and reading over my shoulder.

"I know that one!" he cried. "It brings back my Dartmouth days!" He straightened up, took a position in the center of the corridor floor, placed a hand over his eyes to prove he wasn't peeping, and began to recite, from memory:

"O wild west wind, thou breath of autumn's being. . . ."

Just then my oil executives arrived. The three dignified personages stood open-mouthed, staring at the gigantic Dartmouth alumnus passionately declaiming verse. Sensing their presence, he dropped his hand, opened his eyes, mumbled, "Oh! Excuse me!" and fled.

For a moment the oilmen stood rooted to the spot. Then, in an awed voice, one of them asked, "*Who* was *that?*"

"Oh," I answered, giving the first explanation that popped into my head, "he works in that office next to mine."

The second executive inquired, "Does anyone *else* share that office with him?"

"Yes," I blithely responded, "but they're not as, uh, dramatic as the gentleman. It's really a very sedate office."

Just then the door of the very sedate office flew open and a Great Dane streaked out, pursued by two men and a girl. The dog raced through the lobby, to the accompaniment of hysterical screams of women in his path.

The third oilman stared at the fleeing animal. "Er, young lady," he said in a hushed voice, "this *is* the public stenographer's office, isn't it?"

I explained that the Great Dane was brought to the hotel by the wife of the man in charge of the office next door. She tethered him to a chair in that office and went to keep an appointment in the beauty salon. The dog got bored and tore loose. Nothing terribly unusual about that.

My customers always seem to be in a hurry for the work they give me. A heavy-set man presented me with a sheaf of papers to be typed immediately, and inquired as to when he might pick up the work. I recognized him—Elliott Roosevelt, the son of F.D.R. Greeting him by name, I informed him that I had worked in Washington in the New Deal years.

"How interesting!" he murmured. "Well, you can take your time with this."

I had an easier but more extraordinary assignment while still at the Beverly Hills Hotel. Lady Fellows checked in, with her secretary, footman, pantryman and maid (whom she called her lady-in-waiting). The party was quartered in a bungalow behind the main building.

The day she was to check out, I was summoned to the bungalow. The maid admitted me and went back to packing bags. The footman was engaged in a closet room. Lady Fellows sat at her desk, concentrating on a letter she was writing. She did not look up at me; in fact, she gave no indication that she was aware of my presence. I sat down, waiting to be acknowledged.

Servants went in and out. Lady Fellows' pen raced on. I studied my nails, pushed back the cuticles. At last, after half an hour, milady looked up. Pointing three feet from the desk, she asked, very politely, "Would you please hand me that waste-basket?"

I lifted it, transported it one full yard, deposited it at her feet.

"Thank you!" she said. "That will be all."

I shall never know what she had in mind when she called for me. Perhaps she originally meant to dictate the letter she was writing by hand when I arrived. Whatever her intentions, it cost her $5 to have that basket moved.

You meet all sorts of people in this business. Entering the exclusive Marco Polo Club of the Waldorf, I ran into a man I knew and he invited me to join him at the bar. A few minutes later, a nice-looking gentleman, white-haired and very dignified, came in, climbed onto the bar stool next to us, ordered a scotch and soda, and casually turned to me.

"You heard the news?" he asked.

"What news?"

"It just came over the radio. Fidel Castro was assassinated."

"What! By whom?" I inquired.

"His brother Raoul," the stranger replied.

Immediately, it struck me that I ought to call Mr. Hilton's assistant, Mr. Gregory Dillon, for whom I was working at the time. The Hilton Corporation had a hotel in Havana and a turnover in the Cuban government could affect it vitally. I ran to the phone, managed to locate Mr. Dillon at a dinner party, and informed him that Fidel Castro was no more. After a moment of dead air, he thanked me for the intelligence and wondered why he hadn't heard about the assassination. He would check further.

Our informant was gone when I rejoined my friend. I asked the bartender if he knew who the man was, and was told, "I'm just new here, but I heard someone mention he's the owner of a baseball team."

Mr. Dillon's comment produced some skepticism in me. I telephoned the networks, asking for verification that the bearded dictator was indeed deceased. They had heard nothing to that effect. Unwilling to let it go at that, I called the New York Times too, and was told there was nothing about an assassination on the teletype.

Something was cockeyed—that was obvious—and I would have to get to the bottom of the matter; but meanwhile, red-faced and ashamed, I called Mr. Dillon again, telling him that the story could not be substantiated and apologizing profusely. Then I returned and spoke to another barman, who had just come on duty. He shook his head. It was a shame if the rumor caused embarrassment in high places, he said. He knew our story-teller well. He was a wealthy businessman and an inveterate prankster. He took delight in seating himself at the bar and passing out spurious tidbits to a bartender in a voice just loud enough to carry to other customers. In a trice, he would have the place buzzing. He enjoyed the effect he produced.

For my benefit, he worked a little differently, delivering his Castro blockbuster face-to-face. By swallowing his story without question, I could have created a mighty stir in the Hilton office, except for the calmer judgment of Mr. Dillon.

The Castro story was pure fabrication, of course, but it reminded Mr. Dillon of a real one, when we discussed the false alarm. He had visited Cuba shortly after Fidel took over, and the manager of the Havana Hilton, believing he would be interested in meeting the mother of the diminutive ruler, who had so suddenly been catapulted into international fame, arranged an invitation for Mr. Dillon to her home. The manager came along as interpreter. Mr. Dillon was talking to Señora Castro and several others in the room, when they heard the wail of sirens and, looking out, saw a huge limousine pull up. Raoul and Fidel Castro stepped out and entered the house. Mrs. Castro arose, walked across the room, and confronting her sons, addressed them sternly, in Spanish, of course. They listened respectfully, but made no reply. When she finished, they turned on their heels and walked out. The remaining visitors went back to their conversation, but the atmosphere had changed, and the guests soon departed.

On their way back to the hotel, the manager told Mr. Dillon he wished he had had a camera or tape recorder to document that moment of history. What they had witnessed was a dramatic confrontation of mother and sons, in which Senora Castro had told her sons off, bluntly and forcefully, informing them they were a disgrace to the family name, and if they continued their revolution along the lines they were currently following, she would never speak to them again. This is particularly interesting since at that time it was not generally understood, at least in our country, that Fidel Castro was a Communist, determined to re-construct the Cuban government and its economy according to party lines.

Senora Castro has passed away since that episode. And the Havana Hilton is now Fidel's headquarters.

I have had a few mildly zany adventures in England. I upset the equilibrium of a large London office by addressing almost everyone by his first name, including my boss, the top man in the place, whom I had known for years. British employees considered this very odd, to say the least, and the boss himself informed me that although he had worked with the same secretary for more than twenty-five years he still did not know her first name.

A young fellow in the same office told me that in the seven years he had worked for the company he had never met the boss. I relayed this comment to the executive, who said he didn't know he had anyone by that name working for him. Four years later, I happen to know, they still had not met.

I really upset the elderly caretaker who served the staff its tea every afternoon, a custom so ingrained that a man would as soon give up wearing shoes as skip his traditional libation. One particularly raw afternoon I asked for a second cup of tea to get the chill out of my bones. He stared at me as if I were asking him to go out and shoot the Queen. "But no one asks for a second cup!" he said, enunciating each word slowly and distinctly.

"But I would *like* another cup," I said, as sweetly as I knew how. "Will one more cup make so much difference?"

"I only make *so much*," he told me. For years he had brewed exactly the same amount. It had never occurred to him or anyone else that he might now and then, on very raw days, add just a few more drops to his accustomed allotment of water.

My request swept through the offices in seconds. I could see people peeping at me, snickering behind their palms. But the London chill was too much for me, and I meant to have that second cup of tea. After finishing a letter, I went out to a restaurant and ordered tea.

"Why," I was told, "*tea* time is over! *We* don't have any tea *now!*"

I stalked back to the job, more than ever wanting that cup of tea. When the office closed, I went directly to my hotel, called room service, ordered dinner, and suppressing a snarl added. "And be sure and send me a pot of tea."

"TEA! Why, Madam, we don't serve tea in the EVE-NING!"

I had had it. I couldn't buck the British Empire. I would have my tea tomorrow afternoon in the office as usual. One cup. As usual.

The British may be old-fashioned on some subjects but they have some very advanced notions regarding others. I broke through the reserve of Katy, the switchboard operator, and in due course she introduced me to her friend Bob. They invited me to accompany them on a tour of the Shakespeare country. We arrived in Oxford on a Saturday night, so late that the only ac-commodations available consisted of one tiny room. I suggested we push on to another town, and return to Oxford in the morn-ing. Katy thought that would be ridiculous. The innkeeper would bring in a cot for me, she said, and she and Bob would occupy the bed.

I bowed to necessity, the cot was delivered, I quickly un-dressed while their backs were turned, and popped under the covers. With no sign of embarrassment whatever, Katy disrobed, donned an old-fashioned nightcap and flannel nightgown, as Bob got into equally unromantic heavy striped flannel. I was waiting for the lights to go off, when out of his valise Bob pulled a lady's mackintosh. He handed it to Katy without a word. She got into it. And they went to bed!

I didn't have the nerve to ask questions. Not then. Long after our unforgettable excursion I begged Katy to enlighten me. Her boy friend was just a wee bit peculiar, she explained. He had a "thing" about mackintoshes and would not have her in bed unless she wore one. Every birthday he presented her with a new mackintosh—and that was all. She built up quite a collection of mackintoshes, but no jewelry, not even a wedding band.

The last time I saw Katy she had broken off with Bob. She humored him as long as she could, she told me, but finally was unable to take it any longer. Which was just as well, say I. Where was she going to store another mackintosh?

Mackintosh fanciers are not unique. There are all kinds of fetishists. I know a French general who gets sensuous pleasure out of seeing and stroking furs. That isn't his only idiosyncrasy. He was in this country on a government mission, and I was traveling in his entourage, as secretary, while he visited various states. He had to make a brief trip to Arizona. We had connecting suites in the hotel in Phoenix. I retired early and got into bed with a book. I took it for granted that the connecting door was locked, but obviously I was mistaken, for I had no sooner gotten under the covers than the door flew open, and there stood the General, in old-fashioned nightgown and sleeping cap.

"Enough reading!" he commanded, turning off the light and heading for the bed.

What he had in mind would have qualified me for the Croix de Guerre. Since I did not earn it, it seemed eminently appropriate that he presented me with his Legion of Honor ribbon as a memento the following morning, having been enlightened as to the proper functions of public stenographers in the United States.

Going from mackintoshes and furs and old-fashioned nightgowns to bathtubs may seem a flight of ideas, but there is a relationship there. Of all the zany stories I have heard about the sexual customs of the human biped, this one is the zaniest. It was told to me by a frail little man of eighty, for whom I did some work. Let's call him Fred.

He was in the coffee shop, late afternoon, for a spot of tea and a piece of cake. An attractive blonde who appeared to be in her thirties occupied the next seat at the counter, and they began talking. He mentioned that he was retired and that he traveled all over the world for pleasure. She traveled a good deal, too, and when she discovered that Fred had spent three months in Japan, this established a bond between them, for she loved Japan above all other parts of the world, she said, and was simply fascinated by its mystical philosophies.

He was pleased, flattered, and surprised when she invited him to her room. They had no sooner closed the door behind them than the lady pulled him to her and pressed kiss after kiss upon him, at the same time proceeding to undress him. He was a tiny little man and quite fragile, so it didn't take her long. He was in the nude in two minutes flat, he told me. She then stepped back, looked him over and instructed him to wait while she went into the bathroom.

He heard her drawing water into the tub, and figured she was going to take a bath—alone or with him. But no, she emerged from the bathroom, took him by the hand, and led him to the tub. She was much bigger than he was, and before he could recover from his astonishment, she lifted him up and set him into the bathtub as if he were a child. She then took a hard-bristled brush and started scrubbing him so vigorously he squealed with pain. She practically rubbed his skin off. When it was red as a lobster, she helped him out, handed him a towel, and told him to dry himself.

As he did, she opened the medicine cabinet and took out a tape measure. She placed one end of it against his navel and measured the distance from there to his genital parts. She then made similar measurements of herself.

"Oh, no!" she exclaimed in consternation.

She went through the same procedure a second time, measuring him and herself, to verify her findings.

"Oh, no!" she said again. She rushed over to the chair where he left his clothes, and handed them to him, saying, "Here! Get the hell out of here! You're not for me! The distance is not the same!"

As he finished telling me his story, Fred shook his head. "I *still* don't know why she threw me out," he said. The closest he could come to guessing was that it had something to do with a Japanese theory of sexual compatibility he heard about while in Tokyo. He vaguely recalled it somehow correlated navel-genital distance with compatibility.

I have a theory of my own. I suspect the lady in question drank of the same astral wine as the piercing-eyed gentleman who once entered my office.

"Young lady," he said, "I have a very important letter for you to send, yes?" He spoke with a foreign accent but I could not identify it.

"Certainly, sir! To whom is it going?"

"No!" He pointed to the pen in my hand. "No record, please! This is very, very confidential! I am an inventor. I have a wonderful invention. It must be kept secret. All right? Ready?"

Pacing about, he dictated to the typewriter: "His Excellency, the Secretary of War, Washington, D.C., Dear Sir: I have a remarkable idea for setting up defenses behind the enemy lines when next comes the war. I have invented a cement parachute—"

I looked up. "Did you say *cement?*"

"Cement. Yes. Where was I? All right? Ready?"

He had, I learned, perfected a cement parachute for issuance to ground troops. They would be airlifted behind enemy lines, descend by said cement parachutes. On the ground, their parachutes would serve as impregnable barricades, from behind which they would bombard the foe.

"What do you think of my idea?" he asked as I handed him the finished copy.

"Well," I stammered, "I, uh, don't know. Have you, er, invented other things?"

"Why, of course! Thousands and thousands of things! Millions of things! You see, young lady, I am older than you think."

"Oh?"

"Yes, indeed! I am 130 years of age!"

I gulped, wished him luck with the Secretary of War, and bade him Godspeed.

Chapter 11

Of parties, poopers and pushers

Would you like to attend a party in a hotel or in the home of an actress or socialite? I may be able to arrange it.

If I am in charge of sending out the invitations—and I often am—I can simply insert your name on the guest list lying on my desk. So many will be invited that even the hostess will not recognize all of them. And she is resigned to the fact that uninvited guests show up at every social event.

Should I not be handling the invitations, you may still gain admittance. Perhaps I will be at the door, checking off guests' names as they arrive, in which case I can look the other way as you go through. Or I may be invited to the party myself, and you can come with me.

And if I can't help you at all, chances are you can make it anyhow, if you employ the artful dodges of experienced party crashers, who need no intermediary.

/ *133*

Party crashing is a sport. Your first consideration in party crashing is which one to invade. That calls for background on parties in general.

Are you interested in a publicity party or a strictly social event?

To publicize a movie, a book, or a painter, the cocktail-buffet has become an established institution. There is no pretense about it. It is openly and avowedly a public relations production. What is not generally recognized is that there is a *genre* of party, presumably the convening of friends for an evening's sociability, which in reality is a promotion as commercial as the obvious publicity affair.

Let us say a dress manufacturer is introducing a new line. He makes a tie-in with a fashion or movie magazine, which will do a story featuring his line. It is a mutually beneficial arrangement. The magazine has an exclusive feature set up for it. The story it runs will sell the manufacturer's dresses.

They need a scene of operations, a showcase. The sumptuous home of a film star or member of the *beau monde* would be ideal. It would provide the setting for a lush picture layout and display the styles to advantage. They find a person who will open her home to the affair. All she need do is authorize the use of her name on the invitations so the party will appear to be a private gathering rather than a promotion. The manufacturer takes care of the advance preparations, underwrites the expense, and may pay the hostess a substantial sum for her courtesy and the wear and tear on the house and her nerves.

Professional models, movie stars, and up-and-coming starlets are prevailed upon by movie studio publicity departments to attend the party, wearing the items the manufacturer is promoting. Various newspaper columnists and editors of society and women's pages will be present. There will be other guests who are unaware of the commercial undertones of the party. Their hostess is well known in the community, an invitation to her home is coveted, and a party she gives is assumed to be purely social in nature.

Everyone is satisfied. The manufacturer reaps the benefits of the publicity shots showing highly placed guests admiring his creations; the magazine sells more copies when it features the star-studded event; and the hostess is pleased by the flattering publicity she receives as a lavish party-giver. The girls who serve as fashion models are delighted to have their photographs appear. And guests who came for fun, drinks, fine food, and good company, go home feeling they got exactly that.

Occasionally, things do not work as smoothly as expected. Some years ago, a movie magazine arranged to use the home of the then Mr. and Mrs. James Mason for an afternoon style show around which a fashion article was to be written. I assisted the woman in charge. We were at the door greeting incoming guests, when Mr. Mason appeared from somewhere in the house, caught sight of some luggage temporarily deposited in the hallway, containing clothing the models would wear at the showing. Mr. Mason glowered, kicked at a bag, and snapped, "Get that goddamned stuff out of here!"

When the luncheon was in full swing, he appeared again, walked up to a cluster of women and, in a voice audible from some distance, demanded, "When are you all going to leave?" It seemed ungracious, a deliberate affront. He knew why we were there. He authorized our being there, and we could not have gotten past the threshold without his consent. Yet he was petulant. Having delivered his gratuitous thrust, he withdrew to the library and we did not see him again.

The custom of lending one's name to advertising undertakings is so widespread that at least one firm, Endorsements, Inc., does nothing but obtain testimonials and enlist individuals for the promotion of products and special events. Let us say you want to put a shirt on the market and believe it will sell better if John Wayne is photographed in it and asserts that he keeps at least a dozen on hand at all times. How are you going to get his endorsement? If you write him a letter he probably will not even see it; he receives thousands of communications, most of which are taken care of by secretaries. Therefore, you ask Endorsements, Inc. if you can get John Wayne. He may already be on their list of available endorsers. If not, he will be interviewed. If he is agreeable, you get John Wayne. If he is not, another film star is ready to step forward and testify that his happiness would be incomplete without a dozen of your shirts.

A person planning a private party in his own home, entirely as a social function, without a promotion angle, may make use of a different sort of intermediary—the professional party planner who is listed in the classified telephone directory under a special heading: Party Planning Service. These are people who come in and take over all the chores. A suitable guest list is compiled in consultation with the hostess. The professional planner sees that invitations go out in proper form. She engages the caterer and superintends other details.

Probably the best known party planner of our time was the late Elsa Maxwell, whose name was associated with the world's most glamorous affairs for more than a generation. I met her for the first—and last—time toward the end of her career in 1961. I was at the Hotel de Paris in Monte Carlo and had taken a table in the lounge, awaiting the arrival of a friend. It was cocktail time, and as usual this exclusive meeting place on the Riviera was crowded. As I gazed about, I noticed a woman near the entrance seated in a wheelchair. It was Miss Maxwell, speaking to another woman standing beside her.

I took a good look at the famous Elsa. She was chunky, square-built, heavy-jowled. She seemed anything but feeble, despite her being in a wheelchair. (I learned later that she had been very ill, and that she was convalescing at this time.) She was all animation, arms waving, jowls jiggling, carrying on her conversation in what appeared a most forceful manner. Miss Maxwell addressed her companion as if she were accustomed to bossing people. I sensed that Miss Maxwell was a woman who took no monkey business from anyone.

I wanted to meet her, and since I couldn't simply walk up and introduce myself, it occurred to me that my reference point might be Earl Blackwell, a friend of mine. Miss Maxwell would surely be acquainted with him. Both were famous party-givers, both ran society columns, both hobnobbed with the top intercontinental society. Earl runs Celebrity Service, which keeps track of the comings and goings of distinguished personages and lists where they can be reached on any given day.

When there was a lull in the conversation between Elsa and her female companion, I approached the formidable lady in the wheelchair. "Miss Maxwell," I said, "we haven't met, but we have a mutual friend in New York. I saw him just before leaving the States, and he told me to be sure and say hello if I should run into you in Monte Carlo." Blackwell had never mentioned Miss Maxwell's name to me, but it was a harmless deception—I thought.

Miss Maxwell heard me out, unsmiling. In a brusque, rather hoarse voice she asked, "Mutual friend? Who?"

"Earl Blackwell."

She let out a roar. "Him!" she bellowed. "Why, he only wants publicity for himself! I hate his guts!" She waved her arms, shook her chins, bulged her eyes. People turned and stared. I was thunderstruck. I didn't know what she had against Earl, and I didn't care. All I wanted was to get out.

As suddenly as it burst, the storm subsided. Miss Maxwell seemed to be aware of my presence again. Perhaps to make amends, she asked me in curt, clipped tones where I was from and what I did for a living.

Before I could reply, an Italian *comtessa* entered the lounge, headed for Miss Maxwell, and kissed her on the cheek. Completely forgotten, I returned to my table.

Party-planners on either side of the Atlantic do a flourishing business. People from out of town, temporarily residing in hotels, find a professional party arranger indispensable on occasion. A woman I shall call Mrs. Carter, spending the winter in Beverly Hills, wanted to meet the local elite. Since she was a member of the most exclusive circles on the East Coast, it would not be deemed presumptuous if she gave a big party on the West Coast for California society. Inasmuch as she knew few of its members personally or by name, she borrowed a party list of "eligibles" from a friend of a friend who gave many parties locally. I furnished another list, containing the addresses of many movie stars. I also took charge of issuing invitations.

I was curious about a name on the first list. I had never seen it before, and it didn't seem to belong with the others.

"Who is this Admiral?" I asked Mrs. Carter. "Do you know him personally?"

"No, I do not."

"Do you want to invite him?"

"Oh, yes! It's good to have an admiral on the list. We may have a war, you never can tell. He might come in handy."

I put the Admiral down for an invitation, in case of war. To keep the peace, I inserted the name of my friend Flo on the guest list. She wanted very much to attend.

Mrs. Carter proved to be a gracious and experienced hostess. Supposedly, she had met some of her guests before this occasion. About others, she must know something, else why were they invited? She greeted each arrival, said a few nice nothings, sparred for time, and dropped a leading question into the conversation when she could, hoping to be clued on the name.

When my friend Flo arrived, well-dressed but nervous, our hostess greeted her cordially and said she was delighted Flo could come. With that out of the way, Mrs. Carter reached for clues. I could see she was more than ordinarily puzzled over the identity of Flo, who fielded leading questions skilfully. In a final stab, Mrs. Carter stepped back, gazed at Flo's hairdo, and exclaimed, "My dear, you look simply stunning! Wherever did you get that beautiful coiffure? You must give me the name of your hairdresser!"

Flo mentioned the salon in the hotel where Mrs. Carter was staying, which helped not at all in establishing her identity. The hostess finally gave up and turned to greet the next arrival. Later, she approached me. "That woman over there. Her face is familiar, but I can't place her. Do you know who she is?"

I said I did, that she was a hairdresser in the hotel salon she had mentioned.

"Ah!" the hostess exclaimed. "Now I recognize her!" Just before the party, Mrs. Carter had been in that salon. And Flo had been her hairdresser. As this dawned on her, Mrs. Carter looked shocked, then she recovered. "I wonder who invited her?" she murmured.

I did not enlighten her.

There is an artificiality about parties out our way, I think primarily because of the Hollywood spirit. Cinema people have been glorified by publicity buildups. Everybody is somebody, or if he isn't he pretends to be. Guests who seem proudest at Hollywood gatherings are generally the least important. People who don't know each other pretend they do. They can't afford to take chances. If a man fails to recognize an important figure in the Hollywood hierarchy, he loses face since it proves he hasn't been around. If an important person passes unrecognized too many times, it is he who loses face—the inference is that he is slipping.

I am at a party. I smile at a man looking my way. His face lights up. "How *are* you!" he says. "*So* good to see you again, sweetie!" We never have seen each other before.

To a great extent, it is this haven't-we-met-before psychology that insures party crashers against detection. Most of those I know are casuals, people from all walks of life, attracted by spectacles, eager to be among the included. They do not make a habit of crashing, perhaps trying it only once or twice in a lifetime. Despite this, they are a goodly number in the aggregate—I estimate about 10% of all those in attendance at any major function in a large hotel, where it is relatively easy to avoid being found out.

Much smaller in number but infinitely more singular than casual strays are the habitual party crashers—I call them professionals. They are a puzzling lot, interesting as psychological studies. They cannot give a sensible reason for their behavior. They don't understand themselves. They have a kind of sickness which controls them; they cannot control it.

Party crashers are mildly compulsive people, in my estimation. They are psychologically driven to behave the way they do; but this is a benign compulsion, not the fearsome, sinister type. It produces no real injury either to the crasher or the party. But compulsion it is. I can think of no other explanation. Why else will a man sneak into parties every night in the year? He is not particularly hungry, and if he were I'm sure he could afford to buy a meal instead of going on the prowl for it. He could pay his way into a show; he does not have to crash a private banquet in order to see the entertainment. He is not an alcoholic foraging for liquor; if he were, he couldn't carry on successfully as a crasher.

Why do they do it? As I see it, a small minority of crashers is primarily interested in the excellent food and drink provided at parties, but this is not true of the most incorrigible of the breed. They have a quite different motivation. For them, liquor and fine foods are merely the symbols of what they crave. The inveterate crasher has a compulsion to attend every noteworthy social event, simply to have been there. It makes no difference what the party is about, who is being honored, what product will be promoted, what producer is hosting which princess. There will be "names" there, and that is enough. The compulsion is to be among celebrities, to talk with them, eat and drink with them, and—here is the crux of it—to report on the adventure tomorrow. If the crasher could not recount his conquests before an audience, I doubt that he would consider the game worth the hazards. He spends his evening at a party so that tomorrow he may tell his tale to other professional party crashers.

They have certain things in common. They despise each other, yet each needs an audience for his own recital; each is willing to offer an ear for an ear. Telling his tale, the crasher will declare that he was invited, that he did not crash, but his party-crashing associates know better. He describes every dish he sampled, every drink he consumed, all the famous people he met. And his listeners, even as they nod and smile admiringly, tell themselves, "So what? He's nothing but a contemptible party crasher." When they themselves crash, it is a demonstration of gallantry and finesse. When he crashes, he is contemptible.

I looked into a reception that Paul Butler, Chairman of the Democratic National Committee, gave for newsmen during the 1960 Democratic National Convention, and was not surprised to find a girl named Sally at the bar, talking to a CBS commentator. Beautiful, a stunning dresser, she swivels in and out of festivities with religious fervor and without invitation. After a while, when she was alone, I went over to chat with her. At one point, catching sight of a girl we both knew, I said, "Look! There's Helene. Let's go over and say hello."

"Nah!" said Sally. "She's nothing but a party crasher!"

Whether an invader penetrates the defenses depends partly on his finesse, partly on the efficiency of preventive measures. Hotels try to discourage crashing. A uniformed officer or other hotel employee stationed near the door for all to see does act as a deterrent to amateurs. Security men sometimes move about in the crowd unobtrusively. From past experience they may recognize someone who has no right to be there. If so, they speak to him in a low voice to avoid embarrassing him and politely ask him to leave.

The size of the gathering is a factor. At massive hotel affairs, the intruder can step in boldly, mingle with the crowd, and become just another invited guest. Even in private homes where the party is very large it is possible to escape detection. Only at the small and intimate soiree is it virtually impossible for the party pirate to come aboard.

If a ticket or engraved invitation is the passport for a large hotel event, this is not an insuperable barrier. Newsmen cover these affairs and need only show a press card to get in. The crasher carries his own fake press pass.

If there is a girl seated at the entrance admitting only persons whose names are on her list, the freeloader does not despair. He hovers about at the fringes of the incoming crowd, waits for the inevitable traffic jam, and then insinuates himself into the milling group. The girl checks her list as fast as she can, but with so many at the entrance, she cannot get every name for fear of creating an even greater crush. She gives up, and the crasher moves in.

But suppose the buildup at the door fails to materialize as the party gets under way. The crasher departs, spends some time at another celebration on his list, and returns to the first affair later on, by which time, he calculates, all invited guests will have arrived, had several drinks, and be feeling fine. The door is no longer guarded. He moves in on the jostling throng, where identities are by now a little fuzzy. He goes to the bar, orders a drink, turns to the guest nearest him and makes a casual remark. That man assumes the crasher is an invited guest and that they have met either earlier that evening or on another occasion. It's a grand affair, loads of fun, and have another highball with me, old boy!

The first time I really discovered the party crasher—that is, discovered that he represented a type—was when I stood in the lobby of the Beverly Hilton watching Hollywood's sparkling stars promenade in to the Academy Awards Dinner. Someone called my name. I turned and found a writer to whom I had been casually and briefly introduced by a star quite some time ago. He was dressed in tails.

He greeted me effusively. "Edna!" he cried. "Where have you been? I've been waiting and waiting for you!"

That was startling news, but I was even more surprised when he took firm hold of my arm, steered me toward the entrance, and right into the ballroom before I could ask for an explanation. At first I assumed he had imbibed a bit too zealously, but I abandon that theory when I realized he was as sober as an owl. I then concluded he had invited a girl to the event, had been stood up, and he wanted a partner at dinner.

I was forced to revise that notion, too, when, once inside, he did not escort me directly to a table, but instead moved about aimlessly from one to another and another. Obviously, he was "not expected"; there was no place reserved for him. Upon discovering this, I politely detached myself from my self-appointed escort and headed for the lobby. However, I was stopped on the way out by some people I knew who asked if I would care to sit with them. I explained how I got in and why I had better leave. My friends told me to stay; they had an extra ticket because a member of their party had been unable to attend.

Which was why I could observe, from a place at a table, the still puzzling maneuvers of the writer who escorted me into the affair. He leaned against a wall or paced up and down until he spotted a couple going to the dance floor, whereupon he popped into one of the vacated chairs and reached for a stalk of celery.

When the couple left the dance floor, he got up quickly and went prowling for another seat. So it went all night.

I got the picture. He arrived at the ballroom hoping to crash the dinner, tickets to which cost $50. When he spotted me, he figured I was known to many of the stars attending, as well as to the people in charge of arrangements. It was a couple affair. If he pretended he was my escort, he might get through the door on his brass, my protective company, and the tails he wore.

Since that experience, I have taken a great interest in the psychology of the inveterate party crasher and have observed a good many.

I now give you Ed, who in my educated opinion is a four-teen-carat example of the breed. At this writing, Ed is in his early thirties, a short, roly-poly fellow with a pouchy face that makes him look older than he is. His perennially bleary eyes bespeak his dedication to party crashing—he drinks too much and never gets enough sleep.

My first contact with Ed was when he came to my office to ask if I would help him gain access to a list of special events the hotel makes up monthly. It would be a time saver. If he knew well in advance what social functions were scheduled, he could organize his time more efficiently. I happened to have one on my desk, and as he looked at it I could see his antennae rising.

After that first meeting, I saw Ed in the hotel practically every night. There was not an affair he didn't try to crash. Once I asked, "Ed, what's the secret of crashing parties?" His answer was: "Always walk in as though you belong. Hold your head high and your shoulders straight, and look everyone in the face."

Over occasional cocktails at parties that I attended and he crashed, I learned a good deal about the life he led.

At noon—his breakfast time—Ed scans the society pages of the newspapers and makes notes on the parties scheduled for the next few days. He proceeds to the news and business sections, searching for items on the opening of a restaurant or a new branch of a bank or loan company, the arrival of a dignitary—anything and everything leading to a ceremony or fête.

This task completed, he goes to work. It isn't really an eight-hour job of work. He manages to find part-time employment, just enough to pay expenses but not enough to interfere with the real purpose of life. He gets through his working "day" somehow, comes home, dresses for the evening's invasion, perhaps in sports clothes or maybe in a tux, depending upon what he has scheduled for the night.

He is on his way. Ed's peregrinations are fantastic. I walked into a strictly private wedding party for my cousin at the Ambassador Hotel. There was Ed, champagne glass in hand. He caught sight of me, disappeared in the twinkling of an eye. I dropped into a cocktail affair during a political campaign; Ed was there ahead of me, shaking hands with the Governor.

The 1960 Democratic Convention sent Ed into a delirium. He dashed from hotel to hotel, covering the social activities. He passed my desk one afternoon, en route to a celebration, a worn hat pushed back on his head, Front Page style, a fake press card sticking out of his breast pocket. He returned five minutes later, crestfallen. The ruse had failed. Within minutes, he was marching resolutely forward again, this time with a handsome Stetson atop his head.

"Who are you now, Eddie?" I asked.

"Congressman Morris, of Alabama."

They turned him back at the door. He stopped at my desk, sweating with the urgency of it. "*You* get me in!" he begged. It was an accusation as well as a plea. He was sure I could if I would.

"How can I get you in?"

"You can get in to all the things at the hotel."

"Only when there's work to be done or I'm invited."

"All right. Let's go to work. Give me one of your notebooks. We'll walk in together, and you tell them I'm your assistant."

One of Ed's more successful "disguises" is a card bearing the legend *Foreign Press*. It is surprising how seldom he is asked what country or organ he represents. He used his "pass" the night he invited me to a gala affair in a restaurant celebrating the return of its world-renowned chef after a ten-year sojourn on the Continent. Admitted without question, we helped ourselves at the lavish buffet and found seats with two ladies at a table. Six times

Ed went back to reload his plate. In between, he held the women at "our" table absolutely spellbound, rattling off news of the world and predictions of things to come. Casually and inoffensively, he dropped names of Spanish grandees and Papal knights with whom he assertedly hobnobbed. He described his alleged misadventures all over the globe, and they were truly hilarious. He spun his yarns with exquisite delicacy, tempered with just the right degree of modesty, just enough glee in a mission accomplished. His putative adventures were wondrous, awesomely precarious, yet within the limits of credibility. When our foreign correspondent left the table for one more raid on the buffet, one of the women said to me, "Oh, I think your friend is the most fascinating man in the world! With all he's been through, he could write a book!"

"You are so right!" I said.

After polishing off his sixth helping, Ed announced we were leaving, casually remarking, "I'm taking Edna to Joe Pasternak's home—you know, the movie producer. Big party!"

The announcement electrified the ladies. One of them asked if she could possibly come with us. Ed apologized. It was a very exclusive affair, he explained. With a self-deprecating smile he added he didn't quite know how *he* happened to be invited.

I thought Ed's boast that we were going to another party was only an excuse for getting rid of the ladies, but when we drove away I discovered, to my consternation, that for the first time that evening he was speaking the truth. It was his intention to drive to Mr. Pasternak's Bel Air home where, according to his log, a celebration of some sort was in progress.

An innocent—and shaky—victim of his timetable, I endeavored to dissuade him. "Why press your luck?" I asked. I might as well have addressed a cheese blintz. Eyes fixed on his star, Ed kept driving. We arrived on the luxurious grounds. Ed rang the bell. A man came to the door. Whether servant or guest, I did not know. Either he was warned against crashers or knew Ed from previous experience, for the moment he saw us, before my escort could open his mouth, the man in the doorway shook his head and said, "No! No! I'm sorry!"

Ed made as if to offer argument, but you can't argue with a door. It shut with just enough bang to make its point, politely but irrevocably. Ed's shoulders slumped. He turned on his heel and walked away, with me bringing up the rear. There just was no other interpretation to be placed on the incident. He had been set right down on his fundamental principles. In the presence of a witness. I sensed his humiliation, and felt sorry for him.

"Funny thing!" he murmured as we made for the car. "I *did* have an invitation. Look!" He dipped into his pocket, fished out what could have been a crumped telegram, and waved it at me. I didn't ask to read it. His *amour propre* was hurt enough already.

❋

Chapter 12

Another day,
another party

I was in a man's suite one afternoon taking dictation when his phone rang and I answered it. A female voice announced, "Tell the gentleman the package has arrived and it has a red ribbon."

I relayed the message to my client, who thereupon decided we had worked long enough; he would have me back tomorrow.

An hour or so later I stopped at the bar with a friend, and there was my erstwhile client at a table with a very attractive redhead. I could now decode her message. The "package" was a call girl. The "red ribbon" was her hair, by which he would identify her when he came to the lobby.

Any one working in hotels becomes aware of such goings-on. There is something about being away from home that stimulates men's sexuality. It is my conviction that, given the opportunity, 90% of them will cheat on their wives. They ask me, "Don't you have a cute girl friend?" They will jump at anything. All someone need say is, "I know a girl . . ." and the immediate response is, "Give me her phone number!" He doesn't even know what she looks like, but he is ready to call her. If he asks any question at all, it is, "How old is she?" It is curious how preoccupied men are about age. They don't ask whether the girl is good looking, or smart. They want someone young.

Since making a date with a nice, respectable girl is not easy for the traveler, call girls do a good business at being bad. A call girl is just that, a girl who is on "call" by telephone. She usually operates through a phone service. Often she may have a list of clients she has developed herself or "borrowed" from other girls. She generally has a fixed fee—maybe $50, maybe $100—and she feels a man will think less of her if she accepts anything below that.

Many big business firms maintain a file of available call girls, knowing full well that when certain of their esteemed customers come to town they expect to be furnished female company. Additionally, of course, there are out and out panderers, male and female, who supply the market from their own "stables." And girls may make their own deals with hotel employees, who earn money on the side as steerers. Whatever the point of origin, the girl operates through an inside person who has contact with guests.

The procedure has advantages for both customer and girl. He need not waste time sitting at a bar trying to figure which girl is a prostitute and taking a chance on a punch in the snout if he guesses wrong. The girl does not risk getting nabbed by a vice-squad officer. Unlike the prostitute openly plying her profession, the call girl appears only when she is answering a call. Police do not recognize her for what she is. Not even the customer has her telephone number. He must work through the intermediary. He calls and places his order. The intermediary telephones the girl, and the "package" delivers itself.

Call girls are all business. Play girls are, too, but they won't admit it. There is a distinction between the two types. Where the call girl works through an intermediary, a play girl is her own boss. Like the call girl, she will go to a man's room, but she also has her own apartment and may entertain a guest there. At no time is she on call through a central agency. Furthermore, all her income may not be derived from prostitution. Some play girls hold conventional, full-time jobs, pick up extra money on the side by selling their favors.

When she feels like operating, the play girl proceeds to a public place, such as a cocktail lounge, where she expects to find a customer. Unlike the common prostitute, she is not obvious about her intention, nor does she immediately agree to go with the first man who guesses that intention. She determines in advance whether it will be worth her while to spend time with him. Does he have money? Is he flush with it? She is very adept at ferreting out information in conversation with the prospect.

Sometimes, a girl knows an employee of the establishment who will tip her off to a live prospect. An acquaintance told me how she operates in the very exclusive lounge of an elegant hotel. She is known to certain members of the staff. "I'll sit there at a table," she explained, "and a waiter will come over and say, 'That man over there asked me to bring you a drink.' That means the man is O.K. If he says, 'That man asked me to bring you a drink and I told him we didn't allow that here,' it means the man is known as no good, not a good prospect. I should stay away from him."

When she is in the lounge of another hotel the switchboard operator has her called to the phone. She tells her, "I'm going to page a man at Table 28. He's very important." The man is paged. Now the girl knows who he is and can proceed with her campaign.

I asked my acquaintance why employees cooperated, since the hotel itself would be set against it. Her explanation was, "They know I am nice. They want me to meet nice people."

The remark is significant. The play girl has a great deal of self-esteem. She considers herself very nice and she tells herself a nice girl sleeps only with nice gentlemen. A nice gentleman is more than a man with a fat wallet. He must be reasonably attractive to her sexually. Unless in dire need of a new coat or bracelet, she will decline an invitation to bed down with a man who is repulsive to her—either physically or because of his sexual pro-clivities.

Unlike the call girl, the play girl expects to stay with the one man for the evening. Moreover, he must court her. She expertly gets him to invite her to dinner. They may take in a nightclub afterward. The entire proceeding is as it would be if they were friends out on a date. Only after protocol has been taken care of is the girl willing to give what her escort has been wanting all evening.

Of course, after she meets a prospect, she will occasionally discover that she has guessed wrongly about him, that he is so tight that last year's moths are still inside his wallet. In that case, she elects one of a number of available tricks for getting rid of him without acrimony. She remembers she must pick up her mother at a party; or she develops a blinding headache. Or—this one is guaranteed—she looks at her watch, casually remarks that her husband should arrive any moment now, that it has been a most enjoyable evening, and—ah! Isn't that her spouse coming through the door?

The aristocrat of the sex business is neither call nor play girl. She is the party girl, an ultra-clever, highly sophisticated, ex-ceedingly devious feline. I became acquainted with several as they flitted in and out of hotels. Some naïvely asked me to tip them off to wealthy prospects.

What is a party girl? Unlike the call girl, she works for no central agency. Unlike the play girl, she does not accept cash on the line for her services. Nor is she particularly interested in being with a man for one night only. She prefers more or less stable friendships. Regulars constitute a basic guarantee, a steady income.

The party girl looks and acts the perfect lady. She dresses expensively, is a stimulating conversationalist, and is so well man-nered that she can be escorted to a dinner party, the opera, or the racetrack without looking the least bit out of place. A man meet-ing her for the first time might spend the entire evening with her, even go to bed with her, without realizing that she is a profes-sional who eventually expects to be recompensed.

The party girl selects her man—he does not select her, although he believes he does. She knows a good deal about him before they ever speak. At least the first time or two, she indignantly refuses his money—what does he think she is? After a decent "courtship," she graciously accepts an apartment house, a Continental, or a royalty interest in an oil well, but only because he is so insistent and because they have become so very, very cozy. By this time her lover is so hopelessly infatuated he will return time and again and may keep her in a love nest for months and even years. He may or may not believe she reserves her charms for him alone.

The party girls I have met hope to find husbands eventually. They look upon marriage as security, which they desperately desire. If they cannot have marriage and security, they settle for security. Dotty, for example, has resigned herself to the latter. She lives in an expensive hotel, where, she says, "Monday, a new batch of men checks into the place. I come down in the morning and there they are. I never have to buy my own breakfast on Mondays." She decides which arrival is worth bumping into that evening, where, for how long, and how much. She has built up a string of regulars by this process, some good for a night each trip in, some for a week, but all of them "hooked."

Most party girls I know are cold and calculating, figuring angles all the time. My friend Marge is an intriguing exception. As avaricious as any self-respecting professional, she is bird-brained at the same time, which is an impediment to figuring angles. Marge would be the prototype of "the dizzy blonde," except her hair is brunette (in its original state). When I first met her, she occupied a residential suite in a very nice hotel with what I took to be her husband. She had a hired limousine and chauffeur. When she or her husband needed my services, they sent the car to fetch me. Marge could stand a certain amount of privation, but not boredom. When her husband was off on a business trip, she would telephone to ask me up for breakfast, or to ask what perfume did the most for her, or just to talk.

She confessed she was not sure Herbert, her bed companion, was really wed to her. Long ago she had married Timothy. She left him without benefit of divorce to marry Karl, whom she deserted for Peter a year or so before leaving him to go through a ceremony with Herbert. But so far as she knew, she was never divorced from her first husband, or for that matter, from spouses number two and three, and therefore she had a sneaking suspicion that she just possibly might be bigamously married to one or more of the gentlemen, including Herbert. It didn't bother her much, it merely intrigued her, like a puzzle.

One day she announced to me that she was getting bored with Herbert. How would I like to sleep with him and two or three other girls at the same time? He enjoyed that, and she would like to watch. No? Would I like to take him off her hands, period? No? Then perhaps I could put her in touch with a nice, attractive, and of course disgustingly wealthy man whom she might marry next? No? Well. . . .

She made her own connection while Herbert was in Chicago. He returned to an empty suite and memories.

I heard nothing from or about Marge for more than a year. Then she dropped into my office. She formerly dressed in top vogue, but now she was shabby. She handed me a fur. "Please buy it, Edna!" she said. "Give me $25 for it! I'm broke." I wouldn't do that, but I loaned her the money.

She disappeared again. A month later she was back with another tale of woe. To change her luck, she called on an astrologist who told her it was in the stars that he must make love to her. He took her to Las Vegas, took from her a large sum of money she "earned" from a rich playboy the week before, deserted, and she was broke again.

A week after that, she was in the chips, through the generosity of a gentleman she met at the track. She telephoned to notify me of her good fortune and to say goodbye for a while. She was going to Las Vegas again. With the astrologist.

"What for?" I asked. "He cleaned you out and left you stranded in Vegas, didn't he?"

"Yeah! That was nasty. But he's back. And he apologized. I *haffta* go, Edna! He says the stars *say* we *haffta* go!"

Another time she phoned to say, "Gee, Edna, I'm bored! I don't know whether I should get my hair done or get married."

I couldn't help her decide, so she made up her own mind—on marriage. After all, she explained, what risk was she taking? If she didn't like the guy, she could break the news to him that she already had a legal husband somewhere or other.

Bent on contracting still another putative husband, Marge rented a car to do a little reconnoitering. As luck would have it, Joe, the man who delivered it, was an old acquaintance, which is not too strange a coincidence considering that Marge meets quite a few gentlemen every year, and sooner or later is bound to get a repeat.

Joe was handsome. He appealed to her when they met previously, but at that time she was encumbered with a millionaire husband. Now here was good old Joe again, straight from heaven. It was against every principle by which Marge ordered her existence to waste time on a chap who made a living delivering cars, but there was the fact that she was bored; and ennui depressed her more than playing for free. She invited Joe to invite her out on the town, at her expense. They made a tour of the clubs, by which time they knew they were meant for each other. Marge suggested that they drive to Las Vegas that very night and get married. Joe agreed. They took along a friend of Marge's, a girl named Judy, to act as witness at the ceremony.

The three piled into the car and drove for the desert city, stopping for a drink every few miles. By the time they reached Las Vegas, Joe was a bit confused. He remembered he was the prospective bridegroom, but was somewhat fuzzy as to which girl was to be his bride. So Marge set him straight. They located a justice of the peace, the ceremony went off with scarcely a hiccup, and the happy trio repaired to a motel. Somehow it was the witness rather than the bride who spent the honeymoon night with the groom. The next day Judy made her report to Marge, on the strength of which the inadvertence was rectified, the wedded couple picked up where they hadn't begun the night before, and everyone was happy.

To confound the moralists, may I say it turned out to be a good marriage? Joe and Marge remained together for six months.

Between husbands, Marge, again bored, obtained the telephone number of a Hollywood star, famed for his gangster roles. She called and informed him she had always admired him and would be happy to drop over if he were so inclined. It happened that he was bored, too.

He greeted her in a terrycloth bathrobe, not very securely tied. They had a drink, he showed her through his place, and having decided Marge could cure his boredom, the actor promised her a pink refrigerator if she would spend the night with him.

"I wouldn't mind a pink refrigerator," Marge told him, although at the particular time she was "living around," which meant she didn't have a place of her own.

When she told me about this incident, I asked, "What did you want with a pink refrigerator when you had no place for it?"

"Oh," she said, "I can always storage it, or sell it." The important thing, she explained, was that she was really in the mood that night. She liked the actor immensely, and enjoyed the evening, "just for itself, you know what I mean? He was very good. So strong! And that wonderful gangster voice, going on and on while we were in bed!"

Despite her giddiness, Marge had her depressed moments. Once she swore off men for life. "Men!" she said. "The hell with them all! I'd rather have a good massage!"

Marge was acquainted with a party girl who was never depressed, and always seemed enthusiastic about her work. This girl stopped at my desk to ask if I knew where Marge was currently sleeping. I had a male client with me, who stared at her in unabashed admiration, then at me with such a pleading expression there was nothing to do but introduce them. She acknowledged the introduction and walked away. That moment, my client remembered that he needed a certain letter before he could go on with the contract he was dictating. He would bring the necessary papers tomorrow, at about. . . . He was halfway down the hall, in the direction the girl took.

He did return to the office the next day—in fact he came tearing in. There was fire in his eye and a surgical bandage on his ear.

"Look what that crazy girl did to me!" he said. "She almost

bit my ear off!" Clearly, it was my fault for introducing them.

Party girls intrigue me. What makes them tick? What do they want out of life? What do they settle for? Whatever their motivation, they all have one thing in common. At some point in their lives they examined the pros and cons and deliberately took a calculated risk. Like the miner, the airline pilot or the movie stunt man, they know there is a good chance that they will get hurt. But they may not. They gamble on making a fortune, then settling down to a happy marriage before they have been beaten to death by a maniac or have outlived their attractiveness and become of no interest to men.

Aging is a phobia with party girls. They study their bodies, and are terrified if they see the beginning of crows' feet around their eyes or a little bulge around the waist. They have dedicated their lives to serving men, and like all high-grade courtesans, their earning power rests on their sexual allure. When they lose that, they will accumulate no more apartment houses, jewelry or gilt-edge bonds.

This is probably why they are never content with their holdings. They look ahead to when they will no longer command men, and fear grips their entrails. Meanwhile, they acquire and accumulate, and it becomes an obsession. They accumulate on principle whether need exists or not.

I am sure, too, that expensive "presents" have more than their dollar value for the girls. One example is Sandra, a still lovely, slim redhead who daily becomes more neurotic about the inevitable decay of her charms. She could "retire" tomorrow and live in splendid luxury. Despite this, she not only continues meeting men—hoping to marry one some day—but subtly and skillfully gets them to give her all sorts of gifts. When she wants a case of vodka, it must be the very special Yugoslavian brand served at Romanoff's when that establishment still existed. The jewels she gets must come from the finest houses. These exceptional presents have a very special meaning for her. They are affirmations of her real worth, her perpetual beauty, her allure.

I do not look upon party girls either with disgust or disrespect. They are, in the aggregate, as good and as bad, as affectionate and as frigid, as any random selection of people. They happen to be more unconventional than some, but they are human.

I imagine most people have an erroneous impression of the party girl, based on what little information and misinformation they are able to glean. For this reason, I would like to present to my readers two party girls I know. Let their own words speak for them. What follows is excerpted, and in some parts paraphrased, from tape-recorded conversations. Each girl was interviewed separately. Each consented to be tape recorded. Certain identifying features have been altered to preserve their anonymity.

Chris is a willowy blonde, Boston-born, who has been in California the past seven years. She was a minor actress in New York when an agent spotted her and brought her to Hollywood. She won the lead role in a picture produced by a major studio, and for a time seemed on her way to the very top. Then, in that inexplicable way things happen in the movie capital, her career collapsed overnight. As she put it, "Yesterday I'm a star, then all of a sudden—nothing! And it stays nothing. I struggled and fought and persevered. I had faith, tolerance, patience. But it just about petered out."

She scarcely realized when she began the routine of the party girl. "I sort of got wise to what was going on when I first saw all the cosmetics that piled up. Operating in hotels, meeting men in their rooms, you build up a whole bathroom full of cosmetics. I buy what I need in the hotel for overnight. Right now, I've got about six brand new washrags I haven't even taken out of the box yet. I haven't got room for the cosmetics in the medicine chest."

She does not indulge in self-pity, nor is she particularly happy about her work. "Nobody ever does anything to me I don't want to do. I've been fortunate with my men. The men I've chosen to be with I liked. They were usually tender, affectionate lovers."

"I've met some weird ones, though. I knew a man, young, single, handsome, good dresser, and lots of money—that was most important. I wouldn't go with him at first, because I was in love then, and I figured why should I go with someone else? Then, about two or three years later, he called me out of a blue sky, and by this time he's married, just got married about six months ago, and I said, 'What are you calling me for?'" (He told her that he was not really in love with his wife, and that he "just happened to get married." He asked Chris to go out with him.)

"So I says, 'Oh, no, you're a married man now.' He's married, and meantime I'm out of love, and here's a man, young, handsome, money, so suave, so polished. Money. Generous. Free with the way he'd spend his money. And you'd never think that this guy would know anything at all about love-making. So one night I had dinner with him. I didn't have no one. I said, 'Oh, well, I can have dinner with him.' What's wrong? I said, 'I have a girl friend here with me.'"

"He said, 'All right, I'll take you both.' So—I can't go into details. Anyway, he gets drunk, but yet decent, coherent, still very nice. You would never know he's drunk. Just stuttering a little bit. So he starts talking sexy, about these orgies and things. He wants to go to bed with me and my girl friend together. Every man—not every man, but so many men—want two women, and three women. This is very common. But! The things that he wanted to do to us! That he sat and told us! Here's a guy, as I say, that I knew, two, three years ago, I thought was a perfect gentleman. He said that he wants to be married to a woman, that he doesn't want to have sex with her, and he wants some other girl on the side—that would be terrific—that he could do everything with, to her, and also, maybe, bring in another girl friend, or bring in a man, and wants me to beat him, and beat him and beat him, and when he enters the door, he wants me to say, 'Enslave yourself!'"

"So O.K. So I say, 'Enslave yourself! Now! Take your clothes off!'"

"So then he wants me to say, 'Now, Johnny, I have a friend here, this is Jack. Jack is my slave, and Jack's a queer, and now, John, I want you—now, this is what he tells me! And when he's all finished, I'm to say, 'All right, get your clothes on and go.'"

"Now this man, so handsome, so suave, so educated. Why? Why is he like this? There's always the mother."

"So now I can make him become enslaved. I can make him do anything I say, with another man, another woman. Anything. Just anything. Beat him. Bite him. Cut him. The other night, he asked me—well, let's let that one go. He said that any time I would do this he would be willing to pay $1,000. And there was when he wanted me to rip his clothes off, tear his clothes off. And, of course this is common, he wanted me to meet him at the door and have my mink coat on and all my jewelry, and nothing else on. Then—I can't even dream of, I can't even say it honey, he said he would—oh, crap on what he said!"

"There's this other man, he wants you to come into a room, absolutely dark. Then the lights go on and you see him, lying in a coffin, with two candles on each side. And you're supposed to scream. That's the way he gets his satisfaction. Why not? Scream. Pick up a thousand dollars and leave. That's not too uncommon. Lots of men want that. But where are you going to get a coffin?"

I asked Chris whether she still enjoys sex, considering the sordid situations to which she has subjected herself. "Oh, yes!" she answered. "I like a man who likes normal, healthy sex. There's nothing more beautiful than just—what's the word for it?—there's a word for it—normal sex—a man that excites you to the fullest extent. To me, a man who can do that is a man who is tender and gentle. I can tell if it's the right man if he just touches me through my clothes. If he's the right man I have that chemistry feeling toward him."

Once Chris and I were with another girl who remarked that all men were beasts. Chris shrugged, "Men say that about women and women say that about men, so who knows? I will say this. There was only one man I ever worked for, when I was working, that never made a pass at me."

"What was wrong?" the other girl asked. "Was he paraplegic?"

The other girl was Sue, the second party girl I taped. She is intelligent, one of the most successful party girls in the environs, a college graduate, chic, and so beautiful that people turn to look at her when she enters a room. She has a rare ability to project sexuality in a refined way.

Her regular boy friend, whom she has known for years, is a multimillionaire. She is faithful to him in her fashion, but indulges in a little side play more than occasionally. Although she lives luxuriously, when she does go with a man who attracts her physically, it is not for sexual enjoyment alone. There must be negotiable profit in it as well.

Sue has a rather peculiar ethic when one considers her vocation. She shudders at risque stories and rarely employs rough language. She speaks contemptuously of girls who accept money or gifts on strictly a *quid pro quo* basis, yet she owns a lavish home, magnificent furs and jewelry, stocks and bonds, all donated by men.

I asked if she associated with call girls. Her answer was, "I don't know a girl who's a call girl, because who'd admit it? I don't know a call girl who'll admit she's a call girl. There was one girl, a little thing, that I sort of took under my wing because I was sorry for her. She had only one dress, that was all; she had three children at home. She'd park her car three blocks from the hotel and come in and look around, like she was expecting to meet someone. One day I was in the lounge with a boy friend, and she came in, and I asked her to come sit with us, and boy, did she take over! I could tell then that she was a call girl. She wanted to take my boy friend away from me. Now, nobody takes a man away from me if I don't want her to; but this man, I was about ready to get rid of him. I found her slipping notes to him under the table. I pretended not to see, but here she is, slipping a note to him! I left. I haven't the slightest idea what happened after that."

Sue will pick up a man herself, but apparently there is something reasonable and proper about it when she does: "I have a boy friend. When I get mad at him, I'll go to a cocktail lounge or some place. He told me, 'Sue, I don't want you going to bars and picking up men.' Now, how else is a girl going to meet men? It's a tragic thing, but that's the only way a woman can meet a man and a man can meet a woman. At house parties, you see the same people over and over again."

Scraping up an acquaintance need not signify it is for sex. "Sometimes a man, all he wants is just a girl for companionship at dinner. They just don't like to come in a fine restaurant alone. Who in the world ever goes to a restaurant like LaRue's, Chasen's, and gets a table for one? The restaurant always likes to have at least two sitting down to it. And what happens after that is up to the girl. If she wants to. . . ."

Sue selects her dinner hosts carefully. "There are only two kinds of men, so far as where they come from: Men, and Texans. They're just wild, Texans. I love to go with a New Yorker. They're so cosmopolitan, they can talk about so many things. They may have only a cursory knowledge of some subjects, but they can at least talk interestingly. Texans, for God's sake, all they can talk about is their own wealth! And they get so drunk! I like to talk about things. The man who keeps thinking about taking this girl to his room, I steer clear of the subject. I want to talk about other things besides that inevitable thing. I don't want to get straight into bed. The New Yorker isn't so obvious, he doesn't get so angry if he doesn't get you into bed. A Texan, it suffers his ego just tremendously."

She differentiates between the Southwesterner, represented by the Texan, and the Southerner: "Southerners are gentlemen. I met a man from Louisiana, and he was a gentleman."

A lady should act like a lady: "Some girls spoil their chances with a spender; they're too obvious, they work too strong, they come right out and ask for things. I always felt a more subtle approach was better. I have this girl friend, she met a man, he fell for her, but his wife was dying of cancer and he didn't want to divorce her, so he just went with Jane. He gave her loads of jewelry, gowns—she'd sell the gowns. She kept getting things from about five boy friends at one time. Now she's well fixed, she has a monthly amount coming in from some oil stock some-one gave her. But she worked cleverly. She let men feel they want to treat her.

"You need security. Otherwise, it's not good when you get

older. I get so angry with some girls! I say, 'What on earth did you have to go out and buy a new dress for, anyhow? Put the money in the bank!' "

Sue will not ask for things directly. She waits for the man to reach the point where he cannot go another day without giving her a gift. But while she appreciates largesse from the heart, she is a bit shocked by the Good Time Charlie who goes to extremes. "I went out with a man, I met him in this bar, and after a while we went to a strip tease place on the Strip. I don't usually go to those places, but we'd been drinking. Well, that night, he gave me $100 to go to the ladies' room. Stupid me! I gave it back to him. He tipped each of two girls, waitresses, $100. Then we took a cab, and he gave the cab driver a $100 tip. I got the idea this man had a complex. He was spending too much money. He has a complex of, well, he has a speech impediment, so maybe that's the reason. But I don't know whether it's that or whether he's trying to impress me, or what. We went out to the Luau once, and he asked how I would like some perfume he saw at the counter. I said, no, thanks. He whispered, 'You know I want to buy it just to help these girls out.' "

"I said, 'Fine!' But I think there has to be a reason why a man would spend money like that. Insecurity or an inferiority complex, or. . . ."

Spending money on her is no guarantee of respect even if the man doesn't have a complex: "These playboys! They can have money, but some of them are just bums, in spite of it. I knew one, he had his face lifted!"

Usually, Sue is gay, full of life, enjoying herself. But she has her down moods when she talks as if there is nothing quite so cruel or degraded as a man. Her first husband, she says, was selfish and inconsiderate. "I supported him all those three years I was married to him until I got tired of it, because I thought, after seven years of medical college, he ought to go out and be a doctor. And my second marriage, I married strictly through love, and honey, I got very little except aberrations, and I didn't enjoy them a bit. I must say, I should have got a lot of money out of my ex-husband. Oh, honey, he had every aberration!"

"You're not saying every man is like that?" I asked.

"Most of them are."

"So you reach the conclusion that men are pretty lousy creatures?"

"You are so right!"

"There are no good men?"

"My father was a good man, I think."

"If you think all men are terrible, does that mean you don't want to marry again?"

"Well, actually, I don't particularly care if I marry them. Leave me six million dollars, I don't have to have your name, is how I feel. I like the name I have. Men are selfish. Women are selfish, too. They only want money. Or what can you buy me? But there are more selfish men. I don't know. A woman has an emotional disturbance; she has to go somewhere for advice; she goes to a minister, she goes to a doctor, and he wants to rape you. It's ridiculous! So, when I go out with a man, a man takes a beautiful girl out because he wants to show her off, he wants people to see he can take a beautiful girl out. She might as well get something out of it. Why should she spend six hours or eight hours with a man unless she gets something out of it?"

"I met a man I would have married him, because he had two million dollars. He takes me out, wastes my time, and goes off with ———— (an actress). I always am the one that gets taken. I spend two years going with Tracy, and don't marry him. Why go with someone I'm not going to marry? Or at least with someone that's going to give me a million dollars. Or buy me a house or something. I went with this fellow Saunders for two years. He promised me a million dollars, but I haven't got it. . . . I spent four years in the ———— Lounge, and it was a waste of time, so far as marrying was concerned. And the things you have to stand for! The aberrations!"

She tells about a man, "he was worth millions," who saw her in an elegant cocktail lounge and sent a drink over to her table. "If a man sends a drink over and you refuse it, that ends it. If you accept it, that's an invitation for him to come over. I rarely accept because then the fellow considers you're a pushover. So I played hard to get. He kept after me, the next night and the next night, and then he came over and told me he knew a certain friend of mine. I don't know how he found out I knew this fellow. So that made it a social meeting. Well, this fellow, he took me to dinner and places. He was really a stimulating conversationalist. Then, of course, the $64 question. I said he was awfully nice and I liked him and that I'd go to his room.

"He got very embarrassed. He said, 'You have to understand about me.'

"I said, 'That's all right. If I like a man, I'm going to be good to him.'

"He kept saying no, I didn't understand, and I'm beginning to wonder what's wrong with him, is he, you know, a queer, or incapable, or what? Finally he tells me. He'll have another man up there and I'm to make love to this other fellow while he watches. Isn't that disgusting?"

"Did you go?"

"Well, yes! But what's wrong with a man like that?"

For a girl who claims that she looks on men with a jaundiced eye at all times, Sue has had an inexplicable relationship with Leon, the multimillionaire who has been her "regular" for a decade. She sees other men secretly, but she takes more abuse from Leon than she would from any other man; yet she sticks with him. She admits, "He always gets drunk, and when he gets drunk he gets obnoxious. He loves to beat me up. He's tried to choke me. He's pulled his loaded gun out and threatened to shoot me. Not because he's a sadist, but because he's mad. He once hit me over the head with a bottle, over and over. He does it only when he's been drinking. I guess when he loves anybody he wants to hurt them."

She never seriously thinks of leaving him, and I am far from certain that it is solely because of his wealth. I think there is a real bond between them, curious as it may be. Perhaps Sue's cheating on Leon is a form of revenge. She retaliates in other ways, too. He has a charge account at Scandia Restaurant, an elegant spot on the Sunset Strip. After a battle with her lover, she brings her girl friends to the restaurant for dinner. "We order bottles of wine, Oysters Rockefeller, which I can't stand, but I'll order everything, just to charge it to him, because I hate him. I'll ask the waiter how much Leon usually gives him, and I'll give him a dollar more. And I'll tip the bartender, and everybody else, to get even with him. Such a mean man! I just love to spend his money, because he's the meanest, cheapest, tightest . . . oooooh!"

"Why do you stick with him?" I ask.

"Love."

"Love!"

"It has to be. I was analyzed once. What other reason? I've tried to analyze it myself. You get awfully used to somebody, too. I used to read in the papers, I'd say, how in the world will these stupid women allow their husbands to beat them, and then take them back? Well, I'm not even married to the bastard, and he does that. You never know until you've had it yourself. I think I'm getting over him, though."

"What do you see in him?"

"I've asked myself that many times."

Sue keeps saying she looks forward to the time when she can settle down for good. I asked what she looks for, what would induce her to marry.

"I'd have to love somebody. I'd also have to respect him, and also have financial security."

"What yields respect?"

"The way a man is. I can't respect a drunk. At least not a terrible drunk. And he mustn't tell me about how much I drink. I tell Leon, 'I can't stand you *unless* I drink!' "

"He has given me a complex. He says what sort of man would ever want to marry me? We were driving through Beverly Hills, past all those lovely houses, and I said, 'Every one of these houses has got a woman in it, a wife.'

"He says, 'What kind of a man would want to marry you?'

"I said, 'Do you think that nobody is going to marry me?'

"He says, 'Nobody is ever going to marry you, Sue. All they want to do is lay you.'

"He's always tearing me down. I'm actually surprised to have anyone compliment me, because of him. It's a terrible thing to have a man do this to you!"

There have been rare occasions when Sue has taken revenge against Leon. They were in a hotel in Canada, "and he had to beat up on me." She telephoned the desk clerk, cried, "Help!" and hung up. When the clerk called back, she told him that she wanted another room. The place was filled to capacity, so the house detective came up and asked if he could do something.

Sue said, "Yes. I need another room. This man won't allow me to sleep. He just won't leave me alone."

"Is this your husband?"

She had to say yes.

"Well, lady, that's your problem."

She tells me, "There was a choice of getting dressed and going out to sit in the lobby, but it was two or three in the morning, and I was awfully tired. Or I could have hoped that this man would drink himself into insensibility. This night I became so incensed that I took his shoe and I hit him over the head, and I *hit* him over the head, and I HIT him over the head, and all of a sudden I saw he was a mess. So I get a towel and commence cleansing the blood that's coming from his head. It was just awful! I said, 'I'd better call a doctor.'

"He said, 'No, no, no! We don't want any police report!'

"I thought, my God! This is terrible! I wrapped a towel around him, and then after I'd practically killed him, he threw his arms around me and said, 'Oh, I love you so much! Don't ever leave me! I love you!' "

Sue tells of many more battles, in which she received the worst of it. "The only thing I worry about is having my teeth knocked out or my nose broken. I really don't think he'll kill me, because I think he just does it enough to scare me."

Will she marry Leon? She would if he were willing, but he is not.

Then what does she look for—if and when she marries another man?

"I suppose maturity, because this man doesn't have it."

"You want maturity in him. And what do you want out of it for yourself?"

"I want love. I've had these men I could have married and I haven't married, so apparently it isn't just that I want financial security. Because I have to have love along with it."

"What's the difference between love and sex?"

"Oh, my God! All the difference in the world! I could go the rest of my life without sex. Sex is nothing to me. I've already had a lot of it. Love is far more endearing. It's a deeper thing. I've heard of women who can feel sexy with bellboys. That's just sex. People in love are more companionable than they are sexy. I believe in companionship and sitting and watching television. Sex isn't going to last in a marriage. That's one reason why you should never get married for sex. That's why some people get divorces, I think."

She continues: "I know a beautiful woman, and she married the ugliest man you ever saw. She didn't marry for sex. She told me, 'Oh, my God! He's so ugly I cover him up with a sheet!' But she loves him. She's got two children by him. She loves him because she's got about three maids, and an unlimited bank account. She came from a poor family; she never had shoes. She has a mother and brothers and sisters and she supports them. Of course, that's not so admirable. I'd do the same if I had a husband that was generous."

"As you see it, Sue, what is the greatest value in life?"

"That's a difficult thing to ask me, when I'm the most confused, mixed-up person in the world. I remember when I was in Acapulco with this man from New York. I go down there and I live in a little room, with just simple things which don't cost any money. I live in a bathing suit. I think of this man I'm with; I think, you know, if I stay here long enough my values will change. I just came from some people I knew who had tremendous wealth. I come to this place, and I'm happier here than I was with them. My sense of values is so distorted that I don't know what to call the values of life."

"Sometimes I wonder, Sue. You always seem so self-contained, so controlled in your emotions. Do you ever cry? What makes you cry?"

"Oh, honey, I was watching a movie on TV last night, 'A Tree Grows in Brooklyn,' and it took me sixteen Kleenexes to get through it. I thought, this woman couldn't possibly have pictured such abject poverty as this girl went through unless she had lived it herself. I've never been poor, but I felt sorry. I cried and cried. I guess I understood because my mother and father were poor. . . . I remember when I was about five, we lived across from the Catholic Church. There was this man, he had a wooden leg, begging in front of the church. I asked my mother for five cents and I gave it to him. I just can't stand poverty! Can't stand it!"

"Did Jimmy Dunn play the part of a good man in the movie?"

"Oh, sure! He was good. But he was irresponsible."

"Was his wife a good woman?"

"Yes. One of them had to have responsibility."

"Did she understand him?"

"N-no. No, I don't think so. She was in love with him, but she didn't understand him. That was enough. She loved him."

Do you see why no one can tell me that Sue is a bad woman?

❊

Chapter 13

Whatever happened
to the house detective?

"Public stenographer? Can you come to Room 766 right away?"
The voice was male, high-pitched.
"Yes, sir! Right away!"
I knocked.
"It's open! Come on in!"
I stepped into the room. There was no one there.
Suddenly the bathroom door opened. A man stepped out, stark naked except for a pair of women's galoshes flopping at his ankles. In his hand was a pistol. It was aimed right at me.
I stood petrified, a scream caught in my throat. The apparition made two giant kangaroo hops, landed three feet from me, and pressed the trigger.
Something clammy hit me full in the face, and trickled downward. Water, from a toy pistol.
Laughing maniacally, the creature placed a hand on its hip,

crowed, "Isn't that fun*ny?* Har-har-har!" By the third "har" I was down the hall, calling for the security officer from the house phone in the maids' quarters.

Every hotel has its occasional madman, its once-in-a-while theft and scandalous party. Coping with them is the function of the security officer. The large hotels employ more than one. The security officer handles the day-to-day police chores of the hotel. More complicated problems are handled in conjunction with local police.

Hotel operations are so gigantic these days that it is impossible for management to be informed on everything that goes on. It can hope only to prevent loss of guests' property and to protect the hostelry's reputation by curbing blatantly scandalous behavior. Should an incident occur that cannot be ignored, the disposition is to settle it quietly. A girl told me that she visited a man in his suite in a first class hotel. There was much drinking, in the course of which they started brawling. The man pummeled the girl. She escaped and locked herself into an adjoining room of the suite, from which she telephoned for help. A security man arrived, surveyed the disordered sitting room, the girl's bruised face, and informed her that he was sorry but he could not take action against the man. He was the guest, not the battered girl. It was his suite, not hers. What was she doing there?

A girl is only a girl, but the hotel character known as an "operator" is a real headache to security. The hotel operator is after a fast buck. His specialty may be real estate deals or worthless oil wells. He may be trying to unload a corporation on the verge of bankruptcy or to sell one existing only on paper. Whatever his game, it is played by false pretenses.

The successful operator looks like any respectable, well-to-do businessman. He dresses in good taste, is courteous, and fits in well with the surroundings. He possesses an outgoing personality and people take to him at once. His most outstanding asset is plausibility. He can discourse on many subjects and knows which one will interest his "mark," an underworld term for the prospective victim. Even more important, he makes a good listener.

A favorite hunting ground of the operator is the swimming

pool, where informality is the rule and guests are in a relaxed frame of mind. The wily operator sits next to his prospect, remarks about the California sunshine, and he is on first base. Perhaps he introduces himself as an investment broker. Casually, he mentions his home in some city. What a coincidence! The mark comes from the same city! (Naturally. The "broker" checked on that in advance.) Nothing breaks the ice so quickly as discovering that someone is from the old home town.

The operator lets slip that he came to town to activate a certain manipulation that will send an unspecified stock zooming. The mark, of course, wants to hear more. Please forget it, the operator begs; he didn't mean to let the cat out of the bag. That only whets the mark's appetite the more. He coaxes for facts.

The operator makes up a likely story and the mark is salivating. He has got to get in on the ground floor. The operator, following the usual practice of his breed, indicates that he is reluctant to deal him in. After all, there is a chance that something will go awry and he doesn't want to involve anyone. Finally, after much coaxing, he gives in. Money is handed over, and before many weeks have passed the mark realizes he spent good currency on nothing. By this time the man who sold it is in Brazil or Istanbul—anywhere but the "home town."

Petty offenders are more common around hotels than big-time confidence operators. Burglars occasionally steal from guest rooms. Here the occupants are often guilty of negligence, failing to lock their rooms securely. The prowler tries doors until he finds one that gives to his touch.

A burglar may register in a hotel, receive a key to his room, have a locksmith make a duplicate, check out next day, and return another time. He keeps his former quarters under surveillance until the occupant steps out; at that point, the burglar enters.

A classical dodge is playing drunk. The thief registers into, say, Room 202. In the wee hours, he tries Room 302, and 402, finally finds an 02 room unlocked. Should the occupant awaken, and call out, the thief stands in the open doorway, swaying, dangling his own room key. "Wha'?" he asks. "Isn't this 202?

Musta got off on wrong floor. Shorry!" Rarely does the occupant give an alarm.

Curious as it may seem, otherwise perfectly legitimate guests cost hotels more in losses than is taken from the premises by hotel prowlers. Guests go in for a type of larceny that is more of a hobby than a misdemeanor. Vacationers especially are souvenir collectors. It is great fun, and the collectors scarcely consider themselves misdemeanants, which they are in fact. They want something to show the folks back home to prove they have been around, visited the interesting spots, and stopped in the best places. They steal—pardon me, appropriate—anything weighing under a ton that can be carried out inconspicuously. The value of a single purloined article is not great, as a rule, but in the aggregate, what is carried away from large establishments comes to a staggering sum. Towels, ashtrays, washcloths, silverware, soap, glasses, boxes of Kleenex, dishes, and even pillows and small lamps vanish by the thousands. The most popular dish liberated by guests, according to security men I know, is the butterboat, filched from room service trays. It can be impressed into service as anything from an ashtray to a zucchini bowl.

I use a butterboat for a card tray in my office and it is lifted almost weekly, the lifter leaving the cards on the counter. Grrrr!

Where do I get the weekly replacement? Well, it's like this. . . .

Although hotel people don't love souvenir hunters, they are not going to lose a hundred dollars worth of patronage over a fifty cent towel. They cooperate with the inevitable, scarcely attempting to retrieve articles stolen from rooms or other parts of the hostelry.

Not all property carried out by guests can be regarded as souvenirs, however, expendable in the interest of public relations. An astonishing number of otherwise respectable folks steal things of such value that they must be branded downright, money-grabbing thieves. It is fantastic what some travelers travel away with: electric irons, blankets, pictures, portable radios, even small air-conditioning units. What can a hotel do about this? Not very much. In most hotels, management is content to detect the thief and recover the loot or bill the guest for it, provided it can be proved that he took it.

A miniscule percentage of hotel employees also indulges in stealing. Most of them are so meticulously honest that they would turn in a dime found in a room. Some, however, who do have a soupçon of larceny in their hearts, are inclined to look upon their thefts as appropriation of things to which they are halfway entitled. A kitchen man takes possession of half a ham or a leftover pie. So what? The hotel can afford the loss and the employee can use the stuff. Besides, it might otherwise wind up in a garbage can as a leftover, and it would be sinful to waste good food, would it not?

In at least one establishment, closed circuit television is used to curb employee larceny. A monitor observes as workers punch the time clock in and out. Some rather remarkable increases in weight have been noted between arrival and departure. Employees have been apprehended with steaks, poultry, and canned goods, secreted under their clothing. One woman was caught with four New York cut steaks in her panties—New York cut, mind you, not rump steaks!

The security man in a New York hotel saw a waiter punch out for the day, go out the back exit, stop at a garbage can, and rummage about inside. Inasmuch as the waiter's earnings scarcely suggested he need rely on refuse for subsistance, this piqued the guard's curiosity. He kept the area under surveillance the following night, and this time observed four employees who apparently had a predilection for garbage. Next evening, the security man beat the departing staff to the lift of the lid. Just before that shift was to go off duty, he inspected the receptacle himself. Atop the refuse lay three neatly wrapped packages, each containing steaks and chops. A kitchen employee, it was discovered, was carrying good meat out with the garbage, depositing both in the can, the expensive brand on top, to be picked up by his friends.

As if tracking down thieves and greedy steak-eaters were not enough, security men must cope with merrymakers and not-such-merrymakers. There was the man who took his wife on a second honeymoon, reserving the same bridal suite they occupied the first time. They ordered champagne and clinked glasses as they had thirty years before. This reminded the wife that in the thirty years of marriage her mate never brought home a bottle of bubbly champagne. When she called his attention to the fact, he remembered something he often intended telling his wife but never got around to in the same three decades. Whatver it was, she was not amused. To accent the fact, she heaved a table lamp at her husband. He retaliated with a wine glass. She riposted with a hairbrush, which glanced off his forehead and smashed the glass of a wall picture. By the time the security officer arrived on the scene he found chairs upended, glasses and lamps smashed to smithereens, and walls and drapes spattered with pink champagne and red blood.

The husband puffed, "She got what she's been asking for all these years!"

It was a rash remark, for he overlooked a vital fact. The empty champagne bottle lay at his wife's feet. She picked it up and wrapped it around her helpmeet's head, laying him out cold.

The manager came up to restore tranquility. The shame-faced husband, awakened from his nap on the floor, offered to pay for the damage. It was his fault, he asserted; in thirty years he should have learned to duck. The manager beamed, the maid swept up the debris, husband and wife made up, and swore it would never happen again.

The night before the loving couple were due to check out, the manager, intending to demonstrate all was forgiven, sent up a note saying he looked forward to having the guests visit his hotel on their third honeymoon.

This time it was he who made a fatal error. He attached the note to a bottle of champagne. The honeymooners began reminiscing again.

Proceeding from pummeling to prankstering, there was the inebriated wiseacre who paid a visit to the pool late one night. Early the next day, some guests dived in and emerged purple as eggplants. Since California never gets that cold, an investigation was instituted. The water of the pool had been impregnated with dye.

And there were the effervescent convention delegates who took over an entire hotel, one floor being occupied by a Cleveland contingent. When two couples left their rooms for an evening session, merry fellow townsmen picked up their keys at the desk and went to work. One husband and wife returned to find their room without a stick of furniture. Not even a picture remained on the wall. The second couple discovered their quarters transformed into a warehouse. It was stacked, wall to wall, floor to ceiling, with furniture from the first couple's room.

Anyone who needs a reason for going on the wagon might consider the Case of the Not So Dead Corpse. During a convention in Buffalo, a group of delegates made the rounds of the local bars. They returned to the hotel and had one more drink before the tap room closed. One man passed out on that final highball. His friends carried him to his room, undressed him, put him in his old-fashioned nightgown, and laid him gently on the bed. A local delegate, who happened to be an official of the Park Department, was struck by what seemed a brilliant idea, in his inebriated state. He rousted a Park Department employee out of bed and had him deliver a dozen potted rubber plants from the Department's stock. These were ranged around the sleeping man's bed.

He awoke late the next morning, on his back, in a white shroud, surrounded by vegetation. Soft music, piped into guest rooms, trembled on the air. Uttering a shriek of horror, he bolted out the door, screaming it was a foul mistake, he wasn't dead, he wouldn't lie in a funeral parlor, and damned if he were going to be embalmed.

As George MacDonald said, "We die daily. Happy those who daily come to life as well."

Chapter 14

Presidents and princes

Not long ago, a shining black limousine was driven up to the front entrance of the Beverly Hilton Hotel. Out stepped a trim woman dressed in a tight Oriental gown of red silk. Her upswept black hair was piled high on her head. Her face was dominated by dark, flashing eyes. She was attractive and she commanded attention.

She swept through the lobby and into the ballroom, where over a thousand people were seated at tables. As she mounted the dais, they applauded enthusiastically. Her smile of acknowledgment was gracious, and regal, too. Clearly, she accepted the plaudits as no more than her due.

This was Madame Ngo Dinh Nhu, come to address the World Affairs Council at a luncheon tendered in her honor. She was then wife of the second most powerful man in South Viet Nam, the brother of the absolute ruler of that war-torn little country. Madame Nhu was herself a highly controversial figure. Rumor had it she was the real power behind her husband and brother-in-law. When native priests set themselves afire in protest against the treatment of Buddhists, it was this charming feminine creature who cynically referred to the self-immolation as "Buddhist barbecues."

Prior to her arrival in California, Madame had delivered many fiery denunciations of our government. She had nothing but scorn for the millions of dollars we poured into her country in foreign aid—it wasn't enough. She showed the utmost contempt for our political and international postures. We were, she vehemently declared, feeble, unrealistic, uninformed, and unsophisticated.

And now here she was, this chic and sinister Madame, about to squirt more venom. And here we were, thrilled to have her in our midst.

I am not guessing about this. I attended the luncheon and sensed the excitement all around me. Everyone was studying the exotic little woman on the platform, commenting on her beauty, her distinguished manner, her beautiful red Chinese dress. They gossiped about her rumored relations with men, speculated whether such a woman could fail to have a few lovers. Not one word did they utter (within my hearing at least) about her politics or the international relations of her country.

From the first sentence of her address, Madame Nhu held the audience spellbound. She projected her personality as effectively and vitally as any professional actress. The words poured out, despite her real or feigned language handicap. She was arrogant, bombastic, tempestuous, and incredibly egotistical by turn. The only way she could have demonstrated more contempt for our government would have been to thumb her nose at the American flag.

I am sure that a few listeners agreed with her ultra-conservative political postulates. I am just as certain that no one in the audience accepted her polemical judgment of our national character. And yet, time after time, she was interrupted by applause. For her sarcasm and vitriol we returned praise and adulation. And I was no exception. I felt that electric thrill at being near a woman who played such a vital role in international affairs. I applauded from time to time. But finally, I stopped. I resented her attitude. Why, then, applaud? Why were others applauding?

When she made still another acidulous comment about our foreign policy I turned to the woman next to me and asked why she was applauding.

She shrugged. "I don't know. Everybody else is. My! Isn't she beautiful?"

That was it. Those people were aware of the hostility the Madame bore us as a nation. They knew she was an arch-authoritarian. But, my! Wasn't she *beautiful!*

We were reacting to something more than physical beauty, too. Madame Nhu's allure lay in her being an important person. She wielded awesome power, and a woman who has and maintains power in government somehow takes on added glamour. Had Madame Nhu been a visiting schoolteacher making the same type of remarks we might have booed or walked out on her.

Just as Madame Nhu fascinated me because of her position in world affairs, so also am I thrilled by kings, princes, presidents, maharajahs. I know little about the political beliefs of King Baudouin of Belgium, but his presence in the hotel had an intoxicating effect on me, as did the visits of Queen Fredericka of Greece, President Macapagal of the Philippines, and King Umberto of Italy.

I was particularly impressed when President Achmed Sukarno of Indonesia visited this country in 1961. It was the first time I had seen a foreign dignitary of his high rank. I witnessed his arrival at the Beverly Hills Hotel. Sukarno wore a petji, the little cap common among Indonesians, and carried a baton as a symbol of his authority. He walked up the red carpet, his aides two-by-two behind him. Of those who followed their leader, one, a tall blond man, seemed out of place among the short, dark Indonesians.

I met him later, when he dictated a speech Sukarno was to give. He was Tom Atkinson, an Englishman, a professor at the university in Djakarta. He received me in bare feet, a colorful batik cloth around his midriff. We developed a sort of intellectual companionship during his stay, discussing poetry and philosophy, in which he was well versed.

The Indonesians were given an elaborate banquet in the hotel, but that evening Tom called my office and blurted out, "We're hungry! We want some plain boiled rice, and don't know where to go. Can you come along and lead the way?" He and his friends had barely nibbled at the fine American food; Indonesian appetites could be satisfied only by the filling bowl of rice. He and I got into my car, the others following in limousines, and I led them to a modest Chinese café in Hollywood.

Tom arranged for me to meet President Sukarno. I was instructed not to shake hands when introduced, but to grasp the staff of office Sukarno would extend. I was also told I had best not be alone with him, because he was quite a ladies' man. As it turned out, I had no opportunity to test this, for Sukarno was surrounded by aides throughout our brief introduction. When he extended the baton, I grasped it. He smiled and spoke a few words in English; I smiled back. He turned to somebody else, and the audience was at an end.

Of the many heads of state who graced a hotel by their presence, none captivated me so completely as President John F. Kennedy. When I think of him, I see him as I did the first time, when he arrived at the Democratic Convention in Los Angeles— young, handsome, vibrant. I have a mental image of him as President, too, leaving the hotel elevator for his car. Velvet ropes were set up in the jammed lobby to create an aisle so he could negotiate the distance to the hotel entrance without being crushed. Men, women and children had been waiting for hours just to catch a glimpse of him. As he proceeded toward the doors, cheers and greetings rang out. Pleased, he responded with smiles and hand-waves. Occasionally, he reached over the ropes to shake hands. A friend of mine in the crowd remarked, "You have to love him. He has the knack of making every person feel he is *somebody*"

When he got outside, preparing to enter his open car, Mr. Kennedy was surrounded by a surging, pushing, yelling crowd. Understandably, the security force was very unhappy, but Mr. Kennedy was unruffled, showing no annoyance even when the jostling almost knocked him off balance. He smiled broadly and gave himself to the people gladly, shaking every hand he could reach before getting into the car. I got the impression he loved receiving this demonstration of affection. And it was precisely that. Most of these people loved the man. Very noticeable, too, was that an unusually large part of the crowd was composed of young people. John F. Kennedy was their inspiration, the first youthful president they had known. He personified their own, not a past generation.

A charming incident occurred during one of his visits to the hotel. He was landed on the roof by helicopter, and Secret Service agents escorted him to a waiting elevator. The route had been carefully mapped out for security. He was to leave the elevator at the sixth floor and proceed directly to his suite. But chance and Mr. Kennedy ruled otherwise. Walking down the sixth-floor corridor, he spied a girl in bridesmaid's dress outside a suite, the door of which was ajar. Sounds of merriment emanated from the interior. Mr. Kennedy stopped, and asked if there was to be a wedding in the hotel. Stricken dumb by the realization of who was speaking, the girl could only nod.

Mr. Kennedy smiled. "Where is the bride?" he asked.

She was inside the suite, with relatives.

The President told the Secret Service men not to follow, and he walked in, went up to the bride and congratulated her. As she recovered from her surprise, other people recognized the Chief Executive, and crowded around him. The bride's mother, almost overcome, managed to say she would be greatly honored if Mr. Kennedy would drop in at the wedding. He gallantly replied he would certainly do so if he found time, but on one condition—that the charming mother of the bride dance the Twist with him.

John F. Kennedy was a nonconformist where his personal safety was concerned. Visiting his sister Pat Lawford at her beachfront house in Santa Monica, he took a dip in the ocean, and when he came out he was mobbed by well-wishers who could have injured him in the crush. At the hotel, every precaution was taken to make certain his food was above suspicion.

It was prepared under close official scrutiny, which came to naught when Mr. Kennedy decided to have his dinners brought in from La Scala, a renowned Italian restaurant.

One afternoon, a maid, Toni, was in the Presidential suite making up the bed. The President's orthopedic mattress had been installed before his arrival, and Toni was putting a sheet in place when she heard a cheery, "Hello!"

She turned around, and there stood President Kennedy. She managed a weak, "Welcome to the Beverly Hilton, Mr. President!"

He smiled and, noting she had an accent, asked where she was from. She told him she was a native of Germany. He inquired if she was happy living in the United States, and seemed pleased when she said she was indeed.

The following day, he passed her in the corridor as he was leaving, stopped, and thanked her warmly for having made his stay comfortable.

When she told me about this later, she said all she could think about was what a land this was and what a man he was. Here she was, a foreigner, a maid, and the Chief of State had taken time out to chat with her.

But a woman is a woman, for all that. When I asked what particular quality in him she found most outstanding, she said, "Oh, he was so-o handsome!"

More than one President or ex-President has visited the hotel during my incumbency, of course. Former President Harry S Truman made a stop in California a few years ago, at which time he held a press conference in the hotel. I got in through the courtesy of the public relations office. I invited Art, a young reporter for the UCLA school paper, to accompany me.

I found Truman much as I had imagined he would be, crisp, pungent, quick witted. Face to face, I had even greater respect for him than previously. He impressed me as a man of true stature. His voice relayed the same tone and character it did on the radio, and his remarks were alternately sharp-edged and contemplative. He was a lively speaker and had reporters laughing so hard that the conference was interrupted many times. He gave the impression that he enjoyed the proceedings.

My friend Art and I had found seats in the center of the room, which was good-sized and very crowded. Chairs were so close together that we were practically sitting on top of each other. During a brief pause in the question-answer period, Art raised his hand. The ex-President may have been blinded by the TV lights, or perhaps since Art and I were both wearing green sweaters Mr. Truman believed it was my hand he saw. In any event, he said, "Yes, young lady?"

My companion looked around the room, then at me. For a moment I considered asking a question—any question—since the President seemed to be looking at me, but the only one that flashed through my mind was, "Is your daughter happily married?" That wouldn't do at all. I looked at Art, as though to indicate, "Go ahead, 'young lady,' and ask the question!"

He regained his composure and asked Mr. Truman to comment on the growth of ultra-conservative groups on university campuses. The ex-President showed no surprise when the "young lady" addressed him in a deep masculine voice. He answered the question by saying he was not worried about the ultra-conservative groups at all, that the American people had too much common sense to be taken in by crackpots.

Mr. Johnson was still Vice-President of the United States the first time I saw him in the hotel. There was no great interest in his appearance at that time. Naturally, when Mr. Johnson came to California as Chief Executive, it was a different story. There was a crowd outside the hotel when he arrived. It was friendly, but more sedate than the sort Mr. Kennedy used to get. And Mr. Johnson was more sedate than his predecessor. He walked more deliberately and his gestures and facial expressions were less mobile. Undoubtedly he was holding himself in check, since the nation was still mourning the late President.

The only other president of the United States I have seen in Beverly Hills is Dwight D. Eisenhower. He landed by helicopter on the parking lot of a department store adjacent to the hotel and came down a ramp and over to the Beverly Hilton, where a crowd awaited him. Although flanked by two guards his pace was so brisk that he outdistanced them much of the time, waving to the assembled people and calling out, "Hello! Hello!" His expression was genial, his manner unassuming. He was very popular with the crowd. Over and over I heard the remark: "Isn't he wonderful!"

And yet he was not as glamorous as Kennedy in the public eye. People responded to President Kennedy the way fans respond to a movie idol. Kennedy was a glamour boy. He had magic for the people. I have never seen anyone evoke the tremendous emotional reaction he did. His crowds were boisterous, undisciplined. The people liked Ike but were dazzled by JFK. When they looked at Kennedy, they saw the man, the handsome, sophisticated idealist of politics. When they saw Eisenhower, they beheld the President of the United States more than the man.

President Kennedy's assassination has created great interest in measures taken for the security of a chief executive. I asked the hotel security officers about this.

A good way to begin is to quote a memorandum to hotel personnel, on the occasion of President Johnson's 1964 visit to the Beverly Hilton Hotel. I do so with the permission and through the courtesy of the management. I have inserted explanatory notes of my own, in parentheses. The memo is interesting not only for what it reveals concerning security measures, but for what it discloses concerning the logistics of making the stay of a Presidential party comfortable.

*   *   *

TO: Staff Members, Department Heads, and Guest Contact Employees
FROM: Managing Director
SUBJECT: Presidential Visit
President Johnson and his White House party will be staying at the Beverly Hilton on Saturday and Sunday, June 20th and 21st. As of this writing the schedule is as follows:

SCHEDULE OF PRESIDENTIAL VISIT

Sat. June 20th

1:00 — 1:45 P.M. President and party to arrive by three Army helicopters on the 5th floor of Self Park Garage about 1:15. Party and welcoming committee will proceed through #434 to elevators and to 7th and 8th floors. Lynda B. Johnson will join the President sometime during the afternoon.

> (#434 is a suite that has a door going from its patio to the top level of the garage, where the helicopters would land. There is a direct access route to elevators from the heliport atop the garage.)

    •   •   •   •   •

3:00 — 3:30 P.M. Arrival by bus of 75 members of the Press.

6:30 — 7:30 P.M. Preparation for departure from lobby through Wilshire entrance to car and motorcade to Palladium, then from Palladium to Ambassador at 10 P.M.

11:15 — 1:00 A.M. Probable return of Presidential party to Hotel. Will use Wilshire entrance and go through lobby to elevators.

Sun. June 2nd

10:30 — 11:00 A.M. Possibility of Presidential departure for local church. Lobby through to Wilshire entrance.

12:00 — 1:00 P.M. Possible return from church via lobby and Wilshire entrance.

1:00 — 2:30 P.M. Departure via #434, 5th floor of Self Park, by helicopter.

ATTENTION SECURITY OFFICER
PRESS BARRICADE

Chief Engineer is setting up Press Barricade on top of selfpark. Please contact and offer assistance.

> (The press barricade consists of ropes behind which members of the press await the President's arrival.)

RED CARPET

Please supervise positioning of red carpet. Housekeeping will have on patio of #434 by 9 A.M. Saturday June 20.

. . . . .

LOBBY AISLE

Head Banquet Houseman will have stanchions and ropes in lobby near bellstand by 5 P.M. Saturday June 20. Both he and Superintendent of Service will aid you setting up and following the below schedule which you will supervise. To allow free circulation of large number of sightseers expected in lobby, use rope and stanchion aisle only when President will use lobby to get to Wilshire entrance. The aisle will run from elevators to door of Wilshire entrance on side by door to front office.

TENTATIVE LOBBY SCHEDULE

Sat. June 20th

5:30 P.M.	Prepare to assemble. (Refers to Superintendent of Service, others, who will set up the ropes.)
6:00 – 6:30 P.M.	Assemble in coordination with Secret Service requests.
7:00 P.M.	Disassemble after departure of President and store near bell station. (Meaning, store ropes and stanchions near bellmen's station.)
11:00 P.M.	Prepare to assemble.
11:15 P.M.– 1:00 A.M.	Assemble and coordinate with Secret Service or Beverly Hills Police request.
11:30 P.M.– 1:00 A.M.	Disassemble after President has gone upstairs.

Sun. June 21st

10:00 – 1:30 P.M.	Prepare to assemble
10:15–10:50 A.M.	Assemble on request of Secret Service or Beverly Hills Police Dept.
11:00 A.M.	After President departs, take down ropes.
11:45 A.M.	Reassemble at request of Secret Service or Beverly Hills Police.
Noon:	Disassemble after President goes upstairs.

ATTENTION SUPERINTENDENT OF SERVICE

Make available 50 typewriters to be delivered to the Pavillon by 8 A.M. on Saturday June 20.
(This for the convenience of the press.)

PRESS BAGGAGE

Baggage for approximately 75 members of the press expected to arrive by truck at 2 P.M. on Saturday June 20. . . . From your rooming list, you may put room number on name tag and transport to rooms at once. Charge $1.00 per bag to each account for total in-out charge. . . .

ELEVATORS

You will arrange for elevator operators to be available for duration of President's visit, and arrange for pre-inspection of all passenger elevators between Saturday A.M. and Saturday noon.

PRESS ARRIVAL

Members of the Press are expected to arrive on Saturday between 2 and 3 P.M. by bus. Approximately 75 in number. All will be pre-registered. . . .

.   .   .   .   .

ATTENTION DIRECTOR OF FOOD
AND BEVERAGE

SECURITY MEALS

You have a considerable number of uniformed police, provided by the Beverly Hills Police Department, who will be eating in the Employees Cafeteria on meal tickets controlled by Head Hotel Security Officer. Would you advise and handle your departments accordingly.

.   .   .   .   .

ATTENTION FRONT OFFICE

RESERVATION MANAGER

You will be on the 7th floor by 12:30 on Saturday with room list in alphabetical order of all White House Party, together with their keys. You will hand out all keys.

You have pre-registered all Press and they will pick up their keys at Front Desk.

You will provide three rooming lists:

1) White House staff
2) Press Corps
3) VVIP's—Congressmen, Governors, etc.

These are to be checked by Resident Manager and distribution only as he directs.

You will coordinate all billing instructions with Credit Manager.

ATTENTION TELEPHONE DEPT.

You know Lt. ——— is in charge of White House Communications. Telephone calls coming through the Hotel Switchboard for any member of the President's Party should be routed to the White House switchboard. . . .

PRESIDENT'S STAFF

LETTERS, TELEGRAMS, PACKAGES

ATTN: FRONT OFFICE AND TIME KEEPERS

All letters and telegrams to be sent to Secret Service man, who will be in #761.

All packages are to be sent to Secret Service. . . .

ATTENTION SUPERINTENDENT OF SERVICE

FLAGS

Attention Superintendent of Service, and Sales Department—Please raise Presidential flag upon presentation and you know decorum, arrangement of our American, State and Corporation flags. Sales Department to follow up on Presidential flag.

(The Presidential flag travels with the President. It is handed to the appropriate hotel employee by one of the Presidential aides when the party arrives. The "decorum" refers to position of each of the mentioned flags. The Corporation flag is of the Hilton Hotels Corporation.)

ATTENTION ROOM SERVICE HEAD

Please provide a man to be available at 8:00 A.M. Sunday June 21st in the press room "Pavillon" until 10:00 A.M. to serve pre-made Tomato Cocktails.

(Ahem!)

Please have one man available on Saturday from 1:00 P.M. to 5:00 P.M. in event that the President would require a bartender in Room 815. This is to be discussed.

ROOM 761

(This is the White House Security room, where Secret Service men go.)

Please serve coffee in urn for room 761 beginning at 9:00 A.M. on Saturday and continuing until 3:00 P.M. Sunday June 21st. Please serve a selection of sandwiches for 10 persons at 11:45 A.M. on Saturday, at 5:30 P.M. for 10 persons on Saturday, coffee and Danish pastries at 9:00 A.M. on Sunday, June 21st, for 10 persons, and sandwiches for 10 persons at 11:45 on Sunday. Please see Sales Manager for billing instructions.

FOR PRESIDENT'S SUITE

ROOM 815

Full bar set up plus 4 bottles of Cutty Sark, lovely cheese tray for 20 persons, sufficient soda crackers, 4 silver bowls of mixed nuts, 2 VIP fruit baskets, one in parlor, one in bedroom, 4 silver bowls of Fritos, many splits of soda. The above to be on comp. basis.

(Comp., of course, means complimentary.)

For Sgt. ———, President's valet, Room 816: "Hot Pot" from housekeeping, supply of dry Sanka, sugar, and cream, VIP fruit basket. Above to be given on comp. basis.

For Mr. ———, Chairman of Democratic National Committee, VVIP Room 648/50: Bar set up with one Cutty Sark, one bottle of good brandy.

VIP fruit basket—comp.

For Mr. ———, Member of Democratic National Committee, VVIP Room 651/652: Bar set up with one Cutty Sark and one V.O.
VIP fruit basket—comp.

For Mr. ———, Member of Democratic National Committee, VVIP Room 655/56: Bar set up with one V.O., one Cutty Sark, 6 bottles of Heinekens and 6 local beer. 2 silver bowls of mixed nuts.
VIP fruit basket—comp.

You will receive various last minute instructions regarding room service requirements.
You will make yourself available to personally serve the President from 10:00 A.M. Saturday to 3:00 P.M. Sunday June 20th and June 21st.
(The designations VIP and VVIP emphasize the relative importance of the individual concerned, in the mind of the person making up the list.)

. . . . .

ATTENTION KITCHEN
EXECUTIVE CHEF

Please refer to Room Service instructions. No special food requirements. President will order from Room Service menu.

ATTENTION VALET
VALET MANAGER

Be prepared for maximum pressing needs from 1:30 P.M. to 7:30 P.M. on Saturday. The President and Party are attending a Black Tie Dinner. Be open Sunday June 21 and have available one presser and one runner from 8 A.M. to 2 P.M.

ATTENTION ALL PERSONNEL

Secret Service Pins will be handed out to proper employees Saturday morning by the Secret Service.
(These are identifying objects signifying the wearer is authorized to serve the President's Party in some capacity.)
Any personnel finding it necessary to go to the 8th floor to

serve Presidential Party or for any person must call in advance the Secret Service in Room #761 and announce themselves. Those people requiring access to area near President, contact Director of Personnel for identification pins.

ATTENTION HOUSEKEEPING DEPARTMENT
ASSISTANT EXECUTIVE HOUSEKEEPER
ROOM INSPECTION

Assistant Executive Housekeeper will personally inspect all rooms to be occupied by the President, his staff, and the White House party by 10 A.M. on June 20. In the remaining time before the arrival, the Secret Service will inspect these rooms.

Please have bedboard placed in President's bed—#815. Please make certain that the pillows in the President's suite are the firmest we have available.

Please have the "hot pot" for making coffee placed in Sgt. ——'s room #816. (He is the President's personal Valet.)

(The material in parentheses immediately above is by the hotel management. The "hot pot" mentioned here and earlier is equipment for brewing coffee.)

.   .   .   .   .

ATTENTION BANQUET DEPARTMENT
BANQUET MANAGER–SERVICE

Chief Engineer will build barricade on roof of Self-Park to contain the press. Please see him to offer assistance. The barricade to be completed by 5 P.M. June 19. He has details.

.   .   .   .   .

STANCHIONS AND ROPE

Head Security Officer will supervise, with your assistance and the assistance of bellmen, the arrangement of an aisle from the elevator lobby to the Wilshire entrance. The aisle will be of stanchions and rope. Please have available sufficient number of these by 5 P.M. Saturday June 20. Please see attention Head Security Officer for the time table for assembling and reassembling on Saturday and Sunday.

PRESS ROOM

Portable bars, tables set up, etc. For Pavillon for duration of visit. See Headwaiter's copy for details.

ATTENTION GARAGE MANAGER

Please have available 30 identification stickers by 4:00 P.M. to 2:00 P.M. Saturday June 20th only.

Please have available 30 identification stickers by 4:00 P.M. Friday, June 19th—use the red guest stickers; 15 coded for parking on the 4th floor only and 14 coded for valet parking lot only. Send to Director of Sales by 5:00 P.M. June 19th. Please have your men ready to tell any autos arriving from Ford Motor Company to park on the 4th floor only. They will be stickered by the Secret Service.

(An advance party from Washington made arrangements for the automobiles.)

. . . . .

Very obviously, the efforts of the Secret Service, local police, and hotel security force are coordinated for a presidential visit. Well before the Chief Executive is to arrive, every means of entrance and exit is examined and secured. Police and firemen are placed on guard to preserve that security. The kitchen is checked out by Secret Service, and men posted to observe kitchen personnel throughout the President's stay.

The hotel furnishes a list of all employees available to serve the Chief Executive in any direct or indirect capacity. (Even though I am not an employee of the Beverly Hilton, my background was thoroughly investigated.) If there is the slightest doubt over an employee's reliability, he is not allowed to work on the Presidential floor. Only screened and accredited personnel will do any sort of work for the presidential party. Other hotel guests scheduled to occupy rooms on the same floor are checked in advance. Should one constitute a dubious risk, he is moved to another floor; in an extreme case he is asked to check out. In either instance, that person will be kept under observation so long as the President is in town. Ideally, all guests, dubious or otherwise, are moved off the floor, but this is feasible only when the presidential party takes the entire floor, as sometimes happens.

Shortly before the President checks in, Secret Service agents "shake down" his suite once more, to make certain there is no unauthorized person about. Every bed, mattress, pillow is re-examined. The chairs are gone over—who knows, there might be a time bomb strapped underneath one. The bathrooms are checked. Toilet bowls are plumbed. Firemen are posted at the exits, with orders to get the President out in case of a fire, even at the cost of their own lives.

Guards are stationed at all stairways and elevator banks throughout the period of the President's visit to see to it no unauthorized individual gets onto the floor. Security men and all hotel staff authorized on the floor must wear identifying insignia. These are kept secret, to prevent counterfeiting. Each time the President visits that hotel the insignia are changed, in form, shape, size, or color.

In recent years, presidents stopping at the Beverly Hilton have been landed on the roof by helicopter. This is considered the safest method of getting them into the suite, obviating the necessity of coming through a crowd. Several days before a Chief Executive's arrival, a helicopter pilot does a dry run, testing the roof for structural strength, landing space and other features. And just before the Chief is to touch down, other Army helicopters fly in, land, and take off as an added precaution so that the ordinary person will not know which helicopter contains the President. Firemen are stationed on the roof in case of emergency, with hoses ready.

Now the President comes in. Security men meet him on the roof, conduct him to his quarters by a carefully charted course, beginning with the elevator ride from the roof to the designated floor.

When the President goes out, there will be Secret Service agents posing as taxi drivers, keeping the street under observation. Some may be atop telephone poles, acting as linesmen. Some may be mingling with guests in the lobby. No security man lets his guard down for a split second. Agents surrounding the President do not look at him, but out at the crowd. Every sudden movement, any unexplained sound, is cause for concern.

What option has a Secret Service man if a President unpredictably decides to do something or go somewhere not scheduled in advance? I have heard it said that the Secret Service can order the President to follow prescribed security rules and may even forbid him to appear in places considered dangerous. That is a myth. Although most presidents follow the plan laid out by security agents, there is no law forcing them to do so.

Since the assassination of President Kennedy, already stiff security has been stiffened further. Secret Service operatives are now stationed on roofs of the hotel and surrounding buildings during presidential visits. The agents assigned to the President seem tougher, more taciturn. I rode up in an elevator with a man who must have been a Secret Service agent, since he wore the special insignia permitting him to be on the presidential floor.

"Are you from Washington?" I asked, merely to be pleasant.

He brushed me off as if I were a typhoid carrier.

"Isn't it a beautiful day?" I amended.

Considering his nerve-wracking assignment, I couldn't blame him for his response, which was, "Humph!"

Chapter 15

That's Hollywood!

Recently I came across a news item announcing the divorce of a well-known Hollywood actress whose husband had been one of my clients. The dispatch concluded: "He was awarded custody of the couple's two dachshunds, also two horses, while she retains custody of their Siamese cat."

That's Hollywood!

I telephoned the home of a prominent English actor to let him know I had completed typing a manuscript he left with me. His secretary, who spoke with a decided English accent, informed me, "So soddy! He cawn't be disturbed. May I ask who is calling?"

I said never mind, hung up, and went out to deliver the work. A maid conducted me to the actor's secretary. I did a double take. Just two weeks ago, this girl, newly arrived in town, had come to me looking for work. Since I had no overflow at the time, I referred her to an employment agency. Quite obviously, she not only found a post with the English actor, but also developed a polished English accent in those two weeks. When she was in my office, her intonations were strictly Bronx.

That's Hollywood, too.

Hollywood is a contradiction, as everyone knows. It is crazy, sensible, beautiful, ugly, phony, sincere, corny, sophisticated, cheap, luxurious. On the screen, the stars are gods and godesses; off-camera, they are husbands and wives, mamas and papas. They go to church, join the P.T.A., applaud enthusiastically when their children appear in school plays. The most glamorous actress may enjoy housekeeping. I have seen Shelley Winters, who lives across the street from me, emptying trash into a can at the sidewalk, still in bathrobe and with curlers in her hair.

What makes a real star? Not beauty in a woman, not handsome features in a man. The essential ingredient is animal magnetism and the ability to turn it on and off at will, to project it from the screen or before a live public.

I remember my first sight of Elizabeth Taylor, when she visited her father's art gallery at the Beverly Hills Hotel. She was attractive, but not what I would call sensationally beautiful. I recall thinking, "What large feet she has!" Then I saw her in a movie. She was truly glamorous, all of a sudden a star. And genuinely beautiful. She wasn't projecting the first time; she was the second. But it is not just projection that makes the star. Certain other actresses are not real stars, no matter how much is done for them by makeup, lighting and costume. They lack animal magnetism. Elizabeth Taylor is charged with it. When she turns it on, she is glamorous, in court gown or blue jeans.

The first time I saw Marilyn Monroe, at a private party, she was not acting for a public. She sat on a couch, talking to Louella Parsons. I failed to see the sex kitten in her. She had on a high-necked, black wool dress, strands of blond hair adhering to the fabric. She wore no makeup and looked ghostly white. She seemed an ordinary blonde with an extraordinary figure. I could not see her as a sex symbol. Rather, there was a sadness or wistfulness about her that was neither sexy nor kittenish.

The next time I saw her, she was an altogether different

woman, and I do mean woman. It was at the Beverly Hilton Hotel, where she was to receive an award from the Foreign Press Association. She arrived in company of an undistinguished-looking man, who may have been Mexican. Marilyn was spectacular, fully aware that she was on stage. Her green sequin gown hugged her figure. She carried herself with the air of a woman who knew she was alluring. With her amazing body, blond hair, and wiggly-jiggly strut, she was something very special, an authentic star, an original.

She had been drinking quite a bit. It was noticeable as she draped herself around the award in making her acknowledgment. She kept blinking throughout her remarks. Still, you could literally see her magnetism reach out and bring the men in the audience to a boil.

Departing, she walked rather unsteadily, but like a queen nevertheless, smiling, waving to fans, her mouth open in her special manner.

A few months later she was dead.

One of the rewards of working in California has been the opportunity afforded me to see the real Hollywood. Movie people rarely come to my office; they send for me, which gives me a chance to observe them at home. Early in my career, I called on the famous director Rouben Mamoulian. He worked in his library, seated behind a huge, 200-year-old desk, a cat curled up on a divan nearby. The Mamoulians are great cat lovers. Among their favorites at the time were Sugar and Spice. There used to be an Everything Nice, but she strayed or was stolen.

At intervals as we worked, Mr. Mamoulian would call a recess. During these breaks he sometimes sat back in his chair and reminisced. "I once had lunch with Somerset Maugham, at the Ritz, in Paris," he told me. "I was doing the screen version of 'Rain' and we were talking about Sadie Thompson being raped by the minister. I told Mr. Maugham it was unbelievable that Sadie could be raped, because in the first place she was a tart, and in the second place it was in a hotel and she could have screamed."

Mr. Maugham regarded Mr. Mamoulian solemnly for a long

moment, and replied, "You know, I never thought of that. No one ever brought that up before."

"I shall never forget the first time I met F. Scott Fitzgerald," Mr. Mamoulian told me another time. "I was attending a cocktail party in New York. The doorbell rang, and when the hostess opened it I could see no one. I looked down, and there, on all fours like an animal, were Fitzgerald and his wife. They greeted the hostess that way. They crawled into the room that way. And they were introduced to everyone that way, on all fours."

A house call to the Mamoulians is always a treat. I could say the same for numerous other Hollywood personalities. But now and then I receive a call that I would just as soon not answer. An example of this kind of call was when an actress had me come to the house to fire her maid, because she herself didn't have the nerve to do it.

Many jobs, whether at the office or in a private home, have curious aftermaths. Actress Dawn Addams, who was in Rome preparing for her wedding to a prince, sent me a lengthy list of Hollywoodians whose addresses she did not have, instructing me to send them invitations. I worked a whole week to get them out by the stipulated date. As I wearily sealed the last envelope, a friend who was flying home to Australia stopped in to say good-bye. Since the bundle of invitations was large and heavy, and he was taking a cab to the airport, I asked if he would mind dropping the wedding bids into a mailbox. He agreed to do so.

A couple of weeks later, Dawn's father called. Did the invitations go out? Yes? Then why was Dawn complaining she hadn't received a single acknowledgment or wedding present? I could only assure him the invitations were mailed.

Two days later he telephoned again. Was I certain? Dawn had cabled that something must be amiss. She still had no acknowledgments from Hollywood. Since her father was leaving for Rome to attend the wedding, I promised him faithfully I would double check on those invitations myself. I cabled my Australian friend, who cabled back that he had positively without question fulfilled the mission.

Next day, he must have developed doubts, for he cabled:

BEST PRINT MORE MY EXPENSE SORRY. But it was too late to print a new supply and get them out in time. So the wedding in Rome took place, amidst great pomp and ceremony, and I hoped that the presence of hundreds of European guests would compensate for the absence of even a single acknowledgment from Hollywood.

But I couldn't forget the matter, and when my Australian friend was back in town several months later, I kept at him for an explanation. He finally admitted he had had too much to drink the night in question, but he still insisted he had a clear recollection of dropping those invitations into a mailbox.

"Where was it?" I asked. "At what corner?"

"At Wilshire and some other street; I don't know the name of the other, but I can show you."

"Come on!" I said. "Let's go!"

Riding along, I suggested, "Maybe you left the envelopes in the cab?"

"No, no, no!" he said, visibly irritated. "I distinctly remember dropping them into——." He stopped and pointed as we reached an intersection. "There! The box is right over there!" He glanced at me, triumphant.

We pulled up to the curb.

"Great God!" he cried. "That's no mailbox! It's a waste receptacle!"

Receptacles remind me of an incident that almost defeated Superman, that legendary figure who could climb the highest mountain, lift the tallest building, don his magic cape and sail up, up and aWAYYYYYYYYYYYYYY!

I was acquainted with the television Superman, George Reeves, a rather shy fellow in real life, and actually no big-muscle man. He resembled the meek reporter, his other self in the melodrama, more than the powerful and indestructible avenger of wrongs. George was calling on a friend of mine who was leaving for Europe, bidding her bon voyage, when I dropped in for the same purpose. I found Tommy, my friend's little boy, circling Superman with stars in his eyes, paying no attention to anything else, until his mother began struggling with a suitcase which was

jammed so full she couldn't get the lid far enough down to snap
the lock.

"You do it, Superman!" Tommy cried, his eyes shining. "You
can do *anything*, can't you, Superman?"

George got on one knee and pressed down with his hand,
attempting to close the suitcase. That didn't work. He got on
both knees, used both hands, bore down with all his might, but
couldn't quite connect the upper part of the lock with the lower.
At which point, Tommy burst into tears, his dream shattered. Still
hoping this might be only the cliff-hanger before the payoff, the
child wailed, "You can do it, Superman! You can do it—can't
you?"

Reeves nodded, turned around, and in desperation, sat on
the bag. His weight brought the top all the way down. He
snapped the lock and preserved a child's faith in fiction.

There's a less charming fictional aspect about Hollywood,
and a chapter on the movie capital would be incomplete if it
failed to take note of it. I refer to the spurious quality of a part
of Hollywood life. The successful actor must live in a thirty-
room mansion even if he is a bachelor. His agent wouldn't be
seen driving anything less than a Continental. The unemployed
thespian is first to grab the check at a dinner party.

Max typifies the sort of person and life I have in mind. He
is an actor who never quite made the grade, but you would never
know it, watching him in action. He plays bit parts when he can
get them; and when he can't, he works in a high-grade men's
haberdashery. He owns one, at the most two suits but they are
fashioned by the finest tailor in Beverly Hills (who may not
get paid until they are worn thin). When he goes visiting, Max
throws his jacket over a chair just carelessly enough to show the
label.

He pays $15 to have his hair cut by a "gentlemen's hair
stylist," although he has so little of the stuff left he can part it
with a wash rag. It makes an impression when a studio executive
runs into Max at the stylist's.

He drives a car, the latest model, but it is rented, and he will
allow months to roll by, in lean times, before he meets the pay-

ments. The rental company does not press him. It knows he will eventually meet the bill, and that meantime he will refer good customers to the firm.

He can't afford an expensive apartment or big house, but he manages to find someone who is leaving town and willing to have him move in and take care of the premises in his absence. Once ensconced, he throws big parties (on credit) and impresses invitees with his living quarters and disregard for costs.

He never dines in an ordinary restaurant. Even when he is alone, he must eat in the establishment considered the best at the time, and preferably one where it is supposedly hard to get a table. The restaurant may have to carry his checks for months.

I have known when Max, unable to pay the price of a swiss on rye, would pay $100 for a ticket to a charity event because it was important to be seen there.

He is a phony, but it is Max at whom people stare outside premieres. "Who is he?" they ask. "He must be important. He knows everyone!"

Max lives to create that impression.

Happily, for every spurious character, Hollywood has two who are real, genuine, and unaffected by the silly status scramble. Bette Davis, for instance, has always been known as an individualist of great talent who lives the way she wants to live and doesn't care for the frou-frou and mumbo-jumbo of the super-colossal, stupendous life. I knew this only from reading about her until recently, when I was called to Miss Davis' home in Bel Air and met her face-to-face.

She was in an upstairs bedroom, propped up on two pillows and a bolster, a cup of coffee at her side, manuscript in hand, cigarettes in easy reach. The room was charming, with an open fireplace at one end, and cheerful paintings on the walls. It was furnished in Cape Cod style, including a four-poster bed. I thought the decor was exactly right for Miss Davis, since I had read that she was very fond of New England and eventually intended to retire to Maine, which she loved most of all.

She greeted me cordially, invited me to pull up a chair, and asked if I would like some coffee. As we worked, she interrupted herself frequently just to chat, in a very friendly manner. She had her maid bring me lunch, first inquiring whether I cared for corned beef hash.

Errol Flynn's name came up in her dictation. Miss Davis told me he was the handsomest man she had ever seen—in fact, she called him "beautiful." But he was a satyr, particularly where very young girls were concerned. I told her I read his book, *My Wicked, Wicked Ways*, in which he reported that Miss Davis slapped him much harder than was necessary during the filming of "Elizabeth and Essex," and that she wore a large ring on her slapping hand, which intensified the pain.

"He's a liar!" Miss Davis said. I let it go at that.

I asked if she thought Hollywood had changed in the years she worked there. She didn't think so, at least not as to the technology of film making. Naturally, she said, film stories regularly evolved into newer patterns and moods. And the personnel of studios were constantly changing. I expressed the opinion that the more recent people in the studios were rough and "way out" types. She replied, "We've always had those types around."

She regretted never having had a great male star acting opposite her. Her own name was big enough to guarantee the success of a picture, and the studio didn't have to add another big name to the billing.

At one point she dictated the words "leading men" which I heard as "meeting men." When I read it back, she burst out laughing. "Men!" she said. "I want no part of them." She had not been lucky in her marriages, and I understood her feelings.

I was surprised to learn that Miss Davis has a genuine respect for the household arts. Because she felt instruction in home-making very important for a girl, she taught her daughter B. D. to cook. The actress herself loves to prepare food, and whenever time permits, cooks the meals for her household.

We began talking like two housewives and I mentioned that I liked certain frozen foods. Oh, said Miss Davis, some were very good indeed, but they were too expensive, particularly for the larger family, and besides, fresh foods were always better.

As I was about to leave, she invited me to look at a collection of photographs, hanging in the hallway, of friends in and out of motion pictures. President Kennedy was represented by what Miss Davis told me was his favorite photograph, the one reproduced on the cover of *Life* after the President's assassination. Another picture, taken at the inauguration party in Washington, showed Miss Davis and daughter seated at the dinner table with President and Mrs. Kennedy. I asked how she got to know the President. "Well," she said, "he was a New Englander, you know."

She talked about Mr. Kennedy at length, about what a wonderful man he was, and how irreplaceable as a statesman. When she learned of his assassination, she was so overcome that she retired to her bedroom and did not emerge for four days.

On the wall alongside the stairway, amidst framed pictures of Hollywood personalities, hung a poem especially created for Bette Davis by Carl Sandburg. I told Miss Davis that it ought to be published, so the world might cherish it too. It was a thing of sheer beauty. And surely the greatest compliment a poet can pay a woman is to create a poem for her alone.

Passing a picture of Olivia de Havilland, Miss Davis commented that the two of them had been the closest of friends for twenty-five years. I remarked that when I worked for Miss de Havilland's sister, Joan Fontaine, I met the latter's adopted daughter, an Indian girl from Peru. Miss Davis shook her head. "I never could see that," she said, "her adopting an Indian girl. We are not ready for that yet. It will be hard on the girl."

At a point where a portion of the wall was concealed by the back of an open closet door, Miss Davis said, "This is my shit list." Laughing, she closed the door, uncovering about ten pictures of well-known persons.

She impressed me as being a brilliant woman, one of a handful in Hollywood who are unconcerned about the more artificial facets of cinemaland's status system. She knows her worth. She told me that when she visits Warner Brothers studio, she points to its seven sound stages and tells Harry Warner, "I built those for you." She is fiercely proud of the acting talent that made those stages possible. The international acclaim it brought her is all the status she needs. Why compete for the sort of prestige she considers nonsense?

I venture that she would have held the stage very effectively had she been on the airline publicity junket that flew several beauteous actresses to Brazil for Carnival in Rio, and would have held it by the strength of her personality. I was on that junket, courtesy of a friend, along with Kim Novak, Julie London and Zsa Zsa Gabor.

Rivalry developed almost as soon as we landed. When Zsa Zsa wore a low-cut gown at a ball, Kim stole the show by arriving in a high-necked dress. When Julie wore a cotton country-girl frock to an afternoon event, Zsa Zsa swept in, in an ostrich-feather wrap and the type of evening gown she wore in the film "Moulin Rouge." She was a sensation. Julie wasn't happy.

Kim was received by the President of Brazil. This annoyed some who were not.

A special plane was provided to fly us to the new capital, Brasília. Kim decided she wouldn't get up early to make the flight. It was canceled; this didn't please the others.

I was in a group with the stellar attractions one night at the Copacabana Hotel. Miss Gabor introduced me to her escort and to the Turkish Ambassador to Brazil. She conversed with the latter in French, and I followed suit, whereupon Miss Gabor told her escort, "You see? Here is a very ordinary girl, just a secretary, and she speaks French. Why can't you?"

Just before leaving Brazil, I saw Miss Gabor in the beauty salon. A hairdresser was tying ribbons into the hair of her Yorkshire pup, Mr. Magoo.

It is difficult for a woman to do justice to Zsa Zsa. We females are jealous, I suppose. We wish we could be like her, beautiful, effervescent, a femme fatale. Men react differently. They consider her simply delicious.

My friend Barbara tells the following story about Miss Gabor. She was in a restaurant when Zsa Zsa entered. Barbara's escort, who knew the Hungarian beauty, introduced them, adding, "My friend named her baby after you."

Zsa Zsa beamed.

Later, leaving the restaurant, she stopped at Barbara's table. "Did you really name your baby after me?" she asked.

Barbara nodded. "My baby is a little black poodle," she explained. Zsa Zsa frowned, but Barbara followed through with, "I named her after you because she has the most beautiful face in the world."

"*Dahling!*" Miss Gabor cried.

Chapter 16

The emperor
of Hollywood!

I have seen changes in Hollywood even in the comparatively few years I have worked there. The cult of the great star is waning. Studios keep few of them under exclusive contract. Show people seldom affect the grand manner, sweeping into a room as if to a flourish of trumpets.

Mind you, I don't say all these changes in the Hollywood scene are for the better. I myself regret the passing of certain gaudy, frenetic aspects of Hollywood when it was HOLLY-WOOD, and I know others feel as I do. I love it when, on rare occasions, a movie personality has the courage to revert to those days. Attending the premiere of *What a Way to Go*, I was delighted when the star, Shirley MacLaine, who wore pink in the picture, arrived at the theatre dressed all in pink, riding in a pink Cadillac driven by a chauffeur in pink uniform, pink cap, pink shoes and pink gloves.

Hollywood still numbers its colorful, fascinating personalities by the hundreds. What we need is more of the whipped-up flim-flam to make our hearts beat faster. What Hollywood needs, in fact, is to return to that unsurpassed era when Francis X. Bushman was unchallenged ruler of the land of make-believe. He was Emperor of Hollywood and all he surveyed, because he was Francis X. Bushman, first of all, and also because Hollywood was a place for giants.

I can think of no better way of describing the changes Hollywood is undergoing than to describe the Hollywood that Francis X. Bushman knew. It was my great pleasure to have lunch with him and his charming wife Iva not long ago. He made no secret of the fact he was 81, yet he could easily pass for a man in his fifties. He entered the restaurant, where I awaited him, with such an air of authority that there could be no question he was accustomed to it. Not that he was theatrical. He underplayed his role. He walked with a studied but unostentatious step. His straw hat was at not quite a rakish angle. His every gesture and facial expression was animated, vibrant. Extremely handsome, his bright blue eyes took in everyone, but not to see whether he was recognized, as is the habit of some actors. It was noteworthy how many did recognize the dashing Mr. Bushman, however.

With rare modesty, detachment and good humor, he looked back to his earlier years in pictures, at my urging. It was something of a miracle that he ever took the first step toward stardom, for he came from a well-to-do Baltimore family whose blood curdled when he manifested an interest in the stage. "They pointed out," Mr. Bushman chuckled, "that in eleven hundred years there had never been anyone in our family who sullied himself by doing theatrical work." In spite of this, he went into vaudeville, later transferring to the legitimate stage. "To this day, my family shudders at the thought of my being in show business."

In vaudeville he became a headliner and was booked into the best houses. He remembers playing B. F. Keith's in Washington. He looked over the footlights and spied President Woodrow Wilson in a box. Bushman interrupted his act and made a stirring speech honoring the President. When he finished his act, he went to the President's box and knelt at his feet so he wouldn't be seen by members of the audience. Bushman stayed with him throughout the rest of the performance, talking to him, "really listening to him, I should say, because there wasn't a thing I could tell him about vaudeville. He knew everybody in it, and more about each one than I did!"

On the legitimate stage, Francis X. Bushman made another quick ascent to the top. He became a great matinee idol. His handsome profile appeared in newspapers and on bill posters throughout the nation. Fan mail followed him everywhere. Women besieged him.

He arrived in Chicago to play a two-week stand at the Kedzie Theatre in a vehicle called *Squaw Man*, which was later made into a movie. A blizzard was raging, with the drifting snow piling all the way up to the marquee of the theatre. The prospect of filling the house for two weeks was dim indeed, which bothered Bushman as much as the theatre owner, since the actor was not only to receive a salary but also 50 percent of box-office receipts after they reached a specified amount. Mr. Bushman proposed an heroic publicity stunt to save the day. He would focus attention on his presence in Chicago, bring people out despite the blizzard, by "selling" himself as a husband to the highest female bidder.

"Are you crazy?" associates asked.

No, he was dead serious, despite the fact that his wife was in a hotel a block away from the Kedzie. He went down to the office of *The Chicago American*, as he recalls it, and notified an open-mouthed reporter of his intentions. The astonished reporter brought Mr. Bushman to the city editor, who heard him out with the skepticism born of too many experiences with too many publicity hoaxes. The editor asked, "Do you mean this? We don't want to build you up, give you a lot of free publicity, if this is just a stunt. *Is* this just a publicity stunt?"

"Oh, no!" said the actor. "I wouldn't dream of such a thing! I really need money, and I'm offering to sell myself to the highest bidder."

Thus it was that the Hearst papers, delighted to have a juicy scoop, played the story up sensationally in a front-page banner headline. Seventeen thousand letters from women all over the United States poured in, making bids. "All we wanted to do was to keep the thing going for two weeks, then get out of town," Bushman said. The thing did keep going that long; the Kedzie Theatre was packed to capacity throughout; the show closed on schedule; no "buyer" was announced; and the public soon forgot to wonder about that. What the city editor of *The Chicago American* wondered, Mr. Bushman did not consider it judicious to inquire.

The matinee idol moved from the legitimate stage to a motion picture production company in Chicago in 1911. The movies were in their infancy; no one knew much about making or acting in them and there was room for both the pioneer producer and the actor willing to take a chance. Studios were paying $5 for a movie story. An actor playing a lead part received $100 a week. A movie story was not a finished script but the barest outline of a plot. The director and actors worked it over, improvising from line to line, bit to bit, and situation to situation.

This was the motion-picture "industry" into which Bushman stepped. The man who had most to do with getting him to leave the stage was Richard Foster Baker, fondly referred to as Daddy Baker. It was Daddy Baker, according to Mr. Bushman, who many years later originated the formal movie script.

Bushman was an innovator too. His originations began with his first part. At that time, the actors received no billing. There were no "stars." Performers' names were not listed on the screen. Producers arbitrarily assigned them stage names which they were to use in public appearances.

Bushman was handed an improvised script when he showed up for the first day's shooting. Penciled on the cover was a British-sounding name.

"Who is that?" he asked.

"That's you," the director said.

"Nothing doing!" He had come from the stage, where he built a reputation around his family name. He would not give it up. Moreover, in the legitimate theatre every play had a star. He would be a star or nothing.

He stormed into the producer's office, announced he would work only if he got billed, and billed as a star. Either his terms were met or he was through.

The producer was in a spot. "All right, Frank," he said.

Thus, says Mr. Bushman, he was responsible for two innovations. "I was the first star," and that inaugurated the star system. "I got billing," which began the listing of cast of characters on the screen.

He was indirectly responsible for another innovation. In the legitimate theatre, he rehearsed in an absolutely quiet house. The only talking was onstage. Electricians, stage hands, scene shifters, tiptoed around in rubber-soled shoes so as not to disturb the performers. When Bushman showed up for rehearsal in the Chicago movie studio the place was a bedlam, people shouting instructions, technicians scraping furniture across the floor, cameras shifting about noisily. He could not adjust to the unaccustomed environment, revolted again, and refused to continue.

This produced consternation, for to delay a shooting was to waste considerable money. Daddy Baker was summoned. Bushman told him he could not get into the required mood over all the noise. Casting about for an expedient, Baker brought in four musicians who stood to one side of the set, playing just loud enough to drown out extraneous sounds as the actor went through his part. This not only masked external noise but also, Bushman discovered, helped put him in the mood for the particular enactment. Unwittingly, Daddy Baker had invented what became known as mood music, standard in silent picture production thereafter.

The same device was later transported to theatres exhibiting the pictures. Live musicians accompanied the action on the screen. If this was skillfully done, the audience soon became unconscious of the music, because it was in the mood of the action on the screen and the acting was "over" the music. Today, of course, mood music is built into the talking picture itself.

Sometime later, Bushman originated the practice of "talking a picture." He followed his own movies to strategic cities, standing either in the apron of the stage or on a chair alongside it, and as the performers enacted their roles he narrated the action. Often, too, he spoke the lines the silent actors mouthed on the screen, with appropriate dramatic inflections. This practice caught on, and for a while other studios and performers emulated Francis X. Bushman in the closest the movies were to come to "talking" for many years.

"Talking a picture" had its hazards. Many theatres played to newly arrived immigrants for whom the moving figures on the silver screen were magical in themselves. Then the house lights would go on; the flesh-and-blood Bushman would appear and walk down the aisle to greet the patrons. Sometimes this would so startle the more superstitious that they would cut and run, to escape the apparition from the screen stalking through their midst.

Cinema folk had to be prepared for anything. "There were heroes in those days," Mr. Bushman remarked, his eyes off in space. "They have no counterpart today. There are no men in Hollywood like Tom Mix, Bill Hart, so many others." They were rugged, masculine men, with normal, natural interests, which included women, drinking, sports, physical exercise. They could do in real life what they did on the screen—ride horses, climb cliffs, use their fists. Because this was so, many of them disdained stand-ins when "doubles" came into use. The stand-in took the risks for the highly paid star where the script called for jumping off a careening stage coach or rolling down a hill locked in battle with an adversary.

"A lot of the people I worked with considered it sissy to use stand-ins," Bushman remembers. "They took their own risks." He himself never used a double. "Why should I? No one could ever do it as well—I thought."

His role as Messala in *Ben Hur* called for taking part in a chariot race in a tremendous arena. Each chariot was driven by eight horses. They raced around curves at such speed that the animals skidded some twelve feet each time. Bushman remained at the reins all the way. Ramon Novarro, on the other hand, playing the part of Ben Hur, used a stand-in, who was concealed under the chariot seat part of the time. The camera would focus in on Novarro for a few seconds, showing him urging his steeds on to greater effort. Then it panned away, Novarro jumped off, the double emerged, and the camera came in on him just as the horses went around a curve.

In the Chicago years, Bushman met a man whom he came to admire greatly. As the star finished work on the set, a sheep-ish-looking fellow with a deeply corrugated face approached him. Stammering and stuttering, he shyly explained that he just began in movies, that he had been observing Bushman, and had developed such an admiration for his work that he had to give him something as a token of respect. He dug inside the belt of his trousers and pulled a large elephant prod out of a pant leg. Bashfully, he murmured, "That's all I've got."

He was Wallace Beery. Prior to getting into the movies he was a roustabout and general handyman in a circus. The prod was a souvenir of those days. According to Bushman, it was Beery who first trained elephants to follow each other in single file, the trunk of one linked to the tail of the animal ahead.

As the cinema industry burgeoned, the public became addicted. And with the star system an established institution, worship of the luminaries became an American preoccupation. Mr. Bushman was walking through a train on his way to the diner when he heard someone call, "Bushman!" Turning, he saw a man with a huge paunch and a broad smile on his face waving to him. It was President Taft. The Chief Executive called him over and asked him to sit down. "He was so big," the actor recalls, "that it left me about three inches of seat."

Taft said that he was delighted to meet the screen star, that he had long admired his work. In the course of a lengthy chat, the President sighed, "I envy you!"

"Why, Mr. President? Why should a man in your position envy me?"

"Because *everybody* loves you. I can't even get *half* the people to love me!"

When motion-picture production became an industry in fact, most of the companies moved to California, and Hollywood was transformed from a rabbit patch into the world capital of filmdom. New "personalities" were discovered and Bushman worked and played with the greatest of them. There were the three brothers, William, Franklyn, and Dustin Farnum, who enacted romantic cowboy roles. There was Wallace Reid, and Charles Ray, and the exotic Alla Nazimova. There was demure Mary Pickford, and the swashbuckling Douglas Fairbanks; and Charlie Chaplin and King Baggott, Mabel Normand, Constance Talmadge, and that outrageous "vamp," Theda Bara.

As befitted his rank, Bushman lived grandly and flamboyantly, in a mansion atop a towering Hollywood hill, commanding a view for miles around. He had to build an eight-foot wall around the property, despite which avid fans sometimes got over and onto the estate.

As a star of the first magnitude he was expected to live extravagantly, and he did his very best. He ordered a Marmon built to his specifications, with the longest body of any automobile then in existence. Because other cars were black, Bushman's was purple. The door handles and interior trim were of solid gold. A gigantic golden eagle was perched on the hood. A liveried chauffeur was behind the wheel. The actor sat in back, flanked by two Great Danes, trained to remain stiffly at attention.

"I may have started a trend," Bushman told me. "Soon there were a great many spectacular automobiles around. Tom Mix had one all trimmed with fur inside. It had two steer horns on the hood."

The manufacturers of Bushman's Marmon offered to deduct $2,000 from the $22,000 price if he would have his name engraved on the door, figuring it would be great advertising if the world knew that Francis X. Bushman drove a Marmon. He agreed to the proposal, but came to regret it. He parked his car outside an office building, went in to transact business, and emerged to find the vehicle surrounded by a dense crowd. The name on the door had done it. A contingent of mounted police was required to break through the crowd and clear a path so he could get into his car.

The interior of Mr. Bushman's home was not as flamboyant as his Marmon, but other stars were less restrained. William S.

Hart did his house in Western decor, with tomahawks, Indian blankets, lariats and other cowboy paraphernalia in every nook and cranny. A few feet down the hill from Bushman's estate lived his good friend and neighbor Rudolph Valentino. One complete wall of his house was taken up with a giant portrait of the Italian-born actor. Costumes he made famous in pictures were strewn over balustrades and chairs and hung from walls.

"Valentino trusted no man," his former neighbor recalled. "Rudy was gruff with them. Not with me, because we were friends, but with other men. There was a time when we weren't friends. He became jealous of me because I was getting more publicity and fan mail, and seemed to have become a bigger figure than he was. He didn't talk to me for three weeks. But we made it up."

Rudy's gruffness did not extend to women. "Let a pretty girl come into sight, and he became the most charming and romantic person alive. He would kiss her hand, bow to her, and make her feel she was a queen."

It was the era of great parties, and Valentino liked to have people over. "They were mostly drinking parties. Those days I could drink any man under the table." Rudy was a heavy drinker. When he occasionally ran out of stock he would borrow a few bottles of vintage wine from Bushman's cellar. "Wine, that's what killed Rudy. After he died, people used to kid me about his having died from my bad wine, because it was found that his stomach was corroded from alcohol. The newspapers were told he died of a bleeding ulcer, which may have been the fact, but if so, the ulcer was produced by the drinking."

Although Bushman could imbibe with the best of them, he never indulged to such an extent as to impair his health or go flabby. He had a superb physique, and still has. He was "a physical type," he says, keeping in form by regular exercise. Rudy, on the other hand, was not a physical type. He was agile but not muscular, engaging in no sports or exercise. Once, when they were horsing around on the lawn, Bushman threw a baseball to his neighbor. Valentino stood there, helpless, arms at his sides, as it looped through the air and smacked into his stomach. He didn't know how to handle a baseball.

A writer doing a magazine article on Rudy decided to play him as the athletic type. He told the uneasy star he would send photographers to get shots of Valentino in big-muscle activity. Thespian though he was, Rudy knew he could never hit a tennis ball or swing a bat as if he knew what it was about. As the next best thing, he borrowed some bar bells and other physical culture equipment from his neighbor and laid the stuff out on his lawn. When the photographers arrived they found him in the midst of the paraphernalia, listlessly swinging a wooden dumbbell.

Rudy's hobby was auto mechanics. He had a passion for tinkering with cars. He would buy a half dozen from as many countries, disassemble them, spend happy hours putting them together again. One day he and Bushman, who also enjoyed tinkering, were lying underneath the body of a dismantled automobile, dressed in dirty, greasy clothes. Parts of the vehicle were strewn all over Valentino's front lawn. As they tinkered, a sightseeing bus lumbered up and stopped in front of the estate. Passengers dismounted. The tour conductor delivered his singsong spiel. This, ladies and gentlemen, was the dwelling place of Rudolph Valentino, star of *The Sheik*, and other hits. Up above, on the hilltop, was the estate of Francis X. Bushman.

The sightseers wanted to walk through the grounds of the estates, but the guide said it was forbidden.

"Oh, dear!" a lady sighed. "I was hoping we could catch at least a glimpse of them!" The grimy mechanics lying directly at her feet, tinkering with a car, kept tinkering.

I urged Mr. Bushman to tell me about the early Hollywood parties which, legend had it, often ran to the orgiastic. He was reluctant. There were "nude women," he admitted diffidently, but "a woman was more passionate, sensitive, vibrant then. She would offer herself to a man if she felt that way about him. She threw discretion to the wind. She was less restrained than she is today. When she loved, she loved."

Sometimes the drinking parties went on for days. That did not mean every actor and actress drank to excess. Bill Hart, for instance, attended the bibulous affairs but didn't touch a drop. He sat quietly, rarely opened his mouth, enjoying himself as an observer more than a participant. But, Mr. Bushman assured me, "He was a real man. Nothing sissy about him. It wasn't that he couldn't drink, or had moral scruples. He just didn't enjoy it."

The movie-going public didn't seem to mind when stories got around about wild parties in the movie colony. It only enhanced the romantic appeal of the participants. And the studios did their part to sustain the image of Hollywood stars as gay, passionate, virile personalities. They were under strict injunction not to let it become known when they married, lest the knowledge discourage the wishful thinking of moviegoers of the opposite sex.

Mr. Bushman faced this problem when he fell in love with Beverly Bayne. The two comprised the original "love team" in pictures, acting opposite each other repeatedly, where the more common practice was to team a male and female star only once, or intermittently at most. The film lovemaking of the first love team so enraptured their public that a full house was practically guaranteed by the mere billing: "Francis X. Bushman and Beverly Bayne, in . . ." This was fine for box office, but although Francis X. Bushman wed Beverly Bayne on the screen by the final fade-out, they kept their actual marriage secret when it occurred, lest the box office suffer.

Such was the fantasy indulged in by cinema patrons that at one time Bushman had 17 secretaries who did nothing but open and reply to the thousands of fan letters he received weekly, largely from females. Only married women were hired for the task because much of the correspondence was too shocking for immature single girls. The secretarial staff was supervised by Louella Parsons, a story editor for the studio at the time.

It was incredible what some females permitted themselves to write—shameless, sizzling declarations of sexual yearning for the handsome movie star. They went into intimate detail as to what they wanted from him. They gave precise measurements of their figures, some even describing their sexual parts and prowess. They sent photographs, many in the nude. They offered themselves in marriage or for an hour or a week of lovemaking. And it was not uncommon for women to show up at the studio, demanding to see the man of their dreams. When they were told he was not available, many refused to leave voluntarily.

The wishful thinking of female fans had its grim aspects. A husband came across a letter his wife was about to mail to Bushman, in which she recalled to his mind the passionate night they enjoyed together not long ago. The rendezvous was entirely imaginary, a product of her fevered frustration, but the husband was unaware of that. He wrote the actor, promising to come to town to beat him to a pulp.

Another fantasying woman told her husband that she was leaving, that she had found a real lover who abundantly established his capabilities where she was concerned. She described her alleged trysts with this paragon of paramours and triumphantly announced his name—Francis X. Bushman. Several days later, as the star left the studio, he was accosted by the husband, who poked a pistol in his face and promised to blow his head off. It took but a moment for the "physical type" Bushman to immobilize and disarm his assailant, but considerably longer to convince the furious man that Bushman had never even heard of his wife.

Describing these fantastic episodes to me, Mr. Bushman showed no irritation, only quiet amusement. His fans, male and female, were responsible for his long-sustained popularity and he was grateful. He accepted the importunities of some and the risks posed by others as the cost of the huge success they brought him.

Much the same consideration caused him to lend himself willingly to publicity stunts, and the stunts of those days were the gaudiest. He made personal appearances to promote his pictures and went around the world publicizing American films. He appeared at civic gatherings, snipped ribbons opening state fairs, and had himself photographed beside presidents of the United States and foreign monarchs. When the studio wanted to build a starlet into a star, it had the immediately recognizable Francis X. Bushman escort her to a night spot and sit in a dark corner holding her hand—to the utter delight of gossip columnists and editors of movie magazines. The fact that he had a wife and five children made no difference because his marital status was, of course, a well-kept secret. Studio executives warned him, "Don't even go to a movie with your wife! Don't ever go *any-where* with your children!"

Once, Mr. Bushman was approached by the managers of a young opera singer, Carmelle Ponselle. She was not as well known as she hoped to become, and publicity associating her with the actor would greatly advance her career, the managers said. They proposed that it be announced he had become engaged to Miss Ponselle. There would be a tornado of publicity, it would help Miss Ponselle, and it would do him no harm. The story would be milked as long as possible. When it lost its zing, an alleged rift would bring an end to the alleged engagement.

Bushman consented, and the subsequent press coverage exceeded the most optimistic expectations. A sensation a day was engineered, beginning with the modest announcement that the longtime "bachelor" had found the girl of his dreams at last. Then Miss Ponselle welcomed the press to her suite, which they found overflowing with flowers. Yes, the blushing singer admitted, her fiancé was an ardent suitor, very ardent indeed. The third day, Bushman sent his prospective bride a little gift, a huge limousine.

The stunt should have been worth several weeks of jazzy journalism, but it came a cropper. A reporter in Carmelle's home town got the idea of a local human-interest scoop. He went out to interview the singer's mother. How did she feel about becoming the mother-in-law of Francis X. Bushman? he asked.

She stared. An Italian woman not long from the Old Country, she hadn't read the papers and knew nothing about the supposed engagement until the local reporter filled her in. Thereupon she cried, "Oh, no! It cannot be! She cannot be engaged to this Mr. Bushman! She is already engaged! Who is this Mr. Bushman? I never heard of him!"

End of publicity.

When it came to press agentry, Mr. Bushman told me, no one ever surpassed Harry Reischenbach. "Here was the greatest press agent ever to work for the movies."

Bushman was in Hollywood, about to leave for San Francisco to open a fair, when he received a call in the middle of the night from the Chief of Police of that northern city asking if he was safe and sound. When Mr. Bushman assured him he was, the Chief, greatly relieved, asked the exact time the star would arrive in San Francisco. He would have a large contingent of officers on hand to escort him to his hotel.

Why such a heavy escort? Bushman asked. Because, the Chief said, a half hour ago a live bomb was found in the suite Mr. Bushman was to occupy. Someone had the presence of mind to pitch it into a tub of water, rendering it harmless before telephoning police.

"Who would want to harm me?" Bushman asked, mystified.

"That's what we'd like to know," the Chief said. "Have you any idea? Have you got enemies in San Francisco? Someone who would want to murder you?"

"Not to my knowledge."

Bushman proceeded to San Francisco, was met by police, and escorted to the hotel. A huge crowd had gathered outside, news stories about the bomb having alerted the population to Bushman's impending arrival. It was with difficulty that a path was cleared, permitting the actor to get into the hotel lobby where Harry Reischenbach was awaiting him.

"Did you hear about the bomb?" Bushman asked.

Harry nodded solemnly, escorted him to his suite.

"Who would want to kill me?" Mr. Bushman asked the press agent when they were alone.

Reischenbach winked. "Frank," he said, "I planted that bomb, and I dropped it into the tub, and I called police. I wanted to make certain you'd have a good turnout to greet you."

After Bushman was back in Hollywood, the Chief of Police, discovering he had been hoaxed, telephoned the actor. "Mr. Bushman," he said, "you tell that sonofabitch Reischenbach to stay out of San Francisco. If he steps foot in this town, so help me, I'll arrest him myself and lock him up for life!"

Nowadays, Bushman said, Hollywood's publicity stunts are more subtle, but he doubts that they are as effective as in former years.

He sheds no tears over the passing of that era, but his fondest recollections are of those halcyon years when new truths were being discovered about motion-picture production every day, when directors were giants or else they faded from the scene, and when actors received the adulation of the populace as they drove down Hollywood Boulevard in purple automobiles trimmed in solid gold.

Who was the greatest director of those pioneering days? I asked.

"Mr. D. W. Griffith. We didn't know anything until Mr. Griffith came along. For one thing, we used to think we had to show the full figure in every movie shot. Mr. Griffith invented the close-up, he moved the camera closer to the actors, so that only the upper part of their bodies showed. When a man and woman kiss, or characters hate, love, are terrified, the lower part of the figure rarely is important. The expression is in the face. The close-up emphasized that."

Did he know Greta Garbo?

"Garbo? I worked with her. I knew who she was. But no one knew her. She would walk through the studio with her head down, talking to no one, dressed in a long overcoat, striding along like a man. She wasn't mannish. Her interest was in men. But no one spoke to her because she would not be spoken to. I saw her on the street once, with her head down, in her shabby overcoat. I called out, 'Hi!' She didn't even look up."

He related a fetching anecdote about Ben Turpin, the cross-eyed comedian. Bushman first knew him as a stagehand, working as a studio grip most of the time, receiving bit parts only occasionally. The studio was shutting down for the day when a stagehand saw Turpin on an abandoned set, picking up a bouquet of flowers, a stage prop during the shooting. It was worth every bit of $5, but it was not the pilfering that bothered his coworker. He wondered what a man as unprepossessing as Ben Turpin wanted with flowers. Did he have a girl friend?

His associate followed him at a discreet distance. About a mile from the studio, Turpin came to a cemetery, climbed a low fence, went over to a grave, and placed the bouquet on top.

The man trailing him was deeply touched. Going over, he placed his hand on Ben's shoulder, saying, "Turpin, that was a beautiful gesture. You don't have to swipe flowers again. Any time you want flowers for this grave, you just take them right off the set. It will be perfectly all right."

Turpin looked embarrassed. "I didn't swipe these flowers from the set," he said. "I borrowed them from this grave in the morning and brought them onto the set. I was just returning them."

I asked Mr. Bushman which picture he most enjoyed doing. It was *Ben Hur*, exhibited in 1926 and acclaimed everywhere as a great artistic achievement.

"When we were filming it in Rome," he said, "enormous crowds gathered wherever we went. Mussolini was in power. In those days he was still doing good. Sanitation. Efficiency." One day, on the spur of the moment, Bushman decided to go down to the palace where the Fascist dictator worked, to catch sight of him. Still wearing his Ben Hur costume, he proceeded to the palace, saw Benito get out of a car and head for the entrance. The Black Shirt leader spied the actor in the Roman toga, strode over and embraced him warmly. Then Mussolini turned to the people congregated before the palace and made a dramatic, emotional speech informing them it was a great honor to have Francis X. Bushman in the city, doing a motion picture that would depict the glory of Italy. "This is a great Roman, a true Roman!" Mussolini orated, pointing to Bushman. In context, he was saying the actor epitomized Italian masculinity and sexual virility.

The dictator and the actor became good friends during the shooting of *Ben Hur*. Bushman visited Mussolini in the palace, and Mussolini dropped in at the motion-picture lot. He showed an interest in movie production, and even more in the pretty girls. "He loved American women. The big busts. He liked big busts. He appreciated them very much." But he could enjoy lesser endowed girls, also. "You might say Mussolini was very much interested in women," Bushman said, a broad grin on his face.

When *Ben Hur* was completed, Mussolini bade Bushman a warm farewell and urged him to visit Italy again as guest of the dictator. It was a shock, therefore, when the film was banned in that country after its first showing.

"In the picture," Bushman explained, "not only are the Italians defeated, but defeated by a Hebrew!"

The reception *Ben Hur* received in the United States was tumultuous. Audiences identified themselves with the action with passionate intensity. In New York, a well-dressed woman jumped up on her seat as the chariot race got under way, teetered precariously on her high heels, and screamed, "Come on, Bushman! Come on, Bushman!"

That was what he loved about those audiences. They were so much more responsive than nowadays. "They laughed with you and cried with you. I had a picture, I used to go to the theatre to watch it, to see *men* cry! Audiences definitely participated, those days. They were doing the thinking when the actor made his gestures. Today, they're critics. They weren't then!"

I asked, "Looking around, seeing so many of your friends gone, so many changes, does it make you sad?"

His answer was given in a firm but muted voice. "No, my dear. I don't look back and I can't look back. I just live for today. I have no regrets."

As we were leaving the restaurant, the hostess, a trim, chic woman, stopped us to say the establishment was honored to have us, that she had admired Mr. Bushman for years and was thrilled to see him in person.

He seized her hand, squeezed it, looked into her eyes and murmured, "*Shame* on you for being such a good-looking woman!"

There flashed through my mind something he had said at the table: "We weren't great actors those days, but great personalities." I don't think this great personality was acting, that moment.

Chapter 17

My pal Sarah

Several years ago, at the Dorchester Hotel in London, I told Sarah Churchill I was writing a book. She said she would be hurt if I didn't include her in it. When I told her she would have a full chapter, she said, "Dedicate it to 'My pal Sarah.' "

Actually, a chapter on Sarah could be written in ten different versions, because she has so many sides to her personality, or perhaps so many personalities. I love Sarah, as do most who come in close contact with her. She is a wonderful human being.

Naturally, the Churchill name is magic, so when I heard Sarah's cultured English accent on the telephone for the first time, and she asked if I could come to her suite in the Beverly Hills Hotel, my pulse quickened. She herself opened the door for me, a slim, boyish figure with beautiful red hair worn shoulder-length. Her husband, Tony Beauchamp, was with her, and she seemed very happy and gay. There were quite a few visitors in the suite, so Sarah and I went into the bedroom and sat on the bed as she dictated, with papers strewn all around us. We established rapport right from the beginning. She told me she would be going back to England soon but expected to return to Hollywood, when she would call if she needed my services.

I next heard from her when she and Tony had a small apartment at the Garden of Allah Hotel. They were working on the story of Christine Granville, a Polish spy in World War II. Sarah was intrigued with the heroine and wanted to star in a film about her.

I sensed tension in the air, despite the exaggerated politeness with which Sarah and Tony addressed each other. They disagreed on particulars of the script but held themselves in check. At one point, they took a break and went to the pool. I sat with Sarah, talking, while Tony went for a swim. He dived in but didn't come up. Sarah was fidgety, yet said nothing. Finally, when it seemed Tony couldn't possibly be alive, he rose to the surface and got out of the pool. Sarah gave him a strange look but made no comment.

I began seeing a good deal of Sarah after she moved to a Hollywood apartment, high above the Sunset Strip. She had separated from Tony by then. When I visited I almost always found her surrounded by people who, for the most part, did not strike me as being of her caliber—an actress who leaned on her for help, an unemployed actor, and a frustrated writer. I became more of a companion than a secretary to Sarah. We went shopping, and I spent a lot of time in the apartment with her.

She was an enigma, a paradox. She didn't need people and she did. She could be entertaining, witty, extroverted, the life of the party; on other occasions she was withdrawn, introverted. She seemed at odds with herself. Her upbringing and conditioning required her to conform to convention. Her inclinations sometimes made this impossible.

She was and is no snob. She accepts people for what they are, not because of their station in life. Her first husband was a Jewish music-hall comedian from the east side of London; her second, Tony, a British society photographer; her third, an English lord.

She is profound, and an artist all the way. She acts, sings, writes poetry, sketches, paints, dances. Material things mean little to her. She is no business woman, has no sense of the value of money. When she had it in Hollywood, she spent it, generously, absent-mindedly, treating everyone. When she didn't have it, she scarcely was aware of it. Bills were a mystery to her. She would even cable me from London, asking me to straighten out her financial affairs.

Once she wrote from there, "My dear—the Standard Garage—almost the first one after leaving Beverly Hills—before Sunset Plaza Drive, I believe—I owe the man fifty cents for petrol!! I guess there's nothing you can do—except stop at a couple and ask for the owner and just say did you lend fifty cents one early morning two months ago to some one who was out of petrol and had to get to NBC. What can we lose? There can't be many Standard Garages in that short strip."

She was just as happy in a dress from a national chain store as in an original creation. When she moved, she often left clothes behind, never bothering about them again. She was used to disorder. It was part of her life. Once I started collecting the many pairs of stockings scattered all over her apartment, intending to put them away in one place. "Oh!" she said. "If you do that, I won't be able to find the ones I want!"

Basically a shy girl, she is painfully aware of who she is, and that the public expects a great deal from her because she is Sir Winston's daughter. People do not believe she appreciates this sufficiently, she told me. They say if she did, she would not live the bohemian life. "The trouble is," she said, "I appreciate only too much who I am."

She knew very well she had witnessed history in the making. One afternoon while trying on a gorgeous turquoise dress a studio designer made up for her, she remarked, wistfully I thought, "I once had a most unusual suit made for me. It was during the war, when Papa met with Roosevelt and Stalin at Yalta. I was Papa's hostess and the only woman there. I didn't want to be too outstanding among so many aides, so I had the outfit made. Slim trousers and a jacket that was like a short Eisenhower style. I must say it did look nice!"

"Did you meet Stalin?" I asked.

"Of course! Papa introduced us."

She was so conscious of her father's greatness and the place the Churchill family must take in the history of the world that it pained her when individuals attributed her sometimes unorthodox behavior to disrespect for Sir Winston. We were having lunch at La Scala in Beverly Hills when a man sent a pizza over to us, after which he came over to introduce himself. He got off on the wrong foot immediately.

"You should be so happy! You should thank God you are Winston Churchill's daughter!" he said.

Very haughtily, Sarah replied, "And, sir, what makes you think I don't?"

Whether it was of any significance I am not sure, but the only brand of cigarette I ever saw Sarah smoke was Winston. She never indicated to me that she chose it because it bore her father's name, but I always wondered. Once she asked me to buy her a pack of cigarettes.

"Make it Winstons," she said.

"Winstons?" I repeated, my inflection suggesting there must be a reason.

She chuckled, "Yes, Winstons." That was all.

I was with her when she was to give a poetry reading at the Shrine Auditorium. She paced up and down, biting her nails, rehearsing over and over.

I said, "What are you so nervous about? It's only a 15-minute reading. You've done things much more difficult."

She was in agony. "Don't you see?" she said. "They don't see me! They see Sir Winston Churchill!"

When I mention Sarah, it often happens that instead of commenting on her talents and other fine qualities, people say, "Oh, yes! She was in that Malibu thing some time back, wasn't she?"

Unfortunately, the papers were not kind to her during that "thing," and that is understandable. Because of her name, it was inevitable that she should receive a great deal of publicity, even though the episode referred to would not rate a stick of type were a lesser figure involved. It is dishing up cold porridge to go into the matter now, but I was with Sarah then, and I want to put in my own word about the affair.

She was deeply depressed at the time. Tony had committed suicide and although by then he and Sarah were divorced, his death upset her terribly. Other events in her personal life contributed to her unhappiness. Also, she had been rehearsing very hard for a television show, had not been able to sleep, and her nerves were frayed. Because she needed rest and isolation from the hurly-burly, she went to stay in an old, rather decrepit beach house in Malibu, California. She wanted to relax, to hear the waves breaking, to inhale the salt air. When I arrived on the evening in question, I found her lying on the couch with the windows wide open, the cold ocean mist permeating every inch of the room. I shivered and buttoned my sweater, but although Sarah was wearing nothing but a coat she did not seem to feel the dampness and cold.

Something was eating at her. She was in mental agony. I had never seen her in quite such a state. She took the world apart, waxing poetic, philosophic, introspective, lyrical, cynical. I massaged her back and neck to help her relax, and when she finally did complain she was cold I made her some tea and put a hot-water bottle at her feet. Then I left, assuming she would sleep.

I don't know just what happened afterward. Newspapers reported she became irked while trying to put through a telephone call, abusing the operator in such language that the girl notified police. According to officers sent to the beach house, they found Sarah in an inebriated state. That is possible. Sarah drinks. But she was not intoxicated when I left, only moody and depressed. At any rate, police said she became infuriated with them, struck one officer, and, I believe they asserted, tore a button off his uniform.

Sarah told me that the officers mistreated and slapped her before she cut loose on them. She made no official complaint, she said, because the publicity was already very bad, and she did not want to create a situation which would have reverberations in England, embarrassing her family still further.

Despite the unsettling experience, Sarah bounced back, and next day turned in a magnificent performance on a television show. I spent weeks acknowledging the wonderful fan letters she received.

Whenever I visited Sarah in London, she treated me like an old friend. Everywhere we went, people recognized her and asked for her autograph. When we had lunch at the Dorchester Hotel in Hyde Park, the maître d' practically doubled over in a bow, welcoming Sarah. He told her he used to wait on her when she was a little girl, dining with her father.

We had a wild time apartment-hunting in Chelsea once, I remember. Sarah impulsively decided she wanted to stand on the running board of the cab as we drove around. I followed her example, and through London we rolled, like two witches, our hair whipping in the wind. And we were both cold sober; we had not had a drop.

Sarah's brother, Randolph Churchill, took me for a different sort of ride. I had heard stories about his supposed arrogance, and rather expected him to give me a bad time when he sent for me while in the hotel in Beverly Hills. He did not disappoint me.

He dictated rapidly, his speech so clipped I couldn't understand a word. "I beg your pardon," I said. "Would you mind repeating that? Your English accent. . . ."

He glared balefully. "How dare you! Eccent indeed! I'll hev y'know my eccent is altogether c'rrect! It's *you* who murder the King's English!" He didn't specify whether the indictment covered only me or all citizens of these United States.

When I brought him the finished work, he would have none of the envelopes I had used. They must be airmail envelopes. I informed him that the hotel didn't furnish these and suggested I type AIR MAIL on each envelope.

"I want airmail env'lopes!"

"But we don't have any!"

"Get them!"

"But . . ."

"Cahn't y'understend? Get them!"

Luckily, I was able to buy some at the drugstore. When I

brought them to his room, he exclaimed, "Good heavens, girl! Not the small ones! I want the big ones!"

"Mr. Churchill, they don't carry the big ones!"

He fixed me with a stare, and uttered just two words: "Get them!"

I was exhausted, ready to cry. "Mr. Churchill," I said, "your letters will fit into these envelopes very neatly. Can't you use them? What difference does it really make?"

"When I order something, I want it done! Young lady, you're very stupid!"

I controlled myself, and said I would be back. I found a stationery store on Santa Monica Boulevard still open, and returned with my prize. As I inserted and sealed the letters, I realized he knew I was angry and upset. I thought I should leave on more friendly terms.

"By the way, Mr. Churchill," I said. "I know your sister Sarah. I'm her secretary here."

"That's no compliment to you!" he snapped.

"And you're no compliment to Sarah," I retorted, but that was halfway down the corridor.

Next time I saw Sarah I described my strenuous session with her brother. She was very apologetic. "Don't let Randolph upset you, my dear. He is difficult. That's just his way."

Shortly after Sir Winston passed away, I received a note from Sarah, and I may be reading something into it, but I think not. The main portion was typed, dictated to a secretary. It dealt with a business matter. There was a P.S. in longhand: "I know I don't have to explain to you what I feel about the loss of my father—although naturally it was inevitable—the finalness is still unbelievable and sharp."

The P.S. was no afterthought, I am positive, considering the subject. And I believe the fact it was handwritten reveals the pain Sarah felt. She could not bring herself to expose her feelings before a third person, the secretary.

Chapter 18

An unforgettable character

"Edna, I present Emile Gauguin." The speaker was my French friend, Josette Giraud, a writer. The place was a New York hotel room. The man was the Polynesian son of the great painter, Paul Gauguin, whose name is synonymous with Tahiti.

Emile Gauguin was a spectacular sight, Gargantuan in height and girth. His belly was like a medicine ball. He was toothless, his eyes were tiny, his lips tight—almost no upper lip at all—and he had practically no hair. He wore a sport shirt spattered with brilliant colors, and he was barefoot.

Most notable was the expression on his face. Rather, the absence of expression. It was the face of a child too young to comprehend the world around it.

I acknowledged Josette's introduction, in French. Emile came forward, murmured, "*Bonjour!*" I extended my hand. He took it briefly, then sat down, laid his head back, and stared at the ceiling.

Josette explained him to me. She found the 300-pound child-man under a tree in Papeete, Tahiti. He was drunk. His sole garment was a pareu (a sort of sarong). A local tourist attraction, he was reputed to be imbecilic and alcoholic. People plied him with liquor and he ate whatever he could forage—cocoanuts, bananas, and handouts from villagers.

As Josette approached, Emile arose and came toward her, palm outstretched, begging ten francs for something to eat. She refused, knowing he would spend the money on drink. Instead, she took him to her hotel and fed him there. He was not an imbecile at all, she found, but an intelligent, if simple man. Not simple of mind; only his wants were simple.

She undertook to rehabilitate him. Since his only possession was his father's great name, she asked why he didn't try to paint. In the back of her mind was the thought that if he became interested in doing anything at all, it would restore his self-respect. She bought an easel, paint brushes and oils, placed the brushes in his hand, and showed him how to make strokes. He was delighted with his new toy, and began painting every day. She decided to bring him to the United States, manage him, perhaps turn him into a creditable artist. That was why he was in New York.

She had a hard time getting him outfitted, because he was so fat. At her urging, he cut his weight down to a mere 234 pounds, easy enough to do because he quit drinking liquor. He painted every day, delighted by the unaccustomed Manhattan scenery, the parks, bridges, skyscrapers and people. He was a lost soul, a primitive in a highly sophisticated city. He couldn't cross the street by himself. He called Josette *Maman* and she told me, "When we walk on the street, and this great big man calls me *Maman*, nobody understands what is—how you say—what is cooking there."

His semantics were delicious. He called New York a "fat town," meaning a big city. Once, gazing upward at a skyscraper, awestruck, he asked, "*Maman*, how many trees does it make?" That meant, "How tall is it?" An elevator was "the floor that rises and falls." Snow was "sugar."

To certain "civilized" inventions he adjusted immediately.

He adored the movies, but only the type he could understand—jungle pictures and Westerns. He loved to see cowboys and Indians.

When Josette had to be out of the apartment, Emile remained in his room, watching television, but the shows mystified him. He couldn't follow the plots or fathom the emotions the characters were portraying, partly because the situations in which they were involved were beyond the comprehension of a person unfamiliar with Western culture. He simply sat and stared at the screen with a blank expression until something appeared that he could grasp, such as an ancient Tarzan picture.

Food was a problem, too, and Josette was forced to prepare special dishes for him, such as rice, papaya and other tropical edibles. Western foods he distrusted or disliked.

As Josette reviewed all this background for me, Emile sat staring at the ceiling. Now, she turned to him, informing him in French that I was a very dear friend of hers, upon which he got up and went to his room. I asked if I had offended him in some way, but Josette said no, that he undoubtedly was looking for a present to give me. The way to greet a friend in French Polynesia was to present her with a gift.

Josette indicated Emile expected us to come to his room for the ceremony. There, grinning his toothless grin, he placed a strand of white sea shells about my neck. I thanked him profusely, and I could see he was pleased.

The next time I saw Emile, he again gave me a *Bonjour!* but I was not sure he recognized me, although Josette said of course he did. He had a bandage on one hand, having cut it while doing some woodcarving. *Maman* cleansed and bandaged the wound.

Sensing Josette was discussing his injury, Emile held his hand up to me, first the palm, then the other side, like a child asking for sympathy. I commiserated with him, after which he sat down and studied the bandage himself for a long time, first the palm side, then over, then palm, then over. Finally satisfied, he turned his eyes upward and stared at the ceiling. Josette said this was because he realized we were talking about him.

Emile's paintings, many of which I saw, had something of the Grandma Moses simplicity. It was as if he viewed the world through the eyes of a child.

Since Josette travels most of the time, she eventually arranged for Emile to live with a couple in a little house with a garden, on the outskirts of Chicago. Encouraged by Josette, he began creating designs, which she had a factory reproduce on dress material as a commercial venture. He no longer is homesick for Tahiti and never mentions it. Josette visits him as often as she can. He is delighted when she arrives and never asks why she must leave again.

According to Josette, he never was a true alcoholic. Tahitians simply failed to understand him; tourists made fun of him, treated him as a freak; his morale was shattered, and he lost the will to be a mature man. When tourists gave him alcohol so they might be amused by his antics, he drank. He has not had an alcoholic drink since leaving Tahiti.

Josette arranged for two exhibitions of Emile's paintings, one in Paris, one in London. The critics were very kind. She hopes Americans will take Gauguin to their hearts and encourage his talent, which Josette thinks he has. In the meantime, she is taking him to a dentist to be fitted with plates so he may be able to chew Western-type food, which he is about ready to chance.

The last time I saw Emile, in New York, I was able to give him a present, reciprocating for the one he gave me. He had discovered another toy—radio—and he was delighted with the music. I was with Josette when he came out of his room, his portable set in hand, complaining it no longer worked. Josette looked it over and said it would have to be sent out for repairs, whereupon Emile set up a howl, clutched his treasure to his breast, and jumped up and down in irritation. He couldn't be without his radio, he cried.

Fortunately, I had a tiny transistor radio in my handbag and I offered it to the grief-stricken Gauguin. For the first time in my association with him he not only smiled but also beamed.

Chapter 19

Take it from me, girls!

Girls often ask me how to be a successful public stenographer. They want to know how to please the customer, how far a girl should go to please him, and how to cope with the man who demands too much pleasing. Without claiming to be the nation's top authority on such matters, the fact is I have had considerable experience in the business. I learned certain things the hard way, and other stenographers might possibly benefit from what I have learned.

In the course of time, for instance, I evolved two rules that I consider absolutely basic.

Rule Number One: Know nothing, about nobody, nowhere, no time. Never discuss one client with another, or you will soon be looking for a new career. Before I learned that rule, I told an Englishman for whom I was working that I had done some letters for another Londoner a few months earlier. I mentioned his name, and described his wife as a spoiled darling who led him around by the nose. Of course, I said, she married him for his money.

The man to whom I was passing on this tidbit listened carefully, seemed quite amused, and encouraged me to say more. By this time, though, I had a hunch that I had gone too far already and buttoned my lip.

That afternoon, when I delivered the work to my customer's room, the door was opened by a woman—the "spoiled darling!" She had divorced the husband I knew, and was honeymooning with my present client. The experience taught me not to gossip, not to mention the name of a client unless someone mentions it to me first. Play dumb, girls, that's my advice. If you and a client are discussing another of your patrons (because your client brought the subject up) pretend you know absolutely nothing about him except that he gave you some work.

Here is how I handle the situation today. One of my clients is married to a woman who has so much money she could buy the bank in which she stores it. She keeps her adored husband handsomely supplied with cash, but demands that he keep busy. She doesn't want to feel he married her for her wealth, so therefore he must prove he can make money on his own. She keeps after him to sell stocks, to put corporations together. "Be busy!" she tells him.

He tries, in his fashion. He dabbles in various enterprises, but his office is in his hat. When he needs to get a few letters out, he drops in on me, dictates for a half hour, and as I type the communications, telephones his wife. "Listen!" he says, holding the telephone close to the typewriter. "Hear the girl type? Am I busy! We've been at it all morning!" After which he leaves for the bar, where I find him later, sipping a martini.

Do I tell his wife when I see her? I do not. She has called me to work for her at the house, but so far as I am concerned, I don't even know her husband. When she informs me he is at his office, working hard, I smile politely. If he tells her he has an office, who am I to deny it?

I will go to considerable lengths to protect a patron's private life. A well-known playboy was having an affair with a Swedish starlet, whom he kept in a suite in the hotel. He was taking a chance, because his wife, well aware of his low boiling point where women were concerned, kept strict tabs on him. Whenever he left the house, he had to let her know where he was going and for what purpose. Then she would telephone and check the truth of his statements. This, of course, could constitute a serious impediment to his trysts with his sweetheart. To forestall trouble, he hit on a plan.

Leaving his residence, he would tell his wife he was going to the hotel to dictate some business correspondence to the public stenographer. He would check in at my desk, instructing me to take calls he was only too certain would be coming in for him. Then he would go up and visit with his paramour. From her suite, he usually telephoned his spouse, announcing that he had arrived and was about to pitch in and do an afternoon's work. He would be very, very busy, he told her, I am sure truthfully. He gave her my extension and returned to his busy work.

Once when he had gone through this routine, his wife telephoned my extension and asked, "Is my husband there?"

"He just left for the drugstore," I said. "He'll be right back."

An hour later: "Is my husband still there?"

"He was here up to a minute ago, but he stepped out to make a barbershop appointment. He should be back any moment."

Ten minutes went by. Then: "Did he get back?"

"Oh, you just missed him again! He came back, but an agent he knew came by, and they went out together. He said to tell you he'd be home early."

The enamored playboy was so grateful for my discreet services that, in addition to paying me, he treated me to a week in Mexico City.

Now here is *Rule Two* of public stenography: *Take them as they come.* There are all kinds of people. You are not going to make them over. You are working for the client, not psychoanalyzing him.

A dapper San Franciscan used to send for me when he came to town. Invariably, when I arrived at his room, I found scores of pornographic pictures scattered about everywhere, on chairs, end tables, the bed. He placed them about so indiscriminately that I could not fail to see them. As soon as I sat down to work, he would eye me furtively, looking for any indication of my reaction to his art exhibit. He never mentioned it, however.

The first time, I pretended not to notice the pictures, which apparently disappointed him. As he dictated, he kept moving around, so as to get me facing one photo or another. He wanted me to react, but I didn't.

I followed the same procedure on several other occasions, and I could tell he was not only puzzled but also peeved, because I was not cooperating. Finally, one day, as he paced around, he moved over to a position where, in order to hear him, I had to face in that direction, bringing a particularly gaudy photograph into my line of vision. I thought it was about time to make clear whether or not I was going to react. For the first time, I made mention of the pornographic display by remarking casually, "I don't think your pictures are very good. I've seen better."

It deflated him, and that was the end of the erotica.

A man sent for me and, believe it or not, I found him minus pants or bathrobe, in nothing but undershorts, and they were partly unbuttoned. I was nonplused, to put it mildly, but he seemed so altogether unconscious of his attire as he sat down and began dictating that I figured he did not intend putting on a show. It was just possible he was so preoccupied with other things he didn't realize what a spectacle he was making of himself.

And he was all business, scarcely glancing at me as we worked, making no off-color remark. I gave him the benefit of the doubt and we kept working. But then someone pressed the buzzer, and if my customer wasn't embarrassed to be found in the company of a stenographer in his condition, that didn't go for me.

"Don't you think, sir," I said, "you ought to put your robe on? It will look better."

"Came away without one," he said. "Guess I'll put my pants on." Which he did.

He admitted the valet, who delivered a suit and departed. We returned to work. When I left that morning, I thought, "Isn't that disgusting!" But the point is I refrained from saying that to him. I kept my feelings to myself.

The same man telephoned for me again, that afternoon, and this time I asked a girl who was helping me to come with me, just in case. And we found the gentleman in his shorts.

"Gee!" I said. "Did you get undressed again?"

He threw up his hands. "Guess I'd better put my pants back on." He headed for the closet, but looked back at us as he said, accusingly, "But I work better without them!"

We were back in my office, about ready to close up, when the gentleman phoned once more. Would I come up, please?

It was time to be firm. "No, sir!" I told him. "I am not coming up. And I think it would be wise if, before you call some other stenographer, you . . ."

"Oh!" he broke in. "But I did! I did! I'm wearing them right now!"

The capacity of the human being for learning is unlimited.

I think the incident that above all others taxed my ability to take people as they come was the one involving The Man Who Liked Company.

He and his wife were vacationing in Beverly Hills, escaping a particularly brutal Chicago winter. We worked in his suite all afternoon, and when dinnertime arrived and he still hadn't finished his work, he suggested that I accompany him and his wife to dinner at the Brown Derby, where he could finish dictating. His wife thought that would be an excellent idea and urged me to come, so I accepted.

It was a lovely repast, but he embarrassed me by dictating at the top of his voice, causing people to turn their heads and stare. I knew then that he was a show-off, but I had no idea to what degree until we returned to the hotel. My hostess suggested I come up to the suite for a nightcap. As she mixed a highball her husband excused himself and went into the adjoining room. He returned wearing a flapping, wide-open bathrobe and nothing else. I jumped to my feet. Speaking not a word, he strode over and took me in his arms. With his wife there all the time! He pulled me close, fondled me shamelessly, and urged me to caress him in return. I tried to break his bear hug, but finding that impossible, looked over my shoulder at his wife, fully expecting her to be up on her feet, ready to conk us with a whisky bottle. Instead, she sat there, staring.

He caught the direction of my gaze. "Oh!" he said. "Don't pay any attention to her. She won't mind."

And now she was smiling; in fact, beaming. "Go ahead," she told me. "I don't care."

Still struggling in his arms, I managed to say, "I don't understand! Your wife——"

"There's nothing to understand, honey!" said my captor. "I've had Stella bring her boy friends up here. I've seen her with them. She'd like to watch me, with a girl friend. Why shouldn't she?" He tried to nuzzle into my bosom.

Even for a girl who has met all kinds of people this was pretty heady stuff, but I showed neither annoyance nor disgust. Smiling to indicate we were still friends, I made it clear I wasn't in the mood.

He was not a monster, after all, and when he was sure I meant what I said, he unlocked his arms and freed me. I even sat down and finished my drink before taking my leave. That kept matters on an even keel. Besides, I needed that whisky.

The Man Who Liked Company was out of the ordinary; he was unpredictable. The behavior of most clients can be predicted within reason. Which brings me to the subject of how a girl is to know she is working for a Casanova in camouflage. You are with a male client for the first time. How can you foretell whether he is going to invite you to dinner or to bed? Whether these possibilities disturb or titillate a stenographer, it is helpful to understand the symptomatology.

Male patrons run to types. There is the *how-about-a-drink* gentleman. You work, he calls a recess, waves toward a bottle on the dresser or bar, and politely inquires, "How about a drink?" He wants you to believe he is merely concerned for your comfort. You have been hard at it, and need a refresher. To establish that he is not getting personal, he may suggest you pour it yourself while he forgoes one in favor of organizing his papers for the next round of dictation.

That is the more direct approach. If your customer is the

shy type, he will start toward the liquor setup, stop midway, turn to you and, as if it were an afterthought, say, "I was just about to pour myself a drink. Will you have one with me?"

When a man uses either technique, you may be sure he is at least mildly interested in you. I employ stenographers to help me when I am overloaded, and they generally report their experiences to me. If I send an older, rather plain-looking woman to take a guest's dictation, he turns out a teetotaler. When I send a young, good-looking girl, the client is a convivial type. I employed a girl named Clara who was really stunning. Many times she was offered a drink before she even opened her notebook. On more than one occasion she returned to the office unable to type without getting her long nails caught in the keyboard. Once she actually reeled in, placed her notebook on the desk, announced she was going to powder her nose, and disappeared for a week.

Once I took a trip East, and upon returning to the office was gratified to discover business was not only as good as usual but better. Or so it seemed. I answered call after call, went to room after room, and at least half the time the man who sent for me hemmed and hawed and explained he received a call a minute ago and had to change his plans, or gave an equally lame excuse. I was beginning to wonder what it was all about, when one guest blurted out, "What happened to that blond stenographer? She was very good! Extremely competent!"

That was it! Clara had filled in for me. I explained this to the gentleman.

"Oh!" he said. "Well, do you play around, too? Have a drink?"

Not every man has liquid refreshment in his room, hence the *have-you-had-dinner* gentleman. Most clients will interrupt work at the proper hour and ask the stenographer, "Why don't you go out and have your dinner, then come back?" That is no come-on. I am speaking of another kind of man. He asks, "Have you had dinner? Would you care to have a bite with me?" That still may not be a come-on. When a stenographer has worked for the same man several times, a perfectly fine friendship may develop, and he will offer to take her to dinner with no ulterior motive in mind. Is is the first-timer I refer to, in the have-you-had-dinner category. If he issues the invitation, at least half the time he wants more than a dinner companion.

I said about half the first-timers who take a girl dining have romance on their minds. Others take a girl out only for company. Thy don't like to eat alone, but they intend to keep the employer-employee relationship on a relatively impersonal plane. There is also the man who brings the conversation around to his family. His eyes warm as he describes his little girl who is just finishing kindergarten. He remarks that his wife is a most wonderful companion. A man who talks about his wife and kids is not likely to make advances to the stenographer. But don't take that as an axiom. There are exceptions.

Your man with an idea is the one who begins with small talk about business, but quickly brings the conversation around to a personal level. I can tell when a client is going to become personal. It is at the moment when he seems really to "see" me for the first time. He will be in the middle of an entertaining recital of the time he bought a bankrupt Algerian diaper factory and converted it into a billion-dollar corporation selling camels to Arabs. As he speaks, there is a split-second hesitation, a barely perceptible sparkling of the eye. Suddenly he sees *me*, not the public stenographer. He drops his camel corporation, lowers his eyes, exclaims, "Say! That's a beautiful ring you're wearing! May I see it?" He holds my hand lightly, studies the stone, then looks up and into my eyes. The campaign has begun.

If it isn't a ring, it is something else, but it has the same meaning. I am now prepared for him. Should he follow through with an invitation to dinner, my answer is ready. I may say, "I'd love it!" And I may tell him, "Oh, I'm so sorry! My husband is taking me out tonight!" I have invented husbands of all sizes and ages, in every conceivable walk of life, from architect to zither strummer. A husband comes in handy under circumstances like these, especially since I can build him to order for the occasion. I can wriggle out of a luncheon or dinner invitation without much difficulty if I want to, and in any case I enjoy being asked. I am flattered. Moreover, having lunch or dinner with a client gives me a chance to get to know him better, to understand how he likes his work done, to learn something new and interesting. Whether or not I accept, the client is not likely to place me in a difficult position.

This is not as true of another category, the *how-about-it-babe* gentleman. He is sure of himself and of the girl. His approach in effect is: "Look, babe! We know what it's all about. We both are after the same thing—birds and bees stuff, hmmm?" He is direct, brazen and sometimes vulgar. His assumption is that he is a man and she is a woman and she is dying to hoopla with him.

The most outstanding feature of the how-about-it-babe man is his conviction that he is irresistible—why waste time on preliminaries? I have worked for men who, showing no prior interest, walked right over and kissed me. One character telephoned from his room to set up an appointment to have a contract typed. He hung up, called back immediately, saying, "I like your voice, sweetie. Shall we start with cocktails?"

The obverse of the how-about-it-babe customer is the *protest-too-much* gentleman. We are working. He studies me. I can hear the wheels whirring in his brain. He is sizing me up—will I or won't I? His conscience tells him I shouldn't and his libido tells him I should. His conscience says he should be ashamed of himself for what he is thinking and his libido says, "To hell with conscience!" Finally he decides I am that kind of girl, and in announcing his own ideas to me he makes his peace with his conscience by saying, "Look! This is something I don't normally do. BUT." I have bewitched him, and so on. This essentially strait-laced fellow is excusing himself to himself.

Still another ploy is one used by the *message-bearer*. A man telephoned me to say, "I have regards for you from Bill Moore."

"Who?"

"You know, Bill Moore, from the vacuum cleaner company. He told me to say hello."

"Oh, that's nice."

"Why don't you come upstairs and have a drink? I want to meet you. Bill mentioned you a couple of times. Great guy, isn't he?"

"Yes. And thank you very much, but I can't come up just now. I'm working. Perhaps later."

"Oh, I didn't mean just *come up*. I've got some letters I want to give you."

I went up, he dictated awhile, then came over and placed his arm around my shoulder. "Say!" he murmured. "You're not bad! How about going out on the town?" Just like that.

"Gee!" I said. "I'm awfully sorry, but my husband expects me home. He's Italian. Very old-fashioned. You know how jealous Sicilians are!"

The prospect of competing with what he must have thought was a member of Mafia was too much for him. He was unhappy, but only momentarily. "Tell you what," he said, his face brightening. "Get me another dame, then, will you?"

"I don't know any. But you're so good looking, you shouldn't have any trouble finding someone yourself."

When I said earlier that a man who talks about his family is simply lonesome for the home folks and not interested in the stenographer, I did not have in mind those who use family in the *personal-history* method of getting to first base. These gentry, once they "see" you, may open with something like, "Are you married?" That is a giveaway of intentions. A client who wants a document typed and no monkey business on the side doesn't give a hang whether a typist is married, single, or living in sin.

A classical example of the approach:

I was working for the chairman of the board of a large corporation in the communications field. At the time he called he advised he would need me the greater part of the day. We worked incessantly for the entire morning. At noon, he asked if I would mind having lunch in the room, so we might get back to work immediately afterward. There was no special invitation in his invitation; just business.

At lunch my client relaxed, and I caught that flash of recognition, when all of a sudden he "saw" me. He smiled. "You're very efficient," he said. "You *are* married, aren't you?"

"Yes."

"Hmm!" He sipped his tomato juice. "Hmmmm!"

He returned to the lists with, "You're so, uh, vivacious, that I must ask this. Are you *happily* married?"

"Oh, yes! My husband is French. He's a writer. That's why I work. Novelists, well, they make lots of money one year, very little the next. But we're *very* happy."

"I see."

I have learned that when a man gets this far I may expect a fairly characteristic alteration in course. My client did not disappoint me. He launched into an enthusiastic harangue about how wonderful it is, these days, to find couples just old-fashioned enough to believe in the fine, time-tested values, in loyalty and honest affection for each other. "I'm madly in love with my wife," he confided over and over. "We have a perfect marriage."

Well, of course, when a man talks like that he is flying in the face of reality. People may be madly in love with each other, but I wonder if there is such a thing as a perfect marriage. We all know that no human being is perfect. When a man says what my client did, he is making his bow to what he believes I think he should feel. The next move is likely to disprove his assertion.

And in this case it did. He repeated how madly he adored his wife. BUT. Had I ever been to the Cocoanut Grove?

The gambit suggests the change that has taken place in our courting customs. Years ago, judged by novels depicting the period, when a man was wooing himself into adultery, he claimed his wife didn't understand him, and, oh, how he needed understanding! Today the man is much more likely to say, "I love my wife and she loves me. You love your husband. Both of us understand the situation. We don't intend breaking up our marriages. I'm asking you to go out with me. We'll have fun, dinner, a drink, then go to bed. It doesn't mean anything beyond the fact you're an exciting girl. You'll go back to your husband, I'll go back to my wife, and we wouldn't want it any other way, would we?"

That was essentially what my client told me. I smiled. Nodded that he was so very right. But then I remarked, "Gee, I forgot— I have an appointment with my psychoanalyst."

That scares them. An analyst? If she's a mixed-up girl, she might get sticky.

The patron who is easiest to anticipate is the chap who enacts the *babe-in-the-woods* gambit. He wants you to believe that he came out of the backwoods, that he is just getting used to wearing shoes, and big cities confuse him. He asks if the stenographer can give him the name of a good restaurant. When she says she is fond of a particular one, he asks, "Really? Why don't you join me, so you can show me where it is?"

This, then, is my classification of patrons a public stenographer meets. Oops! I completely overlooked one category—the *gentlemanly* gentleman. I may have created the impression that a public stenographer takes a chance every time she enters a patron's room. That is far from the truth. The vast majority of my male clients are altogether gentlemanly. I do their work, they thank me, and usher me to the door.

A final tip for my sisters in the secretarial vocation. Don't take offense when a man asks that hackneyed question, "What are *you* doing, working as a public stenographer?" He doesn't mean he considers public stenography a low vocation. He means he thinks you could do even better for yourself. He is impressed with you.

My advice is, respond as I do. When a man wants to know why I am in public stenography, I say, "So I can meet nice people like you." If he meant his question as a come-on, my riposte shames him into behaving. If he was merely complimenting me out of the fullness of his heart, then I mean it double—I like meeting nice people like him.

Chapter 20

L'Envoi

Rewarding as my work is, it has its depressing aspect. What's bad about a hotel is time. The changes.

When I first went to work at the Beverly Hills Hotel in 1947, Hollywood was still the glamour spot of the world. The studios were prosperous, in full swing. Movie stars were everywhere. All the big names were there. People from all over the world came to California to transact business and to look at the scintillating Hollywood society. It was the great day of Romanoff's and the Mocambo, of fabulous parties costing thousands of dollars, of chauffeurs lined up outside hotels and restaurants, of titled gentry who wore their titles quietly and with dignity.

Guests checked in with a corps of servants, secretaries and valets. They hired employees just to walk their dogs. Hotel maids received more in tips than they got in weekly wages.

There was an excuse for orchids and champagne and lobster every day. Wherever you looked in the fine hotels you saw people of greatness as well as status-seekers, quick-money boys, handsome young men squiring dowagers, and cute and flossy girls. Those were the days of a Renaissance-like explosion. Depression and war were over; new ideas and talents blossomed again.

When I started my career, I was very often paid merely to remain on call, without doing a thing. I received long distance messages from all parts of the globe, many individuals telephoning just to say hello. The monetary rewards for my work were secondary to the pleasure and stimulation I received from being with my glamorous clients.

This was the great day of head turning and neck craning, for there was always someone passing by who was worth it.

The greater part of this sparkling era has gone, along with the best years of Hollywood. Some of it still exists, but the overall aura of excitement and thrill is greatly diminished. It adds up in my mind to both a minus and a plus value. I regret the passing of those beautiful people and events. But just like Hollywood itself, the hotel world today is more real than it was, in a utilitarian sense.

What makes me blue, though, is the unremitting passage of time. You see people year after year, and then they are not there any longer. They are dead. Or they married and decided to live in New York. Or they were divorced and went to Europe to forget. Or they are just gone—you don't know what happened to them. It makes you feel you are standing still and everything and everybody is going by, leaving you where you are. It's depressing and somewhat frightening.

I began thinking the other day, when I was in the Beverly Hills Hotel. In that chair, A. C. Blumenthal used to sit every evening at six, reading his paper. He died several years ago. It was at that desk that I was introduced to Clark Gable. He has passed on. Day after day, year after year, it was at this table in the bar that movie director Edmund Goulding sat with two cronies sipping his Scotch and humming the song he wrote for *The Razor's Edge*. He died on the operating table.

Even the familiar bartenders are no longer serving guests; they have been replaced by men who are strangers to me. People get used to certain desk clerks and maids and bellmen and bartenders. They miss the familiar faces.

I looked about me and saw ghosts sitting in the lobby, the restaurants, the lounge. So many people were God knew where. It was sad. They moved on and I stood still. It scared me. I felt all alone—as if I'd been left behind in a strange land.

But my mood passed. Next day, there were newer faces, to be sure, but they were becoming old friends like those of a few years back. There was fresh excitement, fun, parties, intrigue, and yes, glamour and reflected glory. Not the same glamour, not as much, but still there. Like all life, a hotel has the inborn capacity to replenish itself.

So, goodbye, beautiful people! Hello, beautiful people!